THE NEW GREEN CONSUMER GUIDE

First published in Great Britain by Simon & Schuster UK Ltd, 2007
A CBS COMPANY

Designed by Two Associates

1 3 5 7 9 10 8 6 4 2

Simon & Schuster UK Ltd
Africa House
64–78 Kingsway
London WC2B 6AH

www.simonsays.co.uk

Simon & Schuster Australia, Sydney

A CIP catalogue record for this book is available
from the British Library.

ISBN-13: 978-0-7432-9530-7
ISBN-10: 0-7432-9530-7

Printed and Bound in Italy by
L.E.G.O. s.p.a. on 100% recycled paper

THE NEW GREEN CONSUMER GUIDE

JULIA HAILES

CONTENTS

Foreword

Julia co-wrote the original *Green Consumer Guide* in 1988, and for the first time we were able to see and understand the links between what we buy and how this affects the environment. In those days there weren't that many 'green products' on the market – indeed the seriousness of environmental issues was still very much a subject for debate.

Today, no one can say they're unaware of the crisis. We have to act – and act now – to save the planet from runaway global warming. Too many still believe that the size of the problem is so big that their individual efforts won't make a difference. This is both erroneous and lazy thinking. If enough of us make the right sort of changes to the way we live, shop and spend our leisure time it will have an enormous effect. Not least, it will show politicians and manufacturers that we do care, which will in turn influence their crucial decisions.

But how to start? The market is rapidly becoming crowded with products cashing in on 'green chic'. There's an endless stream of conflicting advice about what we should or shouldn't do, which can be overwhelming. Concerned consumers could be forgiven for throwing up their hands in despair.

And this is where *The New Green Consumer Guide* comes in. In this wonderful book Julia hasn't just listed which products to buy and which to avoid, she's also explained why you should make your decisions. And some of her conclusions are truly surprising.

Take plastic bags: we use a staggering 10 billion bags a year, which is about 200 for every man, woman and child. I'd always assumed that by cluttering up landfill sites indefinitely they were an environmental nightmare. Surely paper ones would be better? Not so, Julia reports. Plastic bags may actually be less of a problem than paper ones – and biodegradable plastics are not the answer (for the full story, see page 35).

Another surprise for me was that Julia doesn't recommend 'green' detergent brands. She says that the biodegradability of these products is not a big issue – far more important is to choose detergents that wash at low temperatures.

I think I'm like many in finding the prospect of giving up air travel one of the hardest parts of being green. Julia is enough of a realist to understand that many feel this way, and so she recommends that flying should become more expensive (instead of relentlessly cheaper) and that we should all limit the number of flights we take. Why not conference-call more often? A lawyer friend of mine in New York said that in the months after 9/11 he didn't fly at all; he just used the new technologies to give him face-to-face contact with clients. Unfortunately, the trend only lasted a few months.

If, like me, you're unclear about which sources of alternative energy really work, then Julia steers you in the right direction. There are now so many companies competing in this market that you'll need to be armed with the very best information before installing a new boiler or, like David Cameron, putting a wind turbine on your roof. But as Julia points out, the future of energy is at home – we actually use only one-fifth of the electricity produced by centralised coal-fired power stations.

As a species we're incredibly wasteful: a staggering 1 million tonnes of food is chucked away every year; we buy an average of eight T-shirts in this time (how many can we possibly wear?); there are now nearly 4 farm animals for every human on the planet. In short, we're greedy and we have too much of everything. It's a state of mind that has to change.

In the future there will have to be limits on how much energy we're allowed to use, so products and services that help us reduce our demand will become indispensable. But we shouldn't wait until we reach such a crisis point. Each of us can start right now to lessen our environmental footprint and learn how to live lightly on this earth. *The New Green Consumer Guide* shows us where to begin. We should act together now, while we still have a choice.

Rosie Boycott

Introduction

In 1989 I was in Newcastle filming a green mini series for Richard and Judy's This Morning programme, but I had forgotten to bring any clean underwear. So I dashed into Marks & Spencer for some multi-packed knickers. I accepted a receipt but refused a bag. The lady at the till was insistent about the bag but I had a real bee in my bonnet so I continued to protest until she called the manager. The queue behind me grew longer, but I stood my ground. When the manager appeared I told her that the bag was unnecessary and wasteful. Eventually she gave up on this difficult customer and allowed me to leave the store clutching my goods.

A few weeks later I told this story to the Today newspaper in a feature about 'greening supermarkets'. They ran a centre-page spread headlined 'Green Princess risks arrest in M&S'. Less than six months on I noticed someone on the tube with an M&S bag on which was written: 'Please reuse this bag for the sake of the environment'. Was that because of me? I don't know.

All Change

How things have changed. Today all the supermarkets have initiatives designed to reduce the number of plastic bags handed out to customers. And that's only a fraction of what's happening on the green front. There doesn't seem to be a product or an industry that hasn't responded to the challenge. Whether it's light bulbs or coffins, computers or mobile phones, batteries or cars, there's a whole raft of new technologies, new ideas and new ways of thinking about how we can minimise our impact on the planet.

This has made writing *The New Green Consumer Guide* both exciting and challenging. And very different to when John Elkington and I wrote the original *Green Consumer Guide* in 1988. Then we had to search for examples of good green practice – now I've had to select the best green options from a myriad of choices.

And in the late 1980s climate change was just emerging as an issue, while the ozone layer was hitting the headlines. Now the ozone layer is barely mentioned as climate change or global warming takes centre stage.

The Scale

It's tempting to think that the scale of the challenge means there's simply nothing that we as individuals can do. You couldn't be more wrong. Of course, if one person replaces their car with a bike or installs solar panels on their roof, the world won't notice. But if millions of people make changes – even relatively minor ones – the impact is enormous.

Even the fact that America is guzzling a huge proportion of the world's resources and economic growth in China is exploding shouldn't put us off doing something.

Remember that we're partly responsible for pollution in China because much of what we buy is made there. Equally, we need to lead the way so that other countries don't repeat our mistakes.

Consumer Power

The really great thing is that our choices as consumers have a triple-pronged effect. First, there's minimising our own individual impact. Second, there's the very powerful message we're sending to retailers and manufacturers about what we want and what we don't want – it's amazing how easy and effective it is to complain. And finally there is the message we're sending to the Government. I'd say our vote as a consumer is far more powerful than our vote in an election once every five years.

Supermarkets today are falling over themselves to demonstrate their eco-credentials – they're immensely keen to appeal to 'green consumers' because apart from anything else it makes very good business sense. Marks & Spencer, for example, has recently come out of the doldrums, and it's thought its pioneering approach to sustainability issues has been a key factor in this. And Asda, which is owned by the world's largest company Wal-Mart, has radically improved its approach to environmental issues over the last year.

Some people worry about whether companies are just 'jumping on the bandwagon'. My view is that the more people on this particular bandwagon the better. They may not be as committed as you or me, but so what? If they're prepared to make changes and reduce their impact, we should be supportive and encourage them to go even further.

We want companies to know how their products are mined, grown or produced – and we should ask them. This is a key part of what this book is about. It explains the issues, advises on solutions, and helps you decide which questions to pose. Remember that whatever you buy or don't buy, you're voting for or against the planet.

Your Choice

The New Green Consumer Guide is primarily concerned with environmental issues. I haven't completely ignored health, ethics, fair trade or animal welfare, however – they're all interlinked and part of what we call 'sustainability'. I've identified the most important or interesting issues and made it clear what I think, what I've done or tried to do – and in some cases where the greenest option was a step too far.

You must decide how far you want to go. My only hope is that *The New Green Consumer Guide* will help you along the way.

LOOKING FORWARD

The New Green Consumer Guide is divided into five chapters. The first, 'Consuming the Future', introduces and explains the issues. These include climate change, nuclear energy and wind power, as well as shrinking rainforests, organic agriculture and over-fishing. It looks at the controversial introduction of GM foods, how we should be dealing with our mountains of waste, and whether biodegradable plastics are all they're cracked up to be.

The remaining four chapters form the main part of the book, and are designed to be used as a shopping guide covering 'Home and Garden', 'Food and Drink', 'Transport' and 'Personal Matters'.

In 'Home and Garden' you can find out how new lighting in our homes and offices will dramatically cut energy demand, why cheap imported lavatories can be huge water-wasters, and whether 'green' detergents are actually better for the environment. It helps you choose which electricity supplier to sign up to and advises you on whether it's worth producing your own heat and power at home. And there's information on a whole host of things, from painting your house, buying new furniture or replacing flooring, to composting, lawn care, chemical-free gardening and getting rid of electrical waste such as computers and TVs.

In 'Food and Drink' I look at the real impact of eating cheap meat, how far our food has to travel, why pesticide residues are still permitted in food, and which fish we should all be blacklisting. I've also compared the performances of seven leading supermarkets on a range of issues.

'Transport' contains information on how to find the 'greenest' car, why biofuels aren't as good as they seem, the new car-free options now available, and why air fares should increase.

In 'Personal Matters' you can see why disposable nappies could be the greenest option, how the cut-flower industry is taking its toll, why we should avoid gold and diamonds, which bank or building society has the best approach to eco-issues, and how to choose the greenest funeral.

And finally, the Conclusion looks at your global footprint, lists top dos and don'ts, identifies my top 20 wish list of things that would make a difference, and encourages you to do the same. The future is in our hands. The future is green!

'Nobody made a greater mistake than he who did nothing because he could only do a little'

Edmund Burke

 Consuming the Future

I stood on a white sand beach, staring into the sunset, when a plastic bag wrapped itself around my leg; as I gazed across a beautiful expanse of rainforest stretching into the distance I heard the sound of chainsaws. It was 1983. I was in Brazil towards the end of a trip across South America from Peru. It wasn't a blinding flash, a sudden conversion, but I was hooked. I wanted to save the rainforests and make the world a better place.

It wasn't until 1986, when I returned from another extensive trip, this time around Central America, that I started working for the good of the environment. I joined a campaigning organisation, working alongside John Elkington, with whom I co-wrote the original *Green Consumer Guide* in 1988, and although I remained passionate about the rainforests, I realised there were other issues to be concerned about.

This wasn't long after the Chernobyl nuclear accident. There were worries about acid rain. And the world was waking up to the fact that there was a hole in the ozone layer. Twenty years on, a lot has changed. On the positive side acid rain is not such an issue and the hole in the ozone layer may actually be getting smaller. But the rainforests are smouldering, nuclear power is expanding and global warming has become a real threat.

The New Green Consumer Guide demonstrates how you can make a difference – some of you may want to skip straight to that. This chapter is about what's really happening to our planet – a sort of bluffer's guide answering such questions as:

- **Will climate change make us warmer or colder?**

- **Are wind and wave power real alternatives to nuclear?**

- **Is recycling worthwhile?**

- **Can we save the rainforests?**

- **Could organic farming provide enough food for all?**

- **Why are chemicals that should be banned still being used?**

CLIMATE CHANGE

In 50 years' time I think we'll look back at the early years of the twenty-first century and see them as a turning point. In particular, 2006 was the year in which the world woke up to climate change. It's been headline news across the world; scientists are reaching a consensus; and most significantly, world leaders are finding climate change harder to ignore.

So what is climate change? What's actually happening? It's all to do with the heat from the sun. The Earth absorbs some of it and sends the rest into space. This is where the green-house effect comes in. Gases trap much of this heat and stop it from escaping – they act like a blanket or greenhouse – and the subsequent warming effect is essential for life as we know it.

So far, so good. The problem is that although many of these gases occur naturally, we're now producing a lot more of them. Greenhouse gases such as carbon dioxide (CO_2) are released by burning coal, running cars, and even via animals' breath. More gases mean the blanket is getting thicker and more heat is being trapped – hence global warming.

A Warming World

It's not as simple as that, however. The effects of global warming, or climate change as it has become known, are numerous and complicated.

Climate change doesn't just mean the world getting warmer; it means more weather extremes, more droughts, more flooding and more storms. Recall the impact of Hurricane Katrina on the city of New Orleans and you won't be surprised to hear that storms are getting more violent. In fact over the past 35 years there has been a near-doubling of the strongest hurricanes around the world.

Bizarrely, in Britain it's not clear if the weather will get hotter or colder. Apparently, ocean warming caused by climate change is slowing down the Gulf Stream. This warm ocean current is responsible for our climate being more temperate than other places on a similar latitude – it's curious to think that Moscow is only a little further north than London, yet commonly has midwinter temperatures of –15°C or below. Scientists fear that a slowing Gulf Stream will mean less heat reaching Europe, and hence more extreme winter conditions.

However, it's at the Poles where the effects of warming are already being felt. In the Arctic, temperatures are rising 20 times faster than in the previous century. Spring is coming earlier, autumn later, summer is getting hotter, and the Arctic Ocean ice cap has shrunk by about 40 per cent over three decades.

You may not know, but when a cube of ice melts in a glass of water, the level of the water won't change. It's the same with icebergs – sea levels won't rise if they melt. But snow or ice that sits on land is another matter: when it melts it will slide into the sea and actually add

to the amount of water there. Apparently, 70 per cent of the world's fresh water and 90 per cent of its ice is in Antarctica, mostly on land. If it were divided equally between everyone on the planet, we would each have a chunk of ice larger than the Great Pyramid.

A rise in sea level of a metre is a real possibility by the end of this century. It's predicted that this would result in a coastline retreat of nearly a mile, and I'm afraid the Thames Barrier wouldn't be much protection against that – so watch out, London. Coastal cities around the world would be devastated.

Of course it's not just humans that will feel the effects of climate change. One scientific study concluded that a quarter of all land animals – that's over 1 million species – could become extinct by 2050. Sea life would also be affected. Coral beds are home to a quarter of all marine life and are very vulnerable to global warming; even a small rise in sea temperature will cause them to bleach and die. At least 5 per cent of the coral in the Great Barrier Reef has already been destroyed in this way, and the fear is that the whole of this rich marine eco-system is at risk.

DID YOU KNOW?

Termites produce 20 million tonnes of methane every year – the gas is made in their gut by bacteria breaking down their food.

TOP 10 GREENHOUSE GAS PRODUCERS

United States
China
Russia
Japan
India
Germany
Britain
Canada
South Korea
Ukraine

? DID YOU KNOW? ?

America is responsible for nearly a quarter of the world's total CO_2 emissions.

What in the World Are We Doing?

There's now a broad consensus that climate change is a reality, but there's still no agreement on what to do about it. One of the most difficult issues is that those countries which will be worst affected, such as Bangladesh, are those least responsible for the problem.

Developing countries produce far less CO_2 than richer nations. On average, everyone in the world produces about one tonne of carbon per year; in the UK the average is more like 12 tonnes, and in America it's 25 tonnes.

Given that America is the biggest polluter, you might think it would be leading the way in sorting out the problem. This is far from the case. Whilst 141 countries signed the 2005 Kyoto Protocol, an international agreement on climate change, America wasn't one of them. Australia also opted out.

But it's China, with one-fifth of the world's population and a booming economy, which is probably the world's biggest worry. It creates a new coal-fired power station every two weeks and is currently second only to the US in terms of oil consumption and greenhouse gas production. It's already overtaken the US in the number of broadband subscribers and it looks like it won't be long before it becomes leader in the pollution stakes too.

There are no easy answers. But we can be absolutely certain that without commitment and support from us as individuals, nothing will happen on the political front – certainly nothing bold. Bizarrely, the solution to this huge global problem is in our hands. It's not a question of 'What are they going to do?' but 'What are we prepared to do?' And the stakes couldn't be much higher.

POLAR EXPLORER PEN HADOW ON CLIMATE CHANGE

According to *Geographical* magazine, Pen Hadow is one of the most accomplished polar adventurers of his day.

In May 2003 he became the first person to trek solo – without resupply – on one of the toughest routes to the North Geographic Pole. The 480-mile journey took 64 days and was a feat of extreme endurance. Not only did he have to haul a 20-stone (130kg) sledge, but he frequently swam through icy water – on one occasion he actually fell in without his protective clothing.

Hadow is energetic and always buzzing with ideas. He says his polar-exploring enthusiasm was inspired at an early age by sharing the same nanny as Peter Scott, the son of Scott of the Antarctic. He also had some fairly adventurous ancestors.

The Arctic has become Hadow's passion, and he's committed to raising public interest in its plight. 'US scientists', he says 'are now predicting that the Arctic Ocean could face its first summer without so much as an ice cube in just fifteen years from now.'

World attention, Hadow points out, has primarily been focused on what's happening in the Antarctic. Yet climate change impacts in the Arctic could be just as serious and happen in a far shorter time. I was horrified to learn that ice in the Arctic is less than 3 metres thick, whereas in Antarctica its average thickness is 2 kilometres, and up to 5 kilometres in places.

During his expeditions, Hadow had to swim, where not long ago he would have been able to walk on hard ice. He's only too aware that the Arctic ice is shrinking fast. Scientists say that 8 per cent is being lost every decade, which amounts to an area roughly twice the size of France since 1980.

And what makes this particularly worrying, Hadow explains, is the importance of snow and ice in reflecting solar energy away from the Earth's surface. Whereas snow will reflect as much as 85 per cent of the incoming solar energy, open ocean only reflects 15 per cent. So more heat is being absorbed and the seas are warming. This not only contributes to rising sea levels, as the warmer water expands, but it slows down the Gulf Stream in a complex series of interlinked reactions.

Increasingly, Hadow is becoming a spokesman on climate change issues. He says he wants to make people in Britain aware that a warming world doesn't just mean more T-shirt weather and sunbathing. He's concerned about what will happen in countries hit by severe drought or flooding and how we'll respond to massive displacement of people.

Having experienced extreme cold in a cross-country skiing expedition in Finland, I'm not tempted by the Arctic, but for those who want to see first hand what's happening, Hadow helps organise expeditions. Everyone going is given an information pack on climate change and will be encouraged to contribute towards the cost of carbon-offsetting the impacts of their travel (page 190).

I'm happy to leave the expeditions to Hadow. His message is that the impacts of climate change are serious and we need to act fast.

www.penhadow.co.uk

Cutting Carbon

Some people are prepared to take draconian measures to reduce their carbon emissions. I heard a leading campaigner declare that he and his wife would not be going to their son's wedding overseas as they'd made a commitment never to fly again. I suspect not many people will adopt such a strict approach to carbon rationing, but there are still many things we can do.

There's a compromise alternative to such drastic lifestyle changes: carbon offsets. The idea is to work out your carbon emissions for annual mileage in your car, for home heating, or even for a flight to Honolulu. Then you (or your company) pay enough money to an organisation to fund tree-planting or energy-efficient technologies to offset these carbon emissions.

Of course this isn't a perfect solution; it could be argued that the idea trades on people's guilt. My view is that as long as it's not used as an excuse to pollute more than before, I don't mind. The important thing is that something is being done.

The main carbon-offset organisations in the UK are as follows:

The C-Change Trust
www.thec-changetrust.com
Set up in 2006, it offers carbon offsets by planting trees in the UK for community benefit.

Carbon Clear
www.carbon-clear.com
Offers packages to offset emissions from your car, flights or home. The money is used to help subsistence farmers in Kenya, Uganda, Tanzania and India to reverse damage caused by deforestation, drought and famine.

The Carbon Neutral Company
www.carbonneutral.com
Formerly 'Future Forests', this is the best-established carbon-offset company in the UK. With support from bands such as Coldplay, it offers an impressive array of gifts, including carbon-free weddings and wind-up mobile phone chargers! And it invests in projects worldwide, such as tree-planting and renewable energy.

Climate Care
www.climatecare.org
Investments include simple technologies that improve people's lives and reduce environmental impacts in developing countries (www.practicalaction.org). The excellent website enables you to work out your own carbon profile.

CO_2 Balance
www.co2balance.com
Sells lots of products, including tree-planting for any kind of special event. Unlike other carbon-offset organisations, it owns the trees and the land on which they're planted.

Personal carbon trading

How good are you at managing money? Whatever the answer to that question, you might need to start keeping tabs on your carbon emissions too – essentially this means your contribution to global warming.

On average each of us produces about 10–12 tonnes of CO_2 a year in this country, around half of which relates to home energy and personal transport. An idea that's gathering pace is that everyone will be awarded a quota for the amount of carbon we're permitted to use. Carbon credits will be deducted each time we pay our household bills, fill up our car with fuel or book a holiday flight. Clearly some of us will run out pretty fast. That's where the trading part comes in. If you're a very high-energy user, you'll be able to buy carbon credits from low users.

The main benefit of a scheme of this sort is that there would be a massive increase in public awareness of the issue, leading to some pretty dramatic lifestyle changes. Just imagine having to choose between holidaying in the Bahamas and having central heating during the winter months. It would also provide a real incentive for innovative and creative energy-saving technologies and schemes.

This radical approach to carbon reduction is being considered seriously by the Government. I suspect there'll be huge opposition once people realise what it will mean for them – particularly the wealthier section of the population. But could it be that carbon trading is our best hope for living in a climate-friendly world?

CLIMATE CHANGE WEBLINKS

BBC Climate Change Excellent website forsimple explanation of all aspects of climate change.
www.bbc.co.uk/climate

Carbon Sense Raises awareness of carbon emissions through arts and drama in an initiative called 'We share the air'.
www.carbonsense.org.uk

Friends of the Earth (FoE) Campaigns on climate change issues.
www.foe.co.uk/campaigns/climate

Greenhouse Gas Online Information on greenhouse gases and scientific developments.
www.ghgonline.org

Greenpeace Highlights leading offenders and pushes for more Government action.
www.greenpeace.org.uk/climate

Intergovernmental Panel on Climate Change
Provides independent assessment of climate
change research and analysis. Set up by the
United Nations and the World Meteorological Office. **www.ipcc.ch**

Stop Climate Chaos Coalition of organisations,
including FoE, Greenpeace, RSPB and WWF,
campaigning for action on climate change.   **www.stopclimatechaos.org**

World Wide Fund for Nature (WWF)
Campaigns on climate change with a particular
focus on what businesses can do.   **www.panda.org**

ENERGY and WATER

Whilst demand for energy soars, the debate over where it's going to come from intensifies. The simple fact is that all energy comes at a cost, whether it's financial, social or environmental – normally it's all three.

Power Hungry

In the first 25 years of this century it's predicted that world electricity consumption will nearly double and demand for oil increase by around 60 per cent. That's assuming we continue more or less as we are. If everyone in developing countries used the same amount of energy as the average consumer in richer countries, global consumption would increase eightfold by 2050 and the consequences would be unthinkable.

To power today's world we are utterly dependent on coal, oil and gas. These fossil fuels were formed from the remains of prehistoric plants and animals that lived up to 300 million years ago. All this time they've been storing carbon below the Earth's surface – it has effectively been locked away – but since the Industrial Revolution we've been burning fossil fuels like crazy and releasing this carbon into the air on a huge scale. As a result, current levels of CO_2 in the atmosphere are higher than at any time in the past 650,000 years, and rising 200 times faster than they ever have before.

New coal-fired power stations are being built at a rate of more than one a week, mostly in developing countries. One problem is that many of these countries can't afford up-to-date technology that will reduce dirty emissions. And even the richer nations don't yet have facilities for storing CO_2, which would stop its contribution to global warming. In fact carbon storage is unlikely to be practical before 2015, and even then there's no certainty it'll make a big difference.

The irony is that there may be enough coal to last 200 years, but in using it we may no longer have a planet that's fit for human habitation. Oil, on the other hand, is running out. Some scientists believe that 2005 was a tipping point, when the world had consumed half of the available supply. Even if they haven't got the date exactly right, it's clear that production from oil fields is declining fast.

New sources are not only hard to find, they're also less productive and more environmentally destructive.

Gas is cleaner than either oil or coal; however, even gas exploration, whether at sea or on land, is not without its environmental impacts. And like the other fossil fuels, it's a finite resource.

Of even more concern at present is political tension over gas supply. With many of Europe's gas pipelines under the direct control of Russia, in the future this could well hold as much sway as a nuclear arsenal. And as we all know, the politics of oil has already proved to be explosive. Many people are absolutely certain that getting rid of Saddam Hussein would not have been such a priority if Iraq didn't have huge oil reserves.

Exploring alternatives to all fossil fuels – or non-renewables as they are also known – is becoming critical. The difficulty is that there are at least as many opinions on how it might be done as there are options.

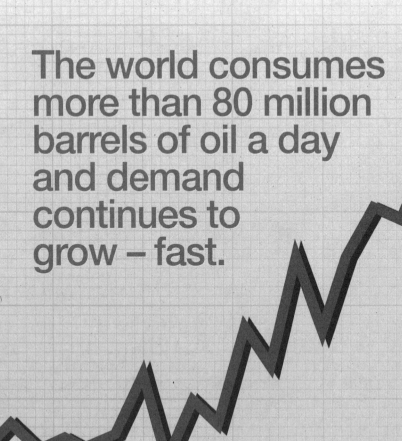

The world consumes more than 80 million barrels of oil a day and demand continues to grow – fast.

Going Nuclear

There's always been a wide divergence of opinion over nuclear power. The interesting thing about the debate today is that the argument is very different.

The key question now is whether nuclear power will be important in the fight against climate change. Certainly, nuclear reactors don't produce CO_2 when they're operating, and it's predicted that by investing in the nuclear option now, annual CO_2 emissions would be reduced by 8 per cent in 50 years' time. Proponents also argue that modern reactors are far safer than those built 20–30 years ago.

A few environmentalists have been persuaded by these arguments, but I'm not one of them. So why not?

First, there's the issue of waste. To dissolve all the 'high-level' nuclear waste produced up to the year 2000, you'd need more than twice the amount of water available on the entire planet. 'High-level' waste is a very small amount of the total waste, but it contains 95 per cent of the radioactivity. In other words, it's the really dangerous bit.

This waste is so hot that it has to be cooled over a 20–50-year period. It's unapproachable for centuries and highly toxic for millennia – so corrosive, in fact, that it has to be moved using robotic equipment, and transported in special flasks chained to trucks and railway carriages. Storage systems have to be utterly safe, yet there's still no proven safe method available for permanent disposal.

5 REASONS TO SAY 'NO' TO NUCLEAR

1 To date there is no long-term solution for storing highly radioactive waste.

2 New nuclear power stations would require a massive public subsidy.

3 There is little to stop other countries developing nuclear material if we do it in the UK.

4 We become locked into a centralised grid system, which is not efficient.

5 It reduces incentives for energy efficiency.

Sustainable Development Commission – 2006

y be unlikely, but how can we
y won't happen? The worrying
uclear material is that the reper-
hy problems are potentially
r more than a decade after the
Chernobyl nuclear accident in Russia, reindeer
in Scandinavia and sheep in Wales were still
judged to be unfit for human consumption.
Even though they were thousands of miles
away, their flesh stored the radioactivity they'd
picked up from eating plants that had been
contaminated by the explosion. And yet in this
case only a small fraction of the radioactive
waste actually escaped.

Terrorism is another threat. It's hard to see
how a determined attack could be prevented,
and the cost of guarding nuclear installations
is already enormous. Equally worrying is the
spread of knowledge about nuclear weapons
in politically unstable countries, an inevitable
consequence of adopting nuclear power. If
we're expanding our own facilities, it's difficult
to argue against others doing the same.

Investing in energy efficiency has the
potential to save far more CO_2 than throwing
billions at the nuclear option. One industry
expert summed it up: 'The brutal truth', he
said, 'is that no one has yet managed to
work out a way of getting nuclear reactors
to burn uranium as effectively as they burn
money.' He continued, 'Nor has anyone
discovered how to make atoms work for
peace without making them available for
war.' Yikes!

Sun, Wind and Waves

If we managed to harvest even one-
thousandth of the solar energy absorbed by
the Earth in just one year, it would be more
than enough to replace fossil fuels. Of course
that wouldn't be practical, but there's far more
potential for solar power than is being realised.

Solar panels on rooftops don't take up
much space, are easy to install and can be
set up in urban areas. The biggest problem is
that they're expensive. This is largely because
the solar industry is still too small to benefit
from economies of scale. However, since the
1970s prices have dropped by as much as
90 per cent as solar technology has become
more popular – further price reductions are
a certainty.

The UK may not be the best country in
which to use the power of the sun, but it does
top the European league in terms of its
suitability for wind power. Unfortunately,
this is not matched by the number of wind
turbines, nor by support for this clean, low-
impact technology.

Over the past few years wind power has
become something of a *cause célèbre* as
people line up on either side of the debate.
Some say they're a terrible blot on the
landscape and don't provide much power
anyway, whilst others are enthusiastic about
the sustainability of the whirling windmills and
want to see more of them. I fall into the
latter camp.

Whilst we haven't been making enough of
the sun and the wind, our support for wave
and tidal power has been pitiful. These technologies have enormous potential and yet
investment in them is about 15 years behind
that of wind power. It's estimated that marine
energy could provide as much as 20 per cent

of this country's electricity and be cost-competitive. But by 2020 it's forecast that only 3 per cent of our electricity will actually come from wave and tidal power.

The huge untapped energy from wave power is mostly offshore, and one of the real benefits is that it can be harvested with relatively little environmental impact. In fact the need to create no-go zones over relatively large areas, where the wave machines are sited, could actually benefit wildlife by creating sheltered habitats.

The advantage of tidal power is that, unlike the wind and waves, it's extremely predictable, which makes it easy to integrate with the existing power supply.

So the combination of wind, wave and tidal power could and should be a far bigger part of the energy solution than is currently pictured. If we are serious about combating climate change, we really need to force this onto the Government's priority list.

I think we should line our motorways with wind turbines!

MORE WIND OR LESS?

Is there enough wind?
There's plenty of wind in the UK for a lot more wind power than we use. It has been calculated that in Scotland, onshore wind farms alone could meet peak winter demand for electricity twice over.

Is the wind too patchy?
The variability of wind speed is less of a problem than is sometimes portrayed. Power companies should be able to make accurate predictions on high and low winds and change the energy mix accordingly.

Is wind power energy-effective?
It takes between three and ten months for a wind turbine to produce the electricity consumed during its lifecycle, from production and installation through to maintenance and decommissioning.

Is wind power too expensive?
By 2020 wind power will be the cheapest of all forms of power generation on its most efficient sites. And this doesn't even take account of the cost benefits of reducing carbon emissions. But electricity prices would increase fractionally if there were a large-scale switch to wind power.

Is wind power bad for birds?
Although there have been wind farms abroad where birds have been seriously affected, there is no evidence that this has happened in the UK.

Is wind power unsightly?
The visual intrusion of wind turbines, particularly in areas of outstanding natural beauty, is highly contentious. But improved efficiency of wind turbines means they can be sited in less prominent positions, which may appease a few opponents.

Are offshore wind farms better?
The problem with locating wind farms out at sea is that they're considerably more expensive than land-based farms. And you waste power in transporting electricity back to where it's needed.

The Future of Energy Is At Home

It's staggering that as much as 60 per cent of the heat produced by large-scale coal and gas power stations is wasted – it simply wafts into the atmosphere through the cooling towers. Yet more is lost distributing electricity around the country. And if you take account of what's then wasted in our homes it means we're using little more than one-fifth of the electricity produced.

That's why there's a rising crescendo of people calling for heat and power to be produced closer to where it's actually used. 'Decentralised energy' or 'microgeneration', as it's known, means lots of small energy-generating operations, including heating systems for small communities, wood-burning boilers, wind turbines, solar panels and heat pumps (see page 114) that extract heat from air, water or earth.

The advantages of decentralised energy are numerous: less waste for a start, but also more support for cleaner energy technologies, more jobs, more independence, and more interest in where and how our electricity is produced. People are far more likely to save energy if they're aware of where it comes from. And the cost of solar and wind power, for example, will come right down once they're produced on a large scale.

Another important factor is safety. Huge power stations or storage facilities have the potential to incur huge accidents. If you have lots of different systems spread all over the country, any accident will have a much smaller impact.

Rather than looking backwards at large and dirty power stations designed for the last century, we have to be bold and look forward to innovative and clean solutions that are also better value for money. But part of that innovation has to be in our approach to using energy more efficiently, thereby reducing demand.

Friends of the Earth asked, 'Why don't we pay power companies more money if they sell *less* power?' In one fell swoop this radical proposal would ensure that there wasn't a loft or cavity wall in the country that wasn't well insulated, a new house built that wasn't designed to be super-energy-efficient, and it would signal the end of energy-guzzling light bulbs.

Even a more moderate change to our electricity bills could make a difference. Have you ever noticed that you pay more for the first lot of units? Why isn't it the other way round: the more units you use, the more you pay for each one?

Whatever the incentive, we need to use less energy. There are lots of ways in which this can be done. Whether you're looking at production or use, I believe that the future of energy is at home, and this book gives you ideas on how to get started.

DECENTRALISED ENERGY IS CHEAPER

Even if you ignore the billions of pounds needed to deal with nuclear waste, decentralised energy would still be £1 billion cheaper.

Water World

Less than one-third of one per cent of the world's water is in lakes and rivers, and only a small fraction of that is readily accessible to us. Yet global water use per person has tripled since 1950, and people in wealthy countries use ten times more than people in poor countries.

Forty per cent of the world's population face serious water shortages, and vast numbers suffer from water-borne diseases, which on average kill one child every eight seconds. The impact of climate change on water supply is hard to predict, but with more storms, floods and droughts it's unlikely to reduce a problem that's already a growing cause of tension.

Even in Britain there are some stark choices to be made. Demand for water is exploding, particularly in the South East, where new water-hungry houses are sprouting like mushrooms. Rivers are being reduced to a trickle, underground water supplies are running out, reservoirs are drying up, and the more we consume the worse these problems get.

Whenever there's a hosepipe ban or water rationing of any kind, there's a public outcry about water leaks and debates over how to transport this precious resource from wetter parts of the country. 'Why don't we simply pipe it from Wales?' people suggest. Or use a tug to tow an enormous plastic bag of water from Scotland? But solutions like this are not practical and are extremely energy-intensive.

Water companies can't take full responsibility for the network of old pipes that are springing leaks – they can't replace them all at the same time. But I do think they should be far more proactive in getting all houses – certainly all new houses – to fit water meters. There's no doubt that if people are charged for what they use, they'll cut consumption. I wonder if the water companies really want us all to use less water – after all, they earn more money if we use more. Is this another case where we should pay the companies more if they sell less?

This is not just an issue for Government and the water industry. We all need to think more carefully about how much water we're using. There are lots of ways to save it – if you want some ideas, see page 74.

? DID YOU KNOW?

? One kWh of electricity is used for every cubic metre of water delivered and disposed of. This means that even running a cold bath will use the same amount of electricity as leaving a one-bar electric fire on for an hour.

WASTE and RECYCLING

WAYS TO CUT WASTE

✔ Avoid disposable products such as napkins, cutlery, plates, batteries, cameras, barbecues, etc.

✔ Reuse as much as you can: bottles, bags, clothes, wrapping paper, envelopes, string, etc.

✔ Use a shopping bag or basket and remember to take it with you.

✔ Complain to companies about over-packaged products.

✔ Drink tap water rather than bottled water.

✔ Plan meals ahead so you don't buy more food than you need which will just go bad.

✔ Learn how to repair your household appliances or find someone locally who can help.

✔ Don't be a slave to fashion and trends. Keep your mobile phone until it stops working.

✔ If you're thinking of buying something new, consider whether you really need it or how much you want it.

✔ Don't go mad with foil and cling film – use plastic or metal containers for storing or transporting food.

✔ Buy fruit and vegetables from a local box scheme – they generally use much less packaging than supermarkets.

✔ Send birthday and Christmas cards by email, or if you can't, make your own.

✔ Buy products made with recycled materials: loo paper, packaging, office paper, glassware and garden furniture.

✔ Stop junk mail by signing up to the Mailing Preference Service: **www.dmaconsumers.org**

✔ Don't buy more clothes than you need.

Waste Mountains

If everyone in the world created as much waste as the average person in the UK, we'd need eight worlds to support us. In fact every one of us throws away the equivalent of our own body weight in less than two months. Along with waste from industry, that's enough to fill the Albert Hall every two hours. And the amount we produce is growing and growing. So what happens to these mountains of waste?

Most of it goes into huge holes in the ground – landfill sites – but one problem is that we're running out of space for dumping our detritus. Another is that these giant pits can be polluting. In fact methane, producedfrom rotting waste, is about 24 times more powerful than CO_2 as a greenhouse gas. There are strict limits on the amount of leakage to air or water permitted, but it's still a problem.

In the Furnace

At the moment just under 10 per cent of our waste is burnt. This is controversial. Friends of the Earth and Greenpeace don't like it, even when it's used as a source of energy. They're concerned, not only about the toxic emissions, but also that large-scale incinerators act as a disincentive to reducing and recycling waste. And people living near proposed new incinerator sites seem to share these concerns.

It has always annoyed me that NIMBY (Not In My Back Yard) is used as a pejorative term. I think that if you're not concerned with what's going on in your back yard, what on earth *are* you concerned about? But I'm not totally against incineration in all circumstances, particularly if it's on a small scale. Recent research clearly shows that if energy is reclaimed, its environmental impact is almost always less than sending waste to landfill. On the other hand, there's a real worry

that the 'techno enthusiasts' see incineration as a quick and easy fix. And big incinerators are like huge, hungry monsters needing food 24 hours a day. If there are too many of them, it will certainly prevent innovative and creative solutions to reducing our waste mountains.

Wasteful Ways

There's a well-known mantra about waste. In order of priority we should: reduce, repair, reuse, recycle, and only then discard. But if we're going to produce less rubbish, we have to change our psyche. We think nothing of buying disposable cameras, barbecues, plastic cups, nappies and packaging of every kind. Everything comes in a disposable bag, very little is reused, and almost nothing is repaired.

It's easy to blame supermarkets and manufacturers for the problem. Quite rightly we ask why everything we buy is packaged in multiple layers and automatically put into a new plastic bags at the check-out; and why products seem designed to fall apart after we've used them only a few times. But how many people actually remember to take a basket or reusable bag when they head off to the shops?

We need to think about what we can do to reduce our own waste mountains. When you're sorting your waste for recycling – as I'm sure you do – why not start by seeing how much you could do without in the first place?

If you're very resourceful you might be able to get down to only one world of waste rather than eight.

Material World

There's an awful lot of rubbish talked about recycling – one horror story about recycled waste ending up in landfill sites goes a long way. But the fact is that recycling makes sense for almost all materials, most of the time.

Whether it's mining for metals, trees for paper or oil for plastics, extracting raw materials for new products can be seriously destructive: often there's many times more waste produced than useful products made. Equally, the manufacturing process uses huge amounts of energy, water and chemicals. The energy and material impacts of recycling are minimal in comparison. And that's before you consider the problem of where we're going to put all the waste we produce.

The UK has taken a long time to get going on the recycling front – even now we're way behind many of our European neighbours – but I know from my own experience that the introduction of doorstep collections of recycled waste has given it a real boost.

I've always been pretty good at recycling bottles, cans and newspapers, but since my recycling box has arrived I've been sorting more materials, including plastic bottles, tin foil, old clothes, cardboard and egg boxes. Anything not taken in the weekly collection gets deposited – at very irregular intervals – in the household recycling depot. (The egg boxes go to a friend with chickens.) The good thing is that I have very little rubbish left after that. Not so good is that there are still a number of things that it's not yet possible to recycle in my area: CFL light bulbs (page 106), batteries and carpets, for example.

Below I've outlined the pros and cons of the most common materials in our bins:

Glass

There's no limit to the number of times glass can be recycled. And recycling just one glass bottle will save enough energy to power all ten energy-efficient light bulbs in my kitchen for nearly an hour.

Well over one-third of all glass bottles are recycled in the UK, but shockingly the recycling rate is no higher for pubs, clubs and restaurants, where they're thrown away en masse. This is because there's some confusion over charging. It's actually illegal for the commercial sector to put bottles in bottle banks because they would be avoiding paying for their waste. This shouldn't be difficult to sort out.

Is there any point in sorting bottles into different colours?

Apparently it *is* worth doing because clear bottles fetch more money than coloured bottles. In the UK we make more things that come in clear glass containers, such as whisky and jam, but we throw away more green bottles from imported wine, for example. Some waste glass is used in road construction, insulation or water filtration. However, the environmental benefits of this aren't as good as making them into bottles again.

Should we be demanding more 'green bottles' made in England?

The main disadvantage of glass is that it's heavy, so in comparison with plastics it takes far more fuel to transport it around the country.

Metals

In the late 1980s we recycled only 2 per cent of cans; now it's nearer 50 per cent. But this still means that more than 10 billion are going to landfill. Recycling both aluminium and steel – which are used in cans – makes a lot of sense.

A new aluminium can takes 20 times more energy to make than a recycled one. In fact, if you recycle 1 tonne of aluminium, you save 6 tonnes of bauxite (the main component of aluminium), 4 tonnes of chemical products and enough electricity to keep an average UK family of four for nearly three years.

Most drinks cans are made from aluminium, whilst food cans are generally made from steel. On average each home gets through 600 of these every year. Recycling them saves 75 per cent of the energy used to make new cans and reduces air and water pollution by even more than that; they're made into new cans, bicycles and car parts.

One type of steel can I've always thought we could do without is the aerosol. Now I discover that 75 per cent of local authorities encourage recycling of aerosol containers – you can throw them in with drink and food cans. This addresses one of my concerns but doesn't make me any more enthusiastic about many of the products that come in aerosols – hair spray and air fresheners, for example. Nor does it get round the fact that aerosols produce about 4 per cent of the UK's VOC emissions (see glossary).

Don't forget that foil can be recycled too. Anything from milk bottle tops, baking and freezing trays and chocolate wrappers to kitchen and cigarette foil.

Paper and cardboard

Paper and cardboard account for about one-fifth of what's in our dustbins – and half of that is made up of newspapers and magazines. Every tonne recycled saves 30,000 litres of water and produces only 5 per cent of the air pollution compared to making it from scratch – and enough electricity to support an average UK family for a year.

There's also the benefit to forests. Contrary to popular belief, recycling paper doesn't directly save trees. In fact paper manufacturers often plant more trees than they cut down. The problem is that these trees will generally come from commercial plantations – rows and rows of conifers – which support very few plant and animal varieties. Even worse, they may actually be replacing old-growth forests, which support a rich, diverse ecosystem. So recycling paper may not save trees, but it could save forests!

We should certainly be doing whatever we can to increase the amount of paper and cardboard that is recycled. But we should also be sustaining the market for recycled end products. Make sure you buy recycled loo paper, notebooks and office paper. And kitchen towels or napkins should be recycled too.

Cartons for orange juice, milk or other fluids are made from a mix of paper, plastic and foil. They're recyclable, but up to now there have been very few collection points. Tetra Pak, one of the companies that make the cartons, is committed to changing this. In 2006 they appointed a recycling officer whose remit is to increase the number of local authorities which collect cartons to 100 per cent by 2008. They're also investing in facilities to convert the waste cartons into useful end products, such as plasterboard building material and furniture.

PLASTICS

The amount of plastics we use in the UK today is nearly as much as was used in the whole world in the 1950s, and it's increasing at an alarming rate. Currently just under 8 per cent of the world's oil is used to make and process these plastics, and only around 15 per cent of them are recycled.

Councils haven't been as enthusiastic about recycling plastic as they have about glass and paper – recycling targets are generally set by weight, and plastics are light. The other problem is that plastics need to be sorted into their different types for recycling. Surprisingly, this is sometimes done by hand, even though machine sorting is more common.

But recycling does reduce energy consumption by two-thirds, water use by 90 per cent, and CO_2 generation by two-and-a-half times. Even with those savings it's far better to reuse plastics, whether it's for shopping bags or bottles to put home-made lemonade in to.

Supermarkets are recognising this, with dramatic increases in their use of returnable plastic crates for transporting and displaying produce. Companies are still exploring the potential for biodegradable plastics. McDonald's, for example, is using them for plastic cutlery, so they can be thrown away and composted with food waste.

I was rather intrigued to discover that exporting plastic waste to China is not such an eco-crime as one might imagine. The amount exported every year nearly quadrupled over the four-year period to 2005, and it appears that China's explosive economic growth means they're prepared to pay good prices for recycled materials, which they use to make new products. The best thing is that these are transported in ships that would otherwise be empty, because they have delivered goods to the UK but have nothing to take back. The downside is that UK companies claim they can't get enough waste plastic to use recycled materials in their products.

SHOULD WE HATE PLASTIC BAGS?

We use 10 billion plastic bags in the UK every year – that's nearly 200 for every man, woman and child. Many people identify these as one of the biggest green offenders. Are they right?

You may be surprised to hear that I think plastic bags are a better eco-choice than paper bags. We all know that paper comes from a renewable resource – trees – and will biodegrade when thrown away, so why isn't it better?

A paper bag is about six times heavier than a plastic bag and takes up to ten times more space in a landfill site as the material is denser. And bag for bag it actually uses about the same amount of fossil fuels as a plastic bag in its manufacture.

Then there's the biodegradability issue. If something is 'biodegradable' it means it's broken down by bugs and bacteria over a period of time. Anything that rots also releases greenhouse gases – either CO_2 or, more problematic, methane. Landfill sites produce an awful lot of these gases, so much, in fact, that there's a European law restricting the amount of biodegradable waste they can take. This means they don't actually want more material that rots.

Biodegradable plastic

So what about biodegradable plastic bags? Contrary to popular belief, they're not such a good idea, either. At this point I have to explain that the world of decomposing bags is a complicated one.

The sort of bags that Tesco is now using are called 'degradable', meaning they break down via a chemical process rather than with help from bugs and micro-organisms. Like other plastic bags they're made from fossil fuels, but chemicals are then added that make the bags break up over time.

What's the point of making bags that rot if they're going to end up in landfill sites where they don't want rotting waste? If, on the other hand, these bags are used in compost, this does make sense – the bags may decompose along with the food and plant matter and will then become a useful soil conditioner.

Another type of 'degradable' bag breaks down in sunlight. This is a nonsense too. It means that the only way for it to work is to have the rubbish lying around in the open air, essentially as litter. It has to be an eyesore for quite some time before it disappears.

Then there are bags made from crops such as corn or potatoes: bioplastics. The manufacturers claim that their main benefit is that they use about one-third less energy to make. If that's true, it is an advantage, but I'm afraid it doesn't give them a clean, green bill of health. To make them even remotely cost-competitive, the crops they're made from have to be intensively farmed, which generally means lots of chemicals or the use of GM technology (page 42).

One advantage of ordinary plastic bags is that they are frequently reused – as bin liners, to take your kit to the gym, for picnics or other everyday chores. They can also be recycled – although not enough of them are. The real solution to the plastic bag problem is to use fewer of them. If you take one, use it again. When it's worn out, recycle it. But don't be tempted to go for alternatives – they're not as good as they seem.

Food and garden waste

If you live in a high-rise block, it's unlikely that you'll be sorting your waste for composting any time soon. For everyone else there may be no option: waste authorities (unfortunately not all of them yet) are being forced to separate food and other biodegradable waste for industrial composting, as there are strict limits on how much can go to landfill.

This is actually rather a good thing. For householders who either haven't got the space or don't feel inclined to make their own compost, it's another recycling option.

And what's more, food waste collectors will accept meat and cooked food, which home composters generally don't welcome in case it attracts rats and other vermin. If, on the other hand, you have a wormery (page 123), the worms relish being given a bit of meat and fish.

We waste about 6 million tonnes of food a year: it makes up about one-third of our rubbish bins. This amounts to 250kg of food waste for each of us – 5kg a week. But for many people it will be substantially more than this. And the catering industry is even worse – they apparently chuck out a little short of half of the food they buy!

Once collected, food waste is taken to a centralised composting facility and shredded. It can then be mixed with green or garden waste and put into a sort of enclosed tunnel. In these controlled conditions it takes less than ten days to decompose enough to be spread outside in what are called windrows. The final 'green waste compost' is then sold to gardeners and farmers, in some cases replacing peat or agro-chemicals.

A WASTED FUEL

In the UK we're missing a trick. Composting food waste is not only a benign way of dealing with what we throw away, it recycles nutrients back to the land. But it could also be used on a far bigger scale for generating electricity and as a vehicle fuel.

Rotting food material produces methane and CO_2, which are known as biogases. As we know, CO_2 is the main greenhouse gas and methane is about 24 times more powerful in its global warming impact, once it's released to the atmosphere. However, if it's used for energy, the methane is converted to CO_2, so its global warming impact actually reduces. The most effective way to produce and collect methane is in anaerobic digesters. They might sound complicated and technical, but they're nothing more than closed compost heaps that don't allow air in. The brilliant thing about these systems is that they stop methane escaping, produce a fuel, and none of the nutrients in the food waste is lost in the process – it can be spread back on the land as fertiliser.

Imagine how much food is thrown away by supermarkets. This could be converted to methane at the back of the store and the fuel used for heating, lighting and vehicles. Food and garden waste from homes could also be converted to fuel. In fact this is already being done in the UK, but there are only a few plants in existence. We should be asking why on earth there aren't more.

This is the sort of imaginative solution to our waste mountains that we need. If you feel inclined to campaign, it's an issue to get your teeth into: lobby your local council, your waste authority, your supermarket or even your MP!

WASTE and RECYCLING WEBLINKS

Aluminium Packaging Recycling Association
Promotes aluminium recycling.
www.alupro.org.uk

British Glass Provides information on glass
and recycling.
www.britglass.co.uk

British Metals Recycling Association
Promotes metal recycling.
www.recyclemetals.org

Centre for Alternative Technology
Provides information on waste and recycling.
www.cat.org.uk

Freecycle If you want to give something away
or find something for free.
www.freecycle.org

Furniture Reuse Network Helps find your
nearest centre for recycling furniture.
www.frn.org.uk

Key Mood UK Recycles CDs, VHS tapes
and other electronic waste.
www.keymood.co.uk

Let's Recycle Provides information on glass
collectors, recyclers and processors.
www.letsrecycle.com

National Household Hazardous Waste Forum
Advises on the disposal of hazardous wastes,
including garden chemicals, paints and oil.
www.nhhwf.org.uk

Oil Care Campaign Enables you to find the
nearest waste oil bank by entering your post code. www.oilbankline.org.uk

Oxfam Makes money by recycling or reselling
a range of items, including mobile phones
and clothes. Clothes are not shipped to
developing countries but sold in their shops,
and must be in good condition.
www.oxfam.org.uk

PlasCan Ltd Sells plastic bottle and can
crushers made from recycled plastic.
www.plascancrusher.com

Prism Project Supplies second-hand books
to prisons.
www.prismproject.co.uk

Rag and Bone Provides a forum for giving things away that are too good to be simply thrown away.

www.rag-and-bone.co.uk

Recoup Industry body promoting plastics recycling.

www.recoup.org

Recovinyl Encourages recycling of PVC, including PVC windows.

www.recovinyl.com

Recycled Products Lists products that are made from recycled materials and the companies that make them.

www.recycledproducts.org.uk

Recycle More One-stop shop for information on recycling.

www.recycle-more.co.uk

Recyclingglass.co.uk Provides educational material on glass recycling.

www.recyclingglass.co.uk

Reuze.co.uk Excellent information source on waste recycling, including links to your local council recycling initiatives.

www.reuze.co.uk

Re-cycle Collects second-hand bicycles and parts and sends them to developing countries

www.re-cycle.org

Saveacup Collects plastic vending cups for recycling.

www.saveacup.co.uk

Steel Can Recycling Information Bureau Promotes can recycling.

www.scrib.org

Tetra Pak Makes cartons and promotes recycling.   www.tetrapakrecycling.co.uk

Waste Online Provides information on waste and recycling.

www.wasteonline.org.uk

Wastewatch Promotes and encourages waste reduction, reuse and recycling.

www.wastewatch.org.uk

Worktwice Arranges collection and recycling of waste electronics, paper and plastic for businesses.

www.worktwice.co.uk

LAND and SEA

Countryside and Farming
Changing times

For most of us the patchwork of fields and hedgerows that covered rural Britain in Victorian times represents an idyll. But the flip side of those times was the back-breaking toil of farm workers and low productivity. In today's industrialised world we produce more food than we can eat. However, miles of hedgerows have been ripped out and wildlife decimated as modern farming techniques require enormous fields to accommodate huge tractors and other agricultural machines.

Traditional farming was based on a rotation of crops, including grass, and on maintaining fertile and productive soil.

Now there's a far narrower range of crops planted, and in some cases just one single repeated crop, with frequent applications of pesticides. Soil nutrition is also deteriorating because man-made fertilisers don't fully replenish the nutrients and trace minerals removed at harvest time.

Dramatic changes have not just affected crop growing. Farm animals are treated like widgets on a factory production line, referred to as 'protein' and measured in terms of volume per square foot.

And rather than their manure being thought of as a highly desirable fertiliser for the fields, the huge lakes of concentrated slurry and mountains of chicken droppings produced are often considered to be a waste management problem requiring treatment and disposal.

The effects of this radical change in approach to our land and countryside have been considerable. Most strikingly, the cost of food, relating to the amount we earn, has plummeted.

Genetic modification (GM)

One techno fix can often lead to another. Modern pesticides have been very effective at killing off crop predators and increasing yields, but in many countries workers have been badly affected by chemical poisoning, for example on banana plantations. And blanket applications of pesticides also result in the killing off of beneficial insects – as well as pests – and pollution.

Genetic modification (GM) can be used as an alternative to spraying food crops with large doses of toxic chemicals that inevitably leave residues in food. Instead, crop genes are altered to resist attack from pests. There are many who are convinced that this will lead to a huge reduction in the use of chemicals and see it as a very positive environmental solution.

GM can also offer other amazing innovations: plants that glow when they need watering, Vitamin D-enriched rice, longer-lasting tomatoes, leaner pigs and super-growing salmon. But it has become clear that this surprising 'goody bag' could also be a Pandora's Box, releasing a host of new problems.

One of the first mainstream uses of GM was in designing crops to resist a *pesticide* rather than a *pest*. Monsanto created what they called 'Roundup Ready Soya'. It was genetically altered so that it could be heavily sprayed with Monsanto's brand of pesticide with no damage to the crop. The first batch of GM soya ingredients reached our supermarket shelves – and an unsuspecting public – in 1997, and has to be one of the best examples of how *not* to introduce a new technology. Once the alarm bell had been sounded there was a public outcry.

The initial response from the GM industry was that the GM soya was no different to its non-GM counterpart, and that it would be impossible to separate it out because it was all part of one huge commodity market. It was fascinating to see how this 'impossibility' was sorted once supermarkets woke up to the fact that consumers didn't want to buy 'GM foods' in any shape or form.

Even today British supermarkets are holding out against the GM tidal wave, both in our food and in animal feed. But with global business and governments piling on the pressure, there's no certainty that GM foods will continue to be kept at bay.

GM ISSUES

Health

There are widespread concerns about the potential for GM foods to cause health problems in humans. This is a highly controversial issue. On the one hand the GM industry says there's no proof of any problem; on the other hand opponents say there hasn't been enough research and that we're all being treated like guinea pigs in a vast GM experiment.

World hunger

It's unlikely that GM technology will help alleviate world hunger, if only because that isn't going to be the priority for companies wishing to profit from their inventions. In reality it will enable rich countries to grow crops that they would previously have imported from developing countries, so it may make the problem worse.

Environment

By creating plants that could survive different climates and soil types, GM could threaten local plant varieties, helping to create global monocultures. There is also concern that plants resistant to weedkiller may become 'super-weeds', impossible to eradicate with any known treatment.

Organic threat

Planting GM crops in open fields means they could cross-pollinate with non-GM crops. For organic producers this could jeopardise their accreditation because organic criteria specify that crops should be non-GM.

Chemicals

Some GM crops need fewer herbicides: for example, there have been dramatic reductions in chemicals used to protect cotton crops. But pesticide-resistant crops may actually result in more chemical spraying.

Efficiency

GM can improve efficiency, so you get more product from less raw material – for example, more tomato purée from fewer tomatoes. And by increasing crop yields on a given acreage of land, GM technology may lower the cost of productivity and result in lower food costs.

Enzymes

GM technology is frequently used to produce enzymes used in food and other products. Some opponents are not so worried about this application because it is carried out in laboratory conditions, which means that no altered genes are released into the environment.

Choice

One of the most worrying aspects of GM technology is how entrenched it has become in world agriculture, despite massive opposition from campaigning organisations and the public. Wherever you live in the world, it appears that it's only a matter of time before GM foods will be unavoidable. We may be able to slow the process down, but it's unlikely that consumer choice will be able to stop this particular train.

ORGANIC IS:
- **less environmentally damaging**
- **less chemicals**
- **less pesticides**
- **less antibiotics**

- **more healthy**
- **more disease-resistant**
- **more wildlife**
- **more animal welfare**
- **more soil fertility**

And no GM.

Organic response

Organic farming may have been around for over 10,000 years, but don't be fooled into thinking that organic enthusiasts are just harking back to the old days. Even in the last ten years there has been a significant change in what it means to be organic. In fact I would argue that this gold-standard system of agriculture is a supremely modern approach to farming.

The basic principle is to preserve soil fertility. Essentially this means farming for the future. There's an old saying that goes, 'Live as if you are going to die tomorrow, but farm as if you will live for ever': this sentiment is pertinent to the debate about the merits of organic systems. It's also central to the challenge of whether organic farming could ever provide enough food for all.

Modern intensive farming practices result in huge quantities of soil being blown away in the wind or washed out to sea, leaving the remainder lacking in vital minerals. In the long term this is unlikely to be more productive than sustainable agriculture, which is spearheaded by the organic movement.

So what do organic farmers actually do differently? Most widely understood is the fact that they use fewer chemicals – both pesticides and fertilisers. It's important to point out, though, that there are a very few chemicals that are permitted – about six ingredients as opposed to 450 for conventional agriculture.

Animal welfare is another differentiating factor. Organically reared animals must be free-range, and there are strict limits on the number of animals permitted on a given area of land. These standards are important to prevent disease, in order to avoid treatment. However, if an animal does fall ill, antibiotics can be used. This is in contrast to mainstream farming, where antibiotics are sometimes given to a whole herd or flock on a daily basis to prevent, as well as treat, disease. They are also used as growth promoters, although this practice is now restricted in Europe.

Wildlife can also benefit from organic practices. Over the last 50 years intensive farming is thought to have been responsible for the decline in birds, butterflies and bees. But many of the species affected are actually valued by organic farmers, for example as predators for pests. Maintaining hedgerows, creating open spaces at the sides of fields, planting a number of different crops close to each other, crop rotation and minimising chemicals all help wildlife revival.

Perhaps the most popular reason for buying organic produce is that people think it is a healthier option. There's little doubt that this has been the driver behind the explosion in organic baby food, which now accounts for over half of that market.

If you're worried about pesticide residues in fruit and vegetables, it certainly makes sense to buy organic, as they'll be non-existent or minimal. There's also a growing body of evidence suggesting that organic produce is more nutritious, with higher levels of vitamin C and trace minerals such as potassium, iron, magnesium and zinc.

Whatever the reason, sales of organic produce rise year after year, even though organic food generally costs more. The annual growth in 2005 was over 30 per cent, in contrast to growth for all UK food and drink of around 3 per cent. What's particularly interesting is that most of the increased demand is coming through farmers' markets and local delivery services. People are not only interested in buying organic, they also want to buy local.

Seeing is believing

The trend for both organic and locally sourced food reflects a growing desire to know where our food comes from and how it's produced. It's recognised that good farming practices not only benefit the environment but also produce good-quality food ingredients. What's more, local food will usually require less energy to transport and bring greater benefits to the local community.

There's even a desire to know more about food that has to be imported, such as tea, coffee, bananas and grapefruit. Consumers want transparency in the food chain, so that we know where produce is grown, whether workers are treated fairly, and what sort of chemicals have been used. Most importantly, we're also keen to know that our supermarket choices are not leading to the destruction of precious habitats and species extinction.

Bizarrely, the overriding message is that cheap food costs more. This means there's less money for conservation and environmental preservation, and pressure is put on farmers to cut corners and introduce shoddy practices. Ultimately we have to pay, not only to subsidise farmers who don't get enough money for what they produce, but also to clean up after them, both in terms of pollution and for disasters such as BSE and foot-and-mouth disease. So the real cost of unsustainable farming practices could actually be much more than you think.

FARMING and COUNTRYSIDE WEBLINKS

Compassion in World Farming
Campaigns for better standards and happier
lives for farm animals.   **www.ciwf.org.uk**

**Council for the Protection of Rural
England (CPRE)** Campaigns to protect
England's countryside and for sustainable
land use.   **www.cpre.org.uk**

Elm Farm Research Centre Supports
sustainable land use and food systems building
on organic principles.   **www.efrc.com**

Friends of the Earth (FoE) Campaigns
against GM and to safeguard food and
sustainable farming practices.   **ww.foe.co.uk**

GeneWatch Monitors GM technologies and
their environmental and social impacts.   **www.genewatch.org**

Greenpeace Campaigns to prevent the
release of GM crops into the environment and
for sustainable farming.   **www.greenpeace.org.uk**

Linking Environment and Farming (LEAF)
Promotes more sustainable farming practices
that are less stringent than organic
production systems.   **www.leafuk.org**

Natural England Replaced English Nature,
the Countryside Agency and parts of the Rural
Development Service, with the objective of
protecting and promoting England's natural
environment.   **www.naturalengland.co.uk**

Organic Farmers and Growers Organic
certification body.   **www.organicfarmers.uk.com**

Organic Food Online organic magazine.   **www.organicfood.co.uk**

Pesticide Action Network Working to
eliminate the dangers of toxic pesticides.   **www.pan-uk.org**

Royal Society for the Prevention of Cruelty to Animals (RSPCA) Campaigns for good animal welfare practices. www.rspca.org.uk

Royal Society for the Protection of Birds (RSPB) Promotes and protects birds and their habitats in Britain and campaigns for wildlife-friendly farming practices. www.rspb.org.uk

Red Tractor British farm assurance scheme. www.redtractor.org.uk

Soil Association Leading organic standards body in the UK, which also campaigns for more sustainable farming. www.soilassociation.org

Sustain Campaigns for better food and farming. www.sustainweb.org

World Wide Fund for Nature Raises awareness of the environmental impacts of food and farming. www.wwf.org.uk

Forests
Forest bounty

If you've ever looked over a view of trees stretching into the distance – to the horizon and beyond – you probably won't need persuading that forests are worth preserving. But forests are not only beautiful, they also play a vital role in sustaining life on Earth. They're home to around two-thirds of the world's land-based plants and animals – in fact rainforests, which cover about 6 per cent of the Earth's surface, house more different animal and plant species than any other place.

The astounding thing is that many of these species are still unknown to man, and only about 1 per cent have been researched in any detail. Despite this, over 2,000 tropical forest plants have been identified as having anti-cancer properties and many others also have valuable medicinal qualities. A huge number of everyday products originate in forest areas, from bananas and peanuts to rubber and rope.

Forests play a vital role in the fight against climate change: they're vast repositories of carbon, which is locked in the trees and soil. And even mature forests absorb more carbon dioxide than they release, at the same time producing oxygen, which is why they're sometimes referred to as 'the lungs of the world'.

Destruction

Having been to many rainforest areas, I find it almost inconceivable that so much has already been destroyed – about half of what existed in 1800. And this destruction continues – indeed in many areas it's actually increasing. We're currently losing natural forests at a rate of 30 hectares every minute – or the whole of Hyde Park every five minutes. This devastation means that on average 50 species of animal are wiped out every day.

Despite world awareness of the plight of the forests, there's still a vast trade in wood and paper coming from illegally logged areas. In fact recent research revealed that nearly 10 per cent of UK wood imports came from illegal sources. Perhaps even more insane is the fact that so much forest is cleared by burning, which means the trees aren't even being used. This isn't just catastrophically wasteful; the practice makes a significant contribution to global warming by releasing CO_2 into the atmosphere.

Forest land is frequently cleared for farming. Whether this is for small-scale subsistence agriculture, huge palm oil plantations or vast tracts of grassland used for rearing cattle, it remains a major contributor to forest destruction. The oil and mining industries can also have devastating consequences for forests. As developers move in, they build long stretches of road right through areas of pristine forest. Within a short space of time the tentacles of development have spread from the road deep into the forest, obliterating the once thriving ecosystem of plants and animals.

The forest is home not only to millions of animals, plants, birds and insects, but also to indigenous human populations. Over thousands of years many of these people have had little impact on their environment. Yet they too have become victims of its demise. At the beginning of the sixteenth century there were around 6 million native people living in Brazilian Amazonia; by 2000 there were fewer than a quarter of a million left.

Before looking at what we can do to save the forests, I'm going to tell you more about arguably the two most destructive crops on the planet: palm oil and soy.

? DID YOU KNOW? ?

Brazil is the world's fourth largest climate polluter and 75 per cent of its greenhouse gas emissions result from deforestation.

PALMED OFF

Most of us wouldn't recognise the plum-sized fruit of a palm oil tree. Yet palm oil from this fruit is in a huge range of products found on supermarket shelves and beyond. It's in lipstick, chocolate, chips and ice-cream, as well as frying oil, soaps and shampoos; it's even used by the metal and leather industries. And worryingly it's being developed as a major fuel replacement for diesel (pages 183 and 187), which could turn an already giant industry into a monster.

Oil palms originated in central Africa, where they're still grown by millions of small-scale farmers, primarily for domestic cooking oil. But nowadays the bulk of this commodity crop comes from vast plantations in Asia – chiefly Malaysia and Indonesia. The tragedy is that many of these single-crop plantations are on land that was previously home to orang-utans, tigers, exotic butterflies and elephants. As the forest cover shrinks, palm oil acreage has more than doubled in the last eight years and demand is still growing.

So should we boycott all products containing palm oil? It's tempting to think this might help even a little bit. Unfortunately, it's not that simple. If we boycotted palm oil, companies would use other oils, such as soya, which are also causing rainforest destruction. Furthermore, we have to accept that with so many small players in this industry, our boycotts might have no more impact than an ant biting a rhinoceros.

Campaigning organisations in the UK have decided our best approach is to promote and support initiatives that are working with all the companies in the palm oil supply chain, to encourage more sustainable practices. Talks have been taking place over the last couple of years and progress is being made. From the outsider's viewpoint, it seems to be unbearably slow, because there are so many players and so many competing interests – and also, at present, pressure from consumers is almost non-existent. We need to encourage supermarkets, manufacturers and other companies to sell only sustainably produced palm oil.

Eating soya

Work is also going on to develop criteria for more responsible soya production. The Swiss Co-op took a lead in showing how this might be done by getting two large Brazilian companies to commit to growing soya in accordance with sustainability criteria.

But like palm oil, demand for soya is exploding: it has doubled in the last 20 years and is expected to increase at a similar rate to 2020 and beyond. South America is where most of this growth is happening, in the Cerrado, the Atlantic Forest and the Amazon Basin, all areas with species-rich ecosystems.

In part, soya is in such demand because it's used in so many processed foods. But an overwhelming 85% of soya grown is used for animal feed for chickens, pigs and cows. According to Swiss figures, we need an area roughly the size of a tennis court per person per year to grow the soya used in the animal feed to supply each one of us with meat, eggs and milk.

WHAT CAN BE DONE?

It's not just the tropical rainforests that would benefit from sustainable forestry practices. In fact the main certification body, the Forest Stewardship Council (FSC), has developed international standards for the production of wood and paper.

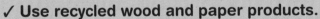

Here are three ways to help forests:

✓ Use recycled wood and paper products.
✓ Only buy new wood or virgin paper that is certified, for example by the FSC.
✓ Ask manufacturers and retailers what they are doing to ensure the use of sustainable palm oil and soya in the products they sell.

There are also more detailed suggestions later in the book in the sections covering wood, paper, biofuels, meat and cosmetics.

FOREST WEBLINKS

Ape Alliance Protects apes, including orang-utans, which are under threat from palm oil plantations.

www.4apes.com

Forest Stewardship Council (FSC) Promotes responsible management of the world's forests and runs a certification scheme to reward good practice.

www.fsc.org

Forestry Commission Protects and promotes Britain's forests and woodlands to increase their value to society and the environment.

www.forestry.gov.uk

Friends of the Earth (FoE) Campaigns on rainforest and biodiversity issues.

www.foe.co.uk

Greenpeace Produced a 2006 report entitled 'We're Trashin' It – How McDonald's is Eating Up the Amazon', to illustrate the threat of soya growing on the Amazon rainforest.

www.greenpeace.org.uk

Living Rainforest Charity and visitor centre educating people about rainforests' eco-systems and sustainability issues.

www.livingrainforest.org

Rainforest Foundation Supports indigenous people from rainforest areas in the fight to protect their environment.

www.rainforestfoundationuk.org

World Wide Fund for Nature (WWF) Campaigns on rainforest issues, working on the impacts of soya and palm oil.

www.wwf.org.uk

Seas and Oceans

If the wind was blowing, rain was in the air and a storm was brewing, my father would say, 'Let's go to the sea.' We'd pack a picnic, coats and hats and pile into the car so we could witness the waves crashing against the rocks and the spray spurting into the air. I also remember crabbing and collecting periwinkles, which we'd cook and prise out of their shells with hairpins.

Almost everyone has memories of seaside expeditions. Apparently 80 per cent of tourism is by the sea, and 60 per cent of the world's population live within 60km of it. Yet the oceans are not only a source of entertainment, they also provide food, transport, minerals and oil; they contain 97 per cent of the water on our planet and 90 per cent of its biomass – they're rich in marine life.

I've already outlined some of the threats of climate change to seas and oceans: rising sea levels, slowing of the Gulf Stream and the threat to coral reefs. Plankton too play a vital role in absorbing as much as 30 per cent of CO_2 that's released into the atmosphere, but the excess is overloading the oceans' capacity to absorb it, making them more acidic and killing off the plankton. We're also having more direct impacts on our seas and oceans through pollution and over-fishing.

Flotsam/Jetsam

Not long ago I saw a film about flip-flops being caught up in the flotsam and jetsam off the coast of East Africa. It was staggering how many were being carried in by the tide and left strewn on the beaches. Some resourceful souls actually collected them for recycling and making into new flip-flops, fencing or other useful products.

Apparently the world produces about 100 million tonnes of plastic every year, and 10 per cent of that ends up in the sea – mostly from land sources rather than shipping. Apart from being visually intrusive, this plastic can be fatal for wildlife. It's estimated that over a million sea birds and about 100,000 marine mammals and sea turtles are killed each year by either swallowing plastic or getting snared by it.

I was intrigued to discover that some areas in the ocean attract floating debris in a vast, slowly rotating vortex of water like a whirlpool. They're called 'gyres' and there's one in the North Pacific that is equivalent to the size of Texas. It's thought to contain 6kg of plastic for every kilo of plankton – presumably more is being added all the time.

Sea dump

Plastics and other rubbish are not the only things dumped at sea. All over the world there are still huge amounts of untreated sewage flowing into the ocean, for example 80 per cent of the sewage discharged into the Mediterranean Sea. Along with fertiliser run-off from farmland, the sewage feeds extra nutrients into the water, resulting in algal blooms, which in turn suck up oxygen and suffocate other marine life.

Another marine killer is oil pollution, the price we pay for shipping millions of gallons of oil across the oceans. The impact of large spills can still be identified decades after the event, and there are surprisingly few effective

measures that can be taken once the spill has happened. Almost worse, in my view, is that lots of ships still clean out their oil tanks with sea water, causing mini slicks on a regular basis. This is wilful pollution rather than the result of an accident.

Toxic shock

Until the 1970s it was accepted waste-disposal practice to dump nearly everything into the sea, including pesticides, chemical weapons, and even radioactive waste. Now we're paying the price. Many chemicals not only stay, they actually accumulate in the body fat of marine life – and of those that eat it. So tiny animals at the bottom of the food chain absorb the chemicals, which then become millions or even billions of times more concentrated when they reach the top of the food chain, in polar bears for example.

Guess who else is at the top of the food chain? The answer is all of us. That's why there's concern about the levels of toxins such as polychlorinated biphenyls (PCBs) and dioxins found in oily fish (page 152).

The shocking fact is that almost all marine life, from whelks to walruses, has been contaminated by these man-made chemicals. And there are still people treating the seas and oceans of the world as if they have an infinite capacity to absorb and disperse our waste.

Fish frenzy

In 1950 18 million tonnes of fish were hauled out of the sea – today it's more like 100 million tonnes. Not only that, but the fish we catch are smaller and younger than they were 50 years ago, which means that fewer of them are able to reach breeding age and so numbers are further depleted.

You only need to look at what's happened to cod over the last 30 years to realise the precarious state of fish stocks. In this time global catches have reduced from over 3 million tonnes to less than 1 million tonnes today. After years of over-fishing and ignoring warning signs, the world's richest cod fishery, in Newfoundland, collapsed in 1992. Between 30,000 and 40,000 people lost their jobs overnight and cod populations have still not recovered over a decade later. North Sea stocks are similarly threatened: WWF estimates that the total volume of cod remaining there would fit into a single North Sea car ferry.

Techno terror

Part of the problem is that fishing has evolved from being something of a gamble, with man pitting his wits against the fish, the weather and the tides, to a highly industrialised and mechanised process. Huge trawlers literally scrape the bottom of the ocean floor, leaving virtual marine deserts behind. Nets large enough to hold 12 large passenger planes are hauled behind boats; lines with tens of thousands of hooks are baited and towed; and for valuable fish that are hard to find, like bluefin tuna, spotter planes are used to direct the fishermen to their target.

One of the worst aspects of fishing on this sort of scale is the waste. Along with what's caught for eating, millions of other fish and marine life are caught in the fray. Known as non-target species or by-catch, some are simply thrown back into the water, whilst others may be turned into fish oil or fish meal, perhaps used in animal feed. Very few live to see another day.

And it's not just fish that become by-catch. Over 300,000 small whales, dolphins and porpoises die from entanglement in fishing nets each year. More than 250,000 endangered loggerhead and leatherback turtles are caught on long fishing lines (known as long lines), and over 300,000 sea birds are similarly killed – the albatross is just one of the species threatened with extinction as a result.

Boats towing nets behind them is bad enough, but drift nets, or 'ghost nets' as they became known, are literally left to float in the waves, snaring and killing millions of fish. They used to stretch up to 50km but thankfully now they're restricted to 2.5km, and are completely banned in EU waters. Greenpeace actually go looking for lost nets so they can pull the deadly mesh out of the water.

Black fish

You'd think that governments would be tackling such an important problem. Of course they're talking about it, but the reality is they're not doing nearly enough. In fact in some cases they're actually making the problem worse. For example, in the EU, at the same time as introducing fishing quotas, some countries are subsidising the building of *more* fishing boats instead of investing money to protect fish stocks and provide alternative employment for fishermen.

There's also an issue with fishing agreements between different countries. It appears that some developing countries are being exploited, as they're paid minimal fees for over-fishing in their waters, leaving very poor pickings for local fishing fleets.

Another wheeze is what are called 'flags of convenience'. Modern-day pirates exploit the 'laws of the high seas', which require them to abide by the law of the country in which the boat is registered. For example, some will adopt the flag of Togo, Belize or Mauritania, who may not have signed up to international fishing agreements, so they can plunder the oceans with impunity. It's estimated that there are 1,300 fishing vessels of a significant size flying flags of convenience, and they seem to have little problem selling their fish onto consumer markets. Governments should not let this happen.

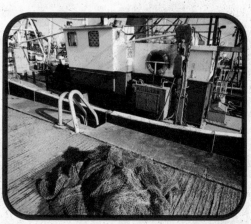

Sea future

Oceans cover 70 per cent of the world's surface and we need to do a lot more to protect them. Environmental campaigners point out that whilst 13 per cent of land has protected status, this applies to less than 1 per cent of water. In the UK, the only protected sea area is a three-mile stretch around Lundy Island in the Bristol Channel.

The idea of marine reserves is to designate large sea areas where marine life is protected. Approaches to this vary from merely banning commercial fishing or mining, to denying access even to tourists. In many cases these no-go zones have given fish stocks vital breathing space and enabled them to recover to previous levels.

Consumers should support marine reserves, push for better pollution controls, and make it clear to the Government that we want to clamp down on over-fishing. We also need to look at our own fish-eating habits (pages 152-161).

SEAS and OCEANS WEBLINKS

Greenpeace Runs the Defending Oceans campaign on a wide range of marine issues.	**www.greenpeace.org.uk/oceans**
Marine Conservation Society (MCS) Protects UK seas, shores and wildlife.	**www.mcsuk.org**
Marine Stewardship council (MSC) Encourages sustainable fishing practices through accreditation and labelling of fish	**www.msc.org**
World Wide Fund for Nature Campaigns against over-fishing, pollution and destruction of ocean habitats and wildlife.	**www.wwf.org.uk**

② Home and Garden

You might imagine that it's easier to be 'green' if you live in the countryside. Actually, I think the reverse is true. The main advantage for urban dwellers is that their homes are often smaller and better insulated than country homes, which means less heat and electricity is used. When I moved out of my London flat in 1994, the old house I rented in Somerset had leaky windows, wind howling under the doors and radiators hidden behind thick curtains. Keeping warm was a real challenge.

A couple of years ago I bought a family home, also in Somerset. Having taken out a huge mortgage I couldn't spend too much on environmental improvements but was really excited by the idea of an eco-renovation. Perhaps even more of a constraint was the issue of time. I had two months in which to get most of the work done. This involved knocking down a couple of walls, pulling out carpets, stripping paper, plastering over Artex, rewiring, replumbing and redecorating throughout.

Apart from lining up a good team of workmen, I had to make some important environmental choices. And I have to admit that I didn't always get it right; if I'd had this book to hand I'd have done a better job. But it's not the end of the road – there are still some things I'm planning to do.

This section is not just about DIY and decorating, it's also about green living: which cleaning products to use; how to save water and energy; what sort of washing machine or fridge to buy; how to recycle your television, mobile phone or computer. And there's information for anyone lucky enough to have a garden.

HOUSEHOLD PRODUCTS

Do you remember the advertising slogan 'kill every known germ'? It appeared to play on people's fears about the hidden bugs lurking in nooks and crannies around the house. Trying to kill them off with harsh chemicals is a bit like using a pesticide to kill all the wildlife in your garden because you're concerned about ants and aphids. You don't need to exterminate all the grease and grime to have a healthy home.

59

Another approach to cleaning is to assume that anything 'natural' is both better for you and better for the environment. It would be preferable – so people think – to make your own household products using lemons, vinegar or bicarbonate of soda. But remember that most companies producing household products employ scientists, and it is in their interests to ensure that these products work and are not harmful to either human health or the environment.

And just imagine if everyone decided to use lemons to disinfect their microwaves or descale their taps. Demand for lemons would soar, and you can be sure that the tonnes of extra fruit wouldn't be grown organically. Then there would be the energy impact of transporting the lemons all over the world. Aside from being vastly more expensive than conventional cleaning products, these lemons certainly wouldn't be environmentally friendly.

In general we use too many cleaning products too often and have difficulty deciding which is the best green solution. With that in mind, here are my views on detergents, cleaners and other household products.

Laundry Detergents

Forty years ago, soapsuds were causing rivers to froth up as well as our clothes. As a result,

Why don't detergent manufacturers work harder to promote:

1. **Lower-temperature washing**
2. **Concentrated products**
3. **Bigger box sizes – minimising packaging overall**

algae blooms, partly caused by cleaning products, were using up oxygen in the waterways, killing off fish as they struggled to breathe.

Since then there have been huge changes in the sorts of detergents we use and widespread interest in their biodegradability. In fact, this is often the key selling point of so called 'green' detergents. But if you ask water authorities today, they're no longer greatly concerned about detergent waste – they get a far bigger headache from water running off farmland, contaminated by fertilisers and animal waste.

If you're looking for the greenest wash on the planet, the most significant issue now is the temperature of your wash. You use much less energy with cooler water. But what else should be on your eco-radar?

Powder power

When a detergent says it's biological, it means it contains enzymes. Sometimes described as nature's miracle workers, these help to break down food in our bodies. In detergents they're used to dissolve fat and stains such as blood and chocolate. They're also pivotal to effective cleaning at low temperatures.

Many people are convinced that enzymes cause allergies or skin irritations but extensive research doesn't support this view. Curiously, this is a far bigger concern in Britain than elsewhere.

Dirty business

The most essential ingredient in any detergent is the surfactant. It's one of the main ingredients for cleaning – lifting dirt off the clothes and stopping it settling back on again. Almost all detergents use palm oil (page 49) in some shape or form. However, detergent manufacturers are either participating in or supporting discussions to make the palm oil industry less damaging to rainforests. Once criteria for sustainable sources of palm oil are in place we have to hope that detergent manufacturers will use only those.

Dosing

More concentrated detergents mean that people use less and therefore create less waste; it cuts down on packaging, transport and chemicals. But when a super-concentrated soap powder was launched a few years ago, it wasn't terribly popular and was subsequently withdrawn. I suspect that because it came in smaller boxes people just thought it was more expensive, and perhaps those who tried it used more than they needed. Surprisingly, the most concentrated detergents on the market today are liquid tablets, which come in dissolvable plastic sachets. Next are powder tablets, then liquid detergents, and the least concentrated are the powders.

Wrapping

A number of detergent products used to come in refill packs, but they were withdrawn because of a lack of consumer interest. Establishing the best packaging for detergents is actually rather complicated. As I have already mentioned, more concentrated products use less packaging. On the other hand, the tablets are individually wrapped, or in the case of liquid tablets have a dissolvable plastic coating. One

TURN TO 30°C

Ariel washing powder is promoting 30°C washing on the box.

thing that is clear is that detergent boxes and bottles are ideal for using recycled materials – whether it's recycled cardboard or plastic, they should be using as much as possible. And they should be recyclable too. Currently plastic bottles are easy to recycle, but plastic tubs are more of a problem in terms of finding facilities that will take them.

Eco-balls

Eco-balls are made of plastic and look a bit like flying saucers. Sold as an alternative to washing powders or liquids, the idea is to put them in your wash – up to a thousand times – and they'll 'lift the dirt away'. If used as recommended they're cheap and they have no harsh chemicals, no palm oil, no enzymes and no detergent residues. The big question is 'Do they work?' I'm not tempted to try them but I've read reports from those who have. Many are positive, but the overriding themes are that they're not effective if your clothes are more than lightly stained, and that they work better at high temperatures – one man said they worked really well at 60°C. I wonder if that was down to the eco-balls or the temperature of the wash! And what about the energy?

My 'green' checklist is as follows:

BUY

biological detergents; the most concentrated detergents you can find; packaging containing a high proportion of recycled materials and that can be recycled itself.

WASH

at the lowest temperature you can for effective cleaning, and check to make sure you're not using too much detergent.

GREEN CLEANING COMPANIES

Ecover is a minnow compared to the big detergent manufacturers, but it's a giant amongst the 'green' cleaners. Founded in 1980 on eco principles, it was the first detergent manufacturer to remove phosphates from its products – they were previously used to soften water. Ecover's eco-policies extend to the whole of its operation.

In 1992 Ecover built a new factory designed to minimise the need for artificial light, by installing windows that let in sunlight throughout the day. They also planted their extensive roof surfaces with drought-resistant vegetation as an innovative approach to regulating the indoor temperature of the building.

But Ecover is not the only 'green' detergent brand. Others include Clear Spring, made by Faith in Nature, and Bio D. Some focus on skin care, but many also claim to be quicker and better at breaking down in sewerage systems – essentially enhancing biodegradability. I'm not convinced this is as significant as they make it appear.

More important, in my view, is reducing the temperature of the wash. Neither Clear Spring nor Bio D offers a biological detergent (with enzymes) – their key target market is people concerned about skin allergies. Ecover, on the other hand, does have a biological detergent, but they say it has a very small market in the UK – roughly 10 per cent compared to 90 per cent for non-bio. Interestingly, in the rest of Europe their biological brand is by far the biggest seller. This is important because it washes better at lower temperatures. None of the 'green cleaners' contain optical brightener, which is the magic ingredient that makes clothes 'whiter than white'.

This made me question whether these detergents are effective at getting your clothes clean. To answer in a roundabout way: 'Do you need a Porsche to drive to the post office?' Probably not. Well, that's what Ecover says about its detergents. Their performance is more comparable to an everyday run-around car rather than a super-charged turbo engine. And for most of us that's probably good enough – in terms of the cleanliness of our wash. But perhaps not in terms of washing at the lowest temperature possible.

My verdict

It's not easy working out which is the greenest wash solution. I think the detergent industry is to blame. Most of us look along the supermarket shelves, completely baffled by what's on offer. There's too much choice and too many conflicting messages.

Dishwasher Detergents

I have to get my son to open the 'child-proof' top of my dishwasher detergent! I buy a powder product in the largest container possible and recycle it. But recently I've found it hard to track down the 3kg plastic bottles and have had to make do with the 1kg size. That's almost three times more plastic waste.

I've now discovered that, despite the individual wrapping, I should be buying dishwasher tablets. Apparently, the recommended dose is half that of powder. But there won't be a choice soon as powders are being phased out.

The issues around dishwasher detergents are similar to those around laundry detergents. Biodegradability of the ingredients is the most highly promoted concern but is less important than the temperature of the wash. However, most dishwashers don't have as much flexibility on temperature as washing machines, so there may not be any compromise in wash performance between the 'eco' and conventional brands.

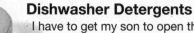

Washing-up Liquid

There's never been a major concern with the environmental impact of washing-up liquids.

And there's no significant difference between brands in terms of their biodegradability.

In terms of packaging, refills are the best approach. Ecover has one of the biggest refill schemes in the country. You take your washing-up liquid bottles to be filled from a 25-litre drum, which is itself refilled from the factory. In one year they saved over half a million 1-litre bottles, which is over 26,000 kilograms of plastic no longer being thrown away. You can also buy 5-litre containers of Ecover and introduce an in-house refill system.

Here's a question: do you buy concentrated or diluted washing-up liquid? If you buy concentrated you benefit from less packaging and waste in transport, but only if you use the correct amount. Don't we all have a tendency to squirt in the same way, whatever sort of liquid we're using? The answer is to buy concentrated solutions and dilute them yourself, to take account of liberal squirting by the washer-uppers in your house.

Looking along the supermarket shelf, I spotted 13 different types of Fairy washing-up liquids. Do we really need so many options? The one that impressed me least was the Fairy Active Foam Pump. It seemed to be designed for extra greasy containers and recommended leaving the tap on while rinsing.

Cleaners and Polishes

Green cleaners promote products principally made from renewable resources, rather than from oil-based materials. This isn't necessarily better for the environment or for your health.

Aerosol producers claim that their technology is efficient because the fine spray allows you to use less product, as well as every last drop in the can. However, their performance benefits are more relevant to hair sprays and deodorants, so I don't recommend them as cleaning products.

If I'm honest, I don't think there are any easy recommendations as to which brand of cleaning product to go for. My advice is not to go overboard with a different type of product for every cleaning job; to minimise packaging; and to use no more than you need. And as I said earlier, don't assume that alternatives such as cleaning with lemons are necessarily better for the environment.

Greenpeace is concerned about artificial musks (page 20), which are used in some household cleaners. They say that these chemicals persist in the environment and eventually get into human beings. On the other hand, the industry is adamant that the musks don't cause problems and so continue to use them.

Air Fresheners

If there were an anti-air fresheners club I'd be tempted to join. With the possible exception of dried lavender heads, I haven't smelt an air freshener I like. What I really hate is getting into a taxi with powerful air fresheners stuck like gruesome little monsters to the door. It's even worse if the sickly aroma is mixed with stale smoke.

What's more, it's often reported that air fresheners are not good for your health. If you have a bad smell in your home, it's far better to eradicate it than cover it up – try opening the window! You can even get air fresheners that plug into electricity sockets – that idea stinks. And remember that aerosols are not so great either.

Toilet Cleaners and Deodorisers

Bicarbonate of soda and vinegar are often suggested as alternative remedies for cleaning your loo. But according to *Which?* magazine they cost three times as much as Ecover and require paper towels or cloths to remove stains, which would eradicate any environmental benefit.

Blue loo deodorisers – the ones that turn the water blue and have a powerful, cloying smell – are on a par with air fresheners on my eco-horrors list. They're unnecessary, and if you have a push-button loo (page 76) they could even be corroding the valve and making it prone to leak.

Many of us feel a bit uncomfortable using powerful bleaches and loo-cleaning fluids. However, they don't cause a problem in the sewerage system because when they come into contact with bacteria, they disintegrate. On the other hand, if you leave brown stains in your loo, they attract nasty germs. So bleaches may not be so bad.

Aluminium Foil

Some people are aluminium foil maniacs. One evening a very nice woman at my sports club arrived with sandwiches – bought from Tesco – on plates covered in foil. That was bad enough. But when she pulled out reams of new foil for the left-over sandwiches, we nearly came to blows. 'At the very least', I said, 'you have to reuse the tin foil you brought the sandwiches in.'

So why worry? Well, aluminium foil is extremely energy intensive to make. It's also made from a material which is primarily found in the rainforest regions of the world – another factor in their destruction. That's two good reasons for not wasting it. Use washable plastic boxes instead.

On the positive side, aluminium can be recycled any number of times. And the energy used to make the recycled material is only 5 per cent of that to make it from scratch.

Many councils will collect aluminium foil as part of your recycled waste. Foil trays, chocolate foil, dairy-product lids and sheets of foil all qualify; you're advised to clean it and pack it into bags. If you're buying new foil, look out for 100 per cent recycled aluminium foil (see Household Products Weblinks). I've bought some and it doesn't look any different.

Rubbish Bags

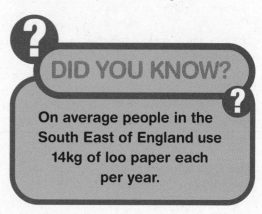

I'm not a great fan of biodegradable rubbish bags. Landfill sites are now restricted as to how much rotting waste they can take because it releases greenhouse gases. Biodegradable compost bags make more sense – at least they rot into a material which can be used again. But why use compost bags at all? Some waste authorities will pour the contents of your compost bin directly into their collection van, so no bags are needed.

My recommendation is to buy rubbish bags made from as much recycled plastic as possible – preferably post-consumer waste: waste that has actually been collected from households and recycled into something useful, rather than just using plastic from factory floors.

Lavatory Paper and Kitchen Towels

Maybe when recycled loo paper first came out it wasn't quite as soft as other brands. Not any more. Look out for brands that are not only recycled but use as much post-consumer waste as possible. Of course, this doesn't mean post-consumer loo paper! Recycled loo paper doesn't cost any more than non-recycled and is easy to find – no green consumer should buy anything else.

Now here's something to worry about. Americans apparently use around double the amount of loo paper as Europeans. And there are many countries in the world that use little or none. Whilst the paper manufacturers see this as a tremendous marketing opportunity, I'm not sure that encouraging everyone to wipe their bottoms as much as Americans would be a good thing!

If you're going to buy kitchen towels they should also be made with post-consumer waste. But use them sparingly. It might be quirky but I can't bear seeing people wipe up a mess with kitchen towel – even worse when they pull off several sheets at a time! Why not use a cloth that you can use again?

DID YOU KNOW?

On average people in the South East of England use 14kg of loo paper each per year.

HOUSEHOLD PRODUCTS WEBLINKS

Bio D Manufactures a range of cleaning products including laundry powder, washing-up liquid and toilet cleaners, sold as 'environmentally responsible' and 'hypo-allergenic'.

www.biodegradable.biz

Clear Spring (Faith in Nature) Started as natural body care company, but extended its hypo-allergenic range to detergents – laundry, dishwasher and washing-up liquids.

www.faithinnature.co.uk

Ecotopia Excellent mail order website selling Ecover detergents and cleaners in bulk.

www.ecotopia.co.uk

Ecover Produces the most extensive range of eco-detergents and -cleaners.

www.ecover.com

Greenpeace Toxics Campaign Campaigns to get rid of toxic chemicals around the home. They give details of which household brands contain chemicals they believe should be banned.

http://greenpeace.org.uk/ products/toxics/campaign.cfm

Lakeland Plastics Sells reusable micro fibre cloths that reduce or eliminate the need for cleaning products and disposable kitchen towels. Beware: it also sells some really wasteful products too. Ones that caught my eye included a rubber glove stand and a banana guard for storing one banana.

www.lakelandlimited.co.uk

If You Care Produces recycled aluminium foil, unbleached coffee filters and baking sheets. You can buy them from Natural Collection.

www.ifyoucare.com

Natural Collection Sells recycled aluminium foil, unbleached parchment paper and other household products.

www.naturalcollection.com

Nouvelle Makes toilet paper from recycled post-consumer waste.

www.nouvelle-environmentmatters.co.uk

WASHING, COOKING and FREEZING

Twenty years ago a washing machine manufacturer told me they could quite easily improve the energy efficiency of their machines, but there was no consumer demand for it. They're not saying the same thing today.

If you've bought a new washing machine, dishwasher or fridge recently, I hope you've been guided by the Energy Efficiency labels. With an 'A' rating for the most efficient appliances and a 'G' for the least efficient, these labels have been really effective in getting manufacturers to make improvements.

Washing Machines

I have three grubby boys (see picture) but still manage to get clothes clean on a 30°C wash. The most significant issue with washing machines is the temperature of the wash, because hot washes use a lot more electricity than cold; washing at 90°C uses twice the amount as washing at 40°C. In the last couple of decades wash temperatures have dropped from 90°C to 60°C, and now 40°C is the most common programme. Soon it will be 30°C.

Water use has also fallen from an average of 80 litres per wash 15 years ago to around 50 litres today. In some countries, such as Japan, Australia and Spain, cold washes are common. But the benefits are offset by the fact that they use much more water, different detergents, and wash cycles take longer.

More exciting is the launch of a new type of washing machine – one that cleans with steam. It looks very similar to any other front-loading washing machine, but its eco-performance is superior: it claims to use 21 per cent less electricity and 35 per cent less water. In fact it may not be quite as good as

that if you compare it with other top-rated machines. But it does have some unusual features, the most significant of which is a sensor that detects how much washing you put in and varies the amount of water and the length of the wash accordingly. More trivial features include an LED monitoring panel, which allows you to check the progress of your wash cycle from any room in the house (it's a pity it doesn't include details of its electricity consumption too), and the option to buy the machine in pink, cherry or aqua blue! It's no surprise that it's at least double the price of an ordinary machine.

Other wizard ideas in the pipeline include ultrasound machines that wash without water and plants that purify the water. But to my

mind most appealing of all is the super-intelligent machine that weighs the laundry, senses the fabric type and works out how dirty it is. Then we won't have to worry about the temperature or how much detergent to put in – just programme it to choose the best green clean.

Here are my tips for washing machines:

Machine type: old-fashioned top-loader machines use more water and are more aggressive on clothes.

Hot or cold fill: if you wash at lower temperatures there's no longer any advantage to hot fill because the water will be piped in hotter than you need.

Load: only use your washing machine when you have a full load. Half-load buttons save energy but they don't halve it.

Timing: set your washing machine to run at night (as long as you won't disturb

your neighbours). It won't be using peak time electricity.

Temperature: use the lowest wash temperature possible – most clothes can be cleaned at 30°C.

Washer dryers: it may be a little more efficient to have two machines rather than one, but not if you take account of the energy used to make the machines in the first place.

Tumble Dryers

Looking out of a train window during my travels in Guatemala, my American fellow traveller said, 'I don't know how they manage without dryers.' Seeing brightly coloured clothes waving in the wind, I couldn't have disagreed more. I'm a big fan of washing lines. If you don't have outside space, an indoor drying rack is the next best thing. A tumble dryer should be a last resort.

Almost all tumble dryers will be C rated or below on the Energy Efficiency label. If you

really must have one, here are some things to think about:

Condensing vs air-vented: there's no big difference in energy efficiency between these two types of dryer. But if you have an air-vented one, you may be letting cold air into the house.

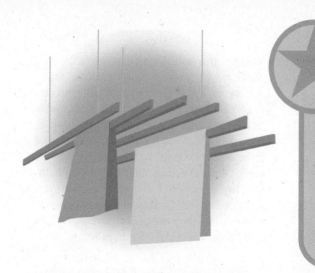

IN PRAISE OF THE PULLEY AIRER

If you haven't got much space for drying clothes, consider getting a pulley system. Once it is loaded you can pull the washing close to the ceiling and out of the way. But don't put it in the kitchen or the clothes might end up smelling of kippers. And make sure it's fixed properly to beams so it doesn't fall on your head.

Sensors: machines with a sensor stop when clothes are dry. This is much more efficient than using timers that rely on guessing how long to set the machine for.

Heat pumps: designed by AEG, heat-pump dryers use waste heat to warm the air going in, which makes them more efficient. As these become more common, prices will tumble.

Gas: these dryers make your clothes fluffier, are cheaper to run and have lower carbon emissions. But they're less energy efficient and difficult to install.

Spin: don't put sopping wet clothes in the dryer – spin them in the washing machine first.

Dishwashers

If you've got more than one person living in the house, I think dishwashers are a real necessity. But washing up by hand will generally use less water and energy, depending, of course, on what sort of washer-upper you are. If you leave the tap running for washing and rinsing, a dishwasher will come out best. Average water use of new models is no more than 45 litres, whereas older models could use as much as 63 litres.

Like washing machines, the amount of energy used by dishwashers is largely determined by the temperature of the wash. You should definitely use the eco-button or low-temperature button, which will generally mean washing at 55°C rather than 65°C. It's also important to load the machine fully before starting it, and avoid opening the door when it's running as this lets heat escape.

? DID YOU KNOW? ?

If half the European households currently using higher temperature dishwashing programmes switched to energy-saving programmes, they could cut greenhouse gas emissions by 388,000 tonnes a year.

AGA TIP

I put my orange peel, egg shells and stale bread in my Aga. The dried orange peel is used for kindling; the egg shells deter slugs; and the bread is used for breadcrumbs.

Cookers and Kettles

I have one of the most inefficient cooking appliances known to man: an oil-fired Aga. Having found out that it uses a substantial 35 litres of oil per week, I looked for some redeeming features. The first is that I really love it. The second is that it means I can do without heating for an extra few weeks because the kitchen is warm. And the third is that I turn it off in the summer when it's hot outside. But if I move house again I won't be getting another one.

Gas vs electric: gas hobs and ovens are more efficient than electric, with the exception of induction hobs – the ones that heat up instantly. And fan ovens are more efficient than conventional ones.

Microwaves: microwaves use less energy than electric or gas ovens, particularly for small quantities of food. Although the digital display panel uses a very small amount of electricity, if you multiply this across all the microwaves in the country it amounts to tens of millions of pounds' worth of electricity. Another issue to be aware of is that microwave meals are often over-packaged.

Kettles: the reason power stations experience a surge in demand at half-time during the TV coverage of football matches is kettles. They use an enormous amount of power, albeit for a relatively short time – between 1,800 and 3,000 watts: that's enough to power 50 ordinary light bulbs or 270 energy-efficient ones. So filling the kettle only with the amount of water you need does make a big difference. Quick-boil kettles use more power when they are on, but are on for less time, so it works out about the same.

ECO-KETTLE

The Eco-Kettle is cleverly designed to allow you to boil only the amount of water you need. Apparently it results in around a 25 per cent saving in electricity. It's widely available on the high street and through mail order:

www.ecokettle.com

Cooking tips

Some of these tips seem obvious, but just in case you need a prompt:

* Match the pan size to the hob.
* Use pans with a flat base.
* Put the lid on saucepans whenever you're boiling something.
* Only use the amount of water you need.
* Don't peer into the oven too often.
* Cook more than one meal at a time.
* Electric toasters are more efficient than grills.
* Avoid the flame licking up the sides of your pan when cooking on gas.

Fridges and Freezers

If you've been aware of fridges in the news in the last few years, it's likely to have been because of 'fridge mountains'. When they're all piled on top of each other it's staggering to see how many we're throwing away. The problem has been that EU laws say that we have to remove the cooling gases – chlorofluorocarbons (CFCs) – rather than let them waft up and play their part in destroying the ozone layer. To be fair, new fridges no

CHEST OR UPRIGHT?

Chest freezers lose less cold air when you open them because hot air rises, not cold. But most people find it difficult to organise the stored food, so they probably have the door open for longer whilst scrabbling around for what they want. Most upright freezers have shelf fronts to stop the air escaping, and they're easier to organise. I think uprights win.

longer use CFCs. But there are still some old ones in the system that do.

Unfortunately, destroying the ozone layer isn't the only problem caused by fridge gases; they can be a significant contributor to global warming too. In fact, the gas that replaced CFCs in most fridges and freezers, hydrofluorocarbons or HFCs, are 1,400 times more powerful than CO_2 as a greenhouse gas.

Greenpeace was so worried about HFCs replacing CFCs that they developed a new type of fridge that didn't use either. This Greenfreeze fridge has been a tremendous success, to the extent that this technology is used in pretty well all domestic fridges and freezers sold in the UK, except American imports. Unfortunately, the picture is not so rosy for fridges and freezers used by supermarkets and manufactures (see box overleaf).

FRIDGE GASES

CFCs: Ozone-destroying but no longer used in new fridges.

HFCs: Huge climate change impact and still used in some fridges imported from America, as well as in industrial refrigeration, for example in supermarkets.

HCs: Ozone- and climate-friendly refrigeration gas that is commonly used in new domestic fridges and freezers.

SUPERMARKET WATCH

Fridges and Freezers

Although domestic fridges and freezers have largely moved away from using refrigerants that are powerful greenhouse gases, other companies, including the supermarkets, have not.

Of course, they are complying with legislation to move away by 2010 from the worse refrigerants currently used, but little more than that. The **Co-op**, **M&S**, **Sainsbury's** and **Tesco** are all researching the most eco-friendly solutions, but at the time of writing none of them had made commitments to introduce these across all their stores in the foreseeable future. **Asda**, **Morrisons** and **Waitrose** did not seem to be thinking about this issue.

This is an area where consumer pressure could really make a difference. Ask your supermarket to set a deadline for moving out of HFCs in their refrigerants and to be more proactive at investigating alternatives.

Cooling power

An iron apparently uses around 1,200 watts of electricity, a kettle between 2,000 and 3,000 watts, and the oven, grill and hob of a cooker a mind-blowing 12,000 watts. In comparison, a fridge or freezer using less than one watt might not seem to be such a big deal. But of course these cooling machines are using power day and night, all through the year. So any energy-efficiency improvements make a difference.

I discovered that my old freezer was costing over £100 a year in electricity, so I've stopped using it. Modern fridges and freezers are far more efficient than that – the running cost of a small fridge, for example, can be as little as £15 a year, although the trend is to have bigger fridges that use more power than this. And beware: 'frost-free' freezers use a lot more energy than those without this feature because they never power down.

On average a new fridge bought today will use a little over half of the electricity of one bought in 1992, and the most energy efficient about a third. If you want to buy one of these, look for an Energy Efficiency rating of A++. The pluses are important because almost all fridges and freezers are eligible for an A rating. Electrolux is leading the way in energy-efficient refrigeration.

The basic design of a fridge has been the same for decades, but change is on the way. OK, it's not going to transform your life. But it will dramatically improve energy efficiency and reduce the amount of space a fridge takes up. Vacuum panels, which are similar in design to a thermos flask, will replace the thick layer of foam in the fridge walls, reducing them from around 10cm to as little as 3cm.

Cool Advice

- Look out for A++ rated fridges or freezers if you are buying a new model.

- If you buy an upright freezer, make sure it has fronts on its drawers.

- Make sure your fridge is not next to your cooker or boiler – it has to work harder to get rid of the heat.

- Don't open and shut the doors of your fridge or freezer more than you need.

- Allow food to cool before putting it into the fridge.

- Defrost your freezer regularly to maximise efficiency.

- Frost-free freezers use more energy than freezers without this feature.

- Don't be tempted by a fridge ice-maker – it's more efficient to make ice in your freezer.

WATERWORKS

Washing and Cleaning

Oh dear. I have a bath almost every night and I am not a shower fan. When I'm travelling, one of the things I miss most is having a bath. The only positive thing to say on this front is that I'm happy to share my bath with my children, my mother and friends who are staying – although not all at the same time! Here are some tips on saving water when washing and cleaning.

Showers

A five-minute shower uses one-third less water than having a bath. But if you use a power shower, there's no water-saving benefit and you'll be using more energy too.

Bathing efficiently

If you're fitting a new bath, choose the smallest one for your needs. Whatever bath you have you don't need to fill it to the top. And if you don't mind sharing your bath water with other members of the household, it makes a lot of sense.

Low-flow taps

If you're buying new taps, look out for ones with water-saving devices: they'll offer different flow speeds. You can also buy inexpensive devices to fit on existing taps that have an economical spray mode.

WASTE DISPOSAL UNITS

I really dislike these gizmos. Not only do they waste water, they discourage composting too. And if more of us had them they would cause serious problems in terms of blocking pipes.

Appliances

If you're buying a new washing machine or dishwasher, look out for one that is A rated. An eco-dishwasher will use about 10 litres less water than older models, and an eco-washing machine 30 litres less per wash. Whatever machine you have, use economy programmes and make sure it's fully loaded.

Kitchen water

Washing dishes and cleaning vegetables should be done in a bowl. The waste water can then be used to water plants if you have them.

Loos

Isn't it crazy that we flush top-quality drinking water down the loo? Apparently, each of us flushes at least six times a day, so if you have an old-fashioned toilet this could use as much as 60 litres of water.

Another Water Life

It's ridiculous that we are still building houses which rely entirely on water piped in from a distance. This all has to be transported, treated and stored. So why not use more of what we can find at home?

Using waste water

Using waste water from your bath in the garden is quite easy; it can be diverted from waste pipes into water butts. I've always wanted to use my bath water for flushing the loo, but this is not as simple. The water has to be chemically treated because it quickly becomes smelly when stored. This uses energy, requires space for storage tanks and is expensive. The good news is that people are working on it, so they might overcome these problems and make it more of an option.

So what to do with your loo?

Water-efficient toilets

Ultra-low-flush toilets can use as little as 2.5 litres of water for liquid wastes and 4 litres for solids. But they cost 2–3 times more than an ordinary loo. I think they're only really worth the extra cost in public places, where they'll be used a lot.

Low-flush lavatory devices

These don't look very spectacular – just a pack of mainly plastic parts that need to be fitted inside your cistern. But they're a great idea because they reduce the amount of water you use for every flush, and they're cheap. Beware, though: they only work on loos with a handle at the front.

Put a brick in it

Putting a brick in your cistern is often recommended as a water-saving measure. Water companies have even produced plastic pouches that swell up and can be used in the same way. This isn't always such a good idea because it can lead to flushing twice, which eliminates the benefit.

Composting lavatories

They're not for everyone, but their eco-credentials are excellent! They don't use any water and the waste can be used to fertilise the garden. In cost terms, with average family use it would take nearly 25 years of saving on your water bill to cover the original purchase price.

You may be surprised at the range of composting loos available, from basic to deluxe. The Rotaloo, for example, is an elaborate device, imported from Australia, that has six compost sections on a turntable. When one is full a new bin is rotated into place, which gives the others time to compost.

STOP PUSH-BUTTON LOOS!

A silent invasion. A national threat. A water-saving disaster. Push-button or valve lavatories reached our shores only in 1999 – that's when they were legalised. But what's wrong with push-button loos? I hear you say.

Let's start at the beginning with the eponymous Thomas Crapper. He invented the siphon lavatory – known at the time as the 'water waste preventer' – in 1866. Ever since, that is until 1999, we have been happily depositing our 'solids' and 'liquids' using his impeccably designed system.

On the surface push-button loos seem better. They generally use less water per flush, and they're cheap. We're importing literally millions from China. Dig a little deeper and you discover that they leak. Not all of them, of course, but an awful lot of them. In America, where they have nothing else, it's estimated that they leak an average of 15–30 litres of water per person per day. If you took the bottom end of that average and applied it to the UK we would be losing 900 million litres of water a day – enough to supply about 6.5 million people.

When I heard about this, I peered into my toilet cisterns to see what I had. I realise now that I need only have checked whether I had handles or buttons. I found that I had two Crapper loos (with handles) and one valve loo (with push-button). And would you believe it, the valve system was leaking! A continuous flow of water was trickling into the cistern and into the toilet pan. I would never have noticed if I hadn't specifically gone to check.

So why are push-button loos prone to leaking? It's because they get jammed opened and because the valve system used can rot when in contact with hard water, grit or blue toilet-flush deodorisers. So after a certain amount of time they'll wear out and let water seep into the pan. Take a look at your loos and check for leaks.

Another advantage of traditional loos is that they work with water-saving devices. I decided to try them out. There are two main ones on the market – Interflush and Peterton's Variflush – and competition between the two is fierce. I preferred Interflush because it allows you to use only the amount of water you need for each flush, rather than set amounts. As soon as you let go of the handle the water stops.

I love it. There's a real satisfaction in saving on every flush! Both gizmos say they're easy to install, although I wasn't entirely convinced, particularly when I realised I needed a cordless drill to fit Interflush. So I asked my plumber, who was already doing work on my house, to set it up. It was worth the trouble.

Rainwater harvesting

If properly collected, rainwater could supply all your household water, except for what you drink. I think rainwater harvesting systems should be compulsory in all new houses – particularly in the South East of England where there are frequent water shortages. But retro-fitting these large storage tanks is more difficult and prohibitively expensive. I was quite enthusiastic to have one at my house until I found out how much it cost – at least as much as a new boiler. And there needs to be space for a large water storage tank – probably underground.

WATER-SAVING WEBLINKS

Centre for Alternative Technology
Provides fact sheet on composting toilets.
www.cat.org.uk

Composting Toilet World Promotes composting toilets worldwide.
www.compostingtoilet.org

Green Building Store Offers water-saving toilets, taps and other devices.
www.greenbuildingstore.co.uk

Interflush Sells water-saving device for toilets. Also available from Energy Saving World.
www.interflush.co.uk

Peterton's Variflush Sells water-saving device for toilets.
www.peterton.co.uk

Reduce Water Bills Advises on reducing water use at home.
www.reducewaterbills.co.uk

Rotaloo Sells innovative composting toilet.
www.rotaloo.co.uk

Tapmagic Offers water-saving devices to fit on taps.
www.tapmagic.co.uk

UK Rainwater Harvesting Association
Trade association promoting rainwater harvesting.
www.ukrha.org

Water Two Supplies valves for diverting bath and shower grey water for use in the garden.
www.watertwo.co.uk

HOME ENTERTAINMENT and OFFICE

Televisions and Set-Top Boxes

We all have far more televisual equipment these days, with videos, DVD players, digi-boxes and remote controls for all of them. And that's before you include computers, MP3 players, Playstations and mobile phones. In the 1960s few people had more than a television, a radio and perhaps a record player. So does it matter? What are the environmental impacts of this tele-explosion?

One of the worst things is that the hardware goes out of date so fast. Digital television, high-definition technology, new and bigger screens are all gathering pace, making millions of electrical goods totally redundant and giving rise to an explosion in electronic waste.

There's also been an explosion in the amount of power needed for our electronic entertainment. Buying a huge screen is like buying a gas-guzzling car. Whether it's plasma, liquid crystal display (LCD) or an old-fashioned TV screen, the bigger it is the more electricity is needed to power it. The average TV screen in the 1990s used about 70–80 watts – now the average is between 140–150 watts. And the biggest plasma screen could use as much electricity in 10 hours as a fridge uses in a whole year.

By 2011 everyone in the UK will need to be able to receive digital signals, because the old analogue system will be switched off. You can get digital either through a separate set-top box – known as a digi-box – or a digital television, known as an integrated digital television (IDTV). Buying a set-top box is preferable to junking your TV, but if you're buying a new system it's definitely worth getting an IDTV, because the digital bit of it won't use any *extra* energy.

Most set-top boxes are designed to be in stand-by mode when not in use. This means they consume between 6 and 20 watts of electricity, 24 hours a day, 365 days a year. You can turn them off at the mains, but few people do. And with some packages, doing this means your programmes will be delayed when you switch the box on again. Sky are working to address this problem, as well as making further energy-efficiency improvements – in fact they're leading the way in reducing power wastage from set-top boxes.

Computers

As more of us work from home, even part-time, we're buying a huge range of equipment, such as large flat screens, laptops, scanners, printers, speakers, routers and keyboards. You don't have to know what

GREEN SKY THINKING

In 2006 Sky became the first media company to go carbon neutral (page 19). In the process they cut emissions from their site by 47 per cent. And they're using 100 per cent renewable energy on all their UK sites.

www.sky.com
www.jointhebiggerpicture.co.uk

all these things do to understand that they make our homes even more power hungry. Have you noticed how many more plugs and wires are needed to support the modern lifestyle? The back of my desk looks like Spaghetti Junction.

LCD screens are far more energy efficient than their predecessors, the bulky cathode ray tubes (CRTs). But that's when you compare them size for size. The problem is that, as with TVs, screens are getting bigger, and that means more energy. But the real energy waste happens when computers and their related attachments are not even being used – when they're in stand-by mode.

I know from my friends and relatives that an awful lot of people leave their computers on all the time. 'It takes ages to power up,' they say. Or 'It's not good for the computer to be switched off and on.' This last excuse is rarely valid because most computers are discarded long before they've had time to wear out.

And some people will turn off their computer but forget about things like their broadband connection, speakers or printer. They're all mini energy guzzlers which, when taken as a whole and multiplied over the entire country, amount to an awful lot. See if you can get them all on one plug system so that you can switch them all off at the same time.

Another life

I feel like one of those people who write to their local newspaper saying 'I'm disgusted': disgusted by how much computer equipment just ends up in landfill – literally millions of tonnes of perfectly good materials being treated like banana skins or soiled nappies. It doesn't make any sense. There are companies in the UK that recycle almost every computer part, and none of it goes to landfill.

Plastic casings can be made into pipes; glass screens into more screens; precious metals can be reused in computer equipment – copper, aluminium, lead, iron and steel can all be recovered; and if there's anything left over after recycling it can be burnt to produce energy. So there's no technical reason why it can't be done. It's simply a matter of political will. Worse than that, recycling companies in the UK are being held back, by the Government dragging its feet and failing to meet EU recycling targets.

If you, as an individual, want to have your computer recycled, you're reliant on your local authority. When I went to my local recycling centre in South Somerset, they said they only recycled monitors, which is slightly bizarre because this is expensive, whereas hard drives will bring some return. For businesses, it's easier to ensure your computer equipment gets another life as there are companies that export them to developing countries – but if they're beyond repair, recycle them.

At this stage I have to sound a cautionary note. One problem with recycling and reuse is fraud. We've all lost documents on our computers that have been impossible to find. In reality it's very difficult to completely eradicate a computer's memory. If it gets into the wrong hands, thieves can steal credit card details, passwords and even your holiday snaps.

LAPTOPS
They're generally more energy efficient than desktops because that's a primary concern for users. But they're getting bigger and therefore more power hungry.

THE THROWAWAY WORLD

From TVs to toasters, mobiles to microwaves, and printers to Playstations, each of us is creating huge amounts of electronic waste. Endearingly known as WEEE – Waste Electrical and Electronic Equipment – this problem is growing and growing.

An average 21 year old in 2003 would produce 3.3 tonnes of WEEE in their lifetime. But someone born in 2003 would generate nearly three times that amount: 8 tonnes.

One of the problems is that products are not made to last. Whether it's your TV, video, washing machine or fridge, it's often cheaper to get a new one than to get it repaired. OK, so products are no longer durable, but are they designed for recycling? Some are, and it makes a big difference. A telephone with six screws, for example, will take half the time to dismantle as one with 12 – this can be the deciding factor in whether it's cost effective or not.

So what are the benefits of recycling? For a start it will prevent highly toxic chemicals and metals leaching into the environment. Forty per cent of all lead and 22 per cent of mercury comes from WEEE. There's also cadmium and a host of flame retardants.

But it's not just the pollution they cause when thrown away, it's the expenditure at the beginning of their life too. For every kilogram of copper produced, for example, 1,176kg of primary resources are consumed. To provide 522,000 tonnes of copper used in WEEE annually, over 600 million tonnes of other raw materials are dug out of the ground.

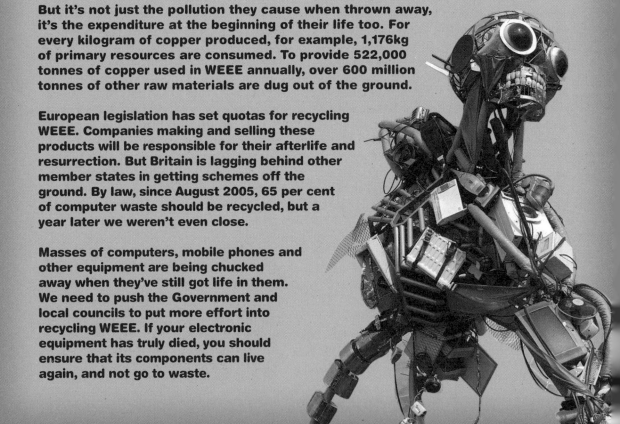

European legislation has set quotas for recycling WEEE. Companies making and selling these products will be responsible for their afterlife and resurrection. But Britain is lagging behind other member states in getting schemes off the ground. By law, since August 2005, 65 per cent of computer waste should be recycled, but a year later we weren't even close.

Masses of computers, mobile phones and other equipment are being chucked away when they've still got life in them. We need to push the Government and local councils to put more effort into recycling WEEE. If your electronic equipment has truly died, you should ensure that its components can live again, and not go to waste.

Apple Mac has effective software that wipes a computer's memory clean. For PCs it's difficult and expensive to get hold of good software to do this. The data eradication programs that are available make it difficult to check whether they've actually worked. Some people resort to driving a nail through the hard disc – but this seems a little radical if the computer could have been reused. It's ridiculous that this problem hasn't been sorted out.

Printers

I've got an Epson inkjet printer – and what do I find? It's just about the only inkjet brand whose cartridges are not recyclable! Like others, I bought it because it was cheap. I've been tempted by cheap cartridges too, but they didn't work well – this proved to be rather wasteful because I had to throw them out before they were used up.

The world of printer cartridges is a bit murky. Many cheap ones claim to be recycled when they're not. And another problem is that some printer manufacturers actually make it difficult to recycle their products. They want you to buy brand new ones from them.

There are a number of charities which make money by collecting waste cartridges to be recycled, and some are beginning to sell recycled cartridges too.

There's no limit on the number of times a cartridge can be refilled, although there'll be some parts that need renewing. Although toner cartridges for laser printers are easier to recycle, they're extremely bulky and therefore wasteful. So I'd recommend an inkjet printer as a greener option.

> ### PRINTING TIP
> Some printers stop you printing in colour once your black ink has run out and vice versa. You can avoid this by checking ink levels and printing documents in whatever colour there is most of.

WEEE WEBLINKS

Cartridge Cashback Takes back printer cartridges for recycling and donates money to environmental charities.	www.cartridgecashback.com
Envocare Useful source of information on electronic waste and recycling, particularly printer cartridges, mobile phones and batteries.	www.envocare.co.uk
Green Agenda Recycles printer cartridges.	www.greenagenda.com
ICER – Industry Council for Electronic Equipment Recycling Source of knowledge and expertise on recycling WEEE.	www.icer.org.uk
Office Green Recycles printer cartridges, mobile phones, fluorescent lights and computers.	www.officegreen.co.uk

RDC The largest computer recycling company in the UK. They reuse two out of three computers and either recycle the remainder or reclaim energy from waste so that nothing goes to landfill.

www.rdc.co.uk

WEEE Man I love the WEEE Man (see pic on page 80). Commissioned by the RSA, he's built from electrical and electronic waste – the amount the average British person creates in their lifetime. He comes with an education pack too.

www.weeeman.org

World Land Trust
Donate your empty inkjet and toner cartridges and help save rainforests.

www.worldlandtrust.org/
supporting/cartridges.htm

Paper and Stationery

Here are some tips for greening your office, paper and other stationery.

- Reduce paper demand by printing double-sided wherever possible.
- Reuse paper that has only been printed on one side.
- Buy paper with the highest recycled paper content possible.
- Look out for FSC certification on paper and wood products.
- Reuse envelopes – put stickers over address labels.
- Organise a paper recycling container.
- Forget disposable coffee cups – bring your own mug.
- Try getting a good-quality pen and keeping it rather than using lots of disposables.
- Buy stationery products made from recycled materials.

RECYCLED OFFICE PAPER

- It takes about twice as much energy to make virgin paper as it does to make recycled paper.

- Throwing paper into landfill sites produces greenhouse gases and wastes resources.

- Getting good-quality recycled paper is no longer a problem as technology has improved significantly.

- Buying recycled paper should be high on the list for any 'green' office.

PAPER and STATIONERY WEBLINKS

Forest Stewardship Council (FSC)
Forestry certification scheme used for paper and wood products.

www.fsc-uk.org

Green Your Office
Supplies extensive range of recycled paper, 'green' stationery and office products, including a recycling service to help you reduce and recycle office waste.

www.greenyouroffice.co.uk

Green Stationery Company
Supplies extensive range of recycled paper and 'green' stationery.

www.greenstat.co.uk

Printed Pen Site Sells pens made from recycled materials such as jeans, tyres and newspapers.

www.theprintedpensite.com

Treecycle Sells recycled office paper and other products.

www.treecycle.com

Trees for Life Sells labels to enable you to reuse envelopes.

www.treesforlife.org.uk

Mobile Phones

Are you tempted by mobile phone upgrades? Well, you're not alone. On average people get a new phone every 18 months, which means 15 million are discarded every year. Often this isn't because our phones are broken but because we like the idea of getting a new model with a few more whizzy features. I had to replace my last one because it fell into a fish pond – apparently 75,000 are dropped in the loo each year!

Our enthusiasm for new phones means there's a flourishing trade in second-hand models. The phones are refurbished and in many cases shipped off to less developed countries, where they're really valued.

If your phone can't be reused, it can be recycled – although less than 5 per cent are. All you have to do is put it in one of the boxes provided in shops or send it through the post (see Mobile Phone Weblinks). Mobile phones and their accessories contain some of the most hazardous substances known to man. Recycling keeps the heavy metals out of the waste stream and saves the mining and manufacturing of new materials.

New mobile phones come with their own plug and charger – so do ipods, digital cameras and a host of other portable electronic equipment. Why on earth don't the manufacturers get together and agree on one type of charger that works for all these things? It would be far more convenient and less wasteful for all concerned – but not so profitable for the companies selling them. As things are, you should send your charger and batteries for recycling with your phone.

Mobile phone masts

Whether they're disguised as trees or attached to church spires, mobile phone masts have proliferated in the last ten years. As a child I loved playing the game of spotting things out of the car window. We'd get one point for a yellow car, a post box, a woman not carrying anything, and of course a

red telephone box. My children are equally enthusiastic, but now mobile phone masts and speed cameras have been added to the list.

Masts are an intrusion, but people seem to complain about them less than they used to. I'd prefer them to remain the focus of people's ire, rather than what's perceived by some as the new countryside scourge – wind turbines. I think mobile phone companies should install wind turbines wherever they put a mobile phone mast – they'd be more visually appealing, with the added benefit of providing clean energy.

MOBILE PHONE WEBLINKS

Cellular Reclamation Company Takes back mobile phones for reuse and recycling.	**www.cellularrecycler.com**
Foneback Takes back mobile phones for reuse and recycling.	**www.foneback.com**
Health Protection Agency Provides information on health issues relating to mobile phones and masts.	**www.hpa.org.uk**
Mobile Phone Recycling Recycles mobile phones for businesses (you need to have more than 20) and donates the money to charity.	**www.mobilephonerecycling.co.uk**
TetraWatch Campaigns against Tetra radio communications masts used by the police.	**www.tetrawatch.net**
Mast Sanity Organisation campaigning against insensitive siting of mobile phone masts.	**www.mastsanity.org**

Batteries
A waste of power

When you buy milk, wine or orange juice there's a label telling you how much you're getting. But finding out the power in a battery is a guessing game. There's no guidance on the pack – and battery makers are fighting to keep it this way. They say it's impossible to give accurate information on the power in a battery, because what you get out of it depends on how you use it. I'm not convinced. For a start, it's already been done for rechargeable batteries.

And this isn't my only gripe with battery makers. In the UK they are selling us nearly 700 million batteries a year, which is an average of about 21 per person. Each of these batteries takes roughly 50 times more energy to make than it provides. But instead of encouraging us all to use rechargeable batteries, which are far more energy efficient, the industry is making a lot of noise about recycling.

Don't get me wrong. I think recycling batteries is a good idea. Everyday non-rechargeable batteries are easy to recycle, but only a fraction of them actually are. The main reason for increasing recycling is not to save resources but to reduce the amount of hazardous waste being thrown into landfill sites – or even worse, into incinerators.

PORTABLE POWER PRIORITIES

1. Avoid battery-operated gadgets.
2. Plug into the mains if possible.
3. Use rechargeable batteries wherever possible.
4. Buy long-life batteries (alkaline) in preference to the cheaper ones (zinc).
5. Recycle all waste batteries if you can.

RECHARGE MORE

If we all switched to rechargeable batteries, we'd save far more than by recycling.

- They save energy. You get 50 times more energy out of a rechargeable battery than it takes to make one. This is the equivalent of 2,500 times more than for a disposable battery.
- They save waste. If you recharge your battery 500 times you save 500 other batteries being chucked away (or 499, to be strictly accurate). Some can be recharged up to 1,000 times, which saves even more.
- They save money. You get the extra money you paid for the battery back after just five charges, so you get the equivalent of 495 charges for free. The cost of recharging them is minimal – about 1p a time.

You should be sorting out your batteries and buying rechargeables. And if you haven't already got one, buy a battery charger too. The cheaper the charger, the longer it takes to recharge the batteries.

My battery charger spent ages lying next to a box of new and half-used disposable batteries. I'm horrified at my own disorganisation, and equally horrified at how many new gadgets the children unwrap at Christmas and birthdays that need batteries. And my suspicions have been confirmed. Labels in many of these products, reading 'no rechargeable batteries', are nonsense. Many of these same products sold in Germany – where there is greater environmental awareness

– actually recommend rechargeables. A guidance note explains not to put the batteries in your pocket because they may overheat; this would hardly seem to be a major hazard.

If you want to power a wall clock or something that needs a small amount of power over a long time, disposables make sense. This is because they release the small amount of energy as it is needed, whereas rechargeable batteries lose their power over a few months. For most other applications rechargeable batteries are the answer. They will out-perform the best long-life batteries by four to one in terms of power in a digital camera, for example. And in less than a decade they've improved their life expectancy at least fivefold.

? WHICH RECHARGEABLE? ?

Do you find it hard getting to grips with different battery types? There are two main sorts of rechargeables: Nickel Cadmiums (Ni-Cds) and Nickel Metal Hydrides (Ni-MHs).

The Ni-Cds are cheap, don't last as long and have less power; they're being phased out. Their main benefit has been getting people to take the plunge and buy rechargeable batteries.

The Ni-MHs are better quality all round. Although they cost more than the Ni-Cds, they still work out much cheaper than single-use batteries.

BATTERY WEBLINKS

British Battery Manufacturers Association
A trade association trying hard to persuade us that batteries have a minimal environmental impact.

www.bbma.co.uk

Uniross Largest manufacturer of rechargeable batteries – they've recently linked up with WWF to promote the benefits of rechargeables.

www.uniross.com

WRAP Helping to make battery recycling schemes viable in the UK by setting up pilot schemes. You can find out whether your local council recycles batteries by inserting your postcode on WRAP's site.

www.wrap.org.uk

Photography

I loved switching from a camera with film to a digital one. There's the joy of instant access and not having to worry about your precious photos getting lost at the printers, as well as the savings from reusing the same disc repeatedly whilst selecting only the good photos to print. Traditional photographic processing was carried out in darkrooms using and disposing of lots of nasty chemicals.

DISPOSABLE BUGBEAR?

One thing that really bugs me is people holding up a disposable camera and saying, 'This is environmentally sound because it can be recycled.' I think single-use cameras are extremely wasteful. You have to consider all the materials used to make them, and then the energy and waste from the recycling process. Sure, if you're going to indulge, make certain it's recyclable, but don't kid yourself you're being eco-friendly!

Digital Camera Tips

But even digital cameras are not without problems. Here's some advice on how to minimise them:

• Use rechargeable batteries.
• Look out for the most efficient battery you can find – that means more shots per charge.

• Don't waste power by previewing every photo, unnecessary zooming and keeping the camera on all the time.
• Use print preview on your computer rather than actually printing.
• Don't use over-size paper for test printing.

DIY and FURNISHING

Paints

Is any paint 'green'?

I've painted my house in wild colours – I even painted my car. I wish I could say that I'd used more 'eco-paints' than I did. So what stopped me?

The first reason was the colour range – my kitchen is vibrant orange with ruby-red cupboards, and my sitting room is beetroot pink, including the ceiling, with black skirting boards. Even if you don't share my taste you might find the colour range of eco-paints limiting, particularly if you're looking for deeper shades. The second reason was more prosaic. Most of the painting was done by my energetic mother. She's in her seventies and was determined to use products she was familiar with. Now I've researched paint issues, I feel I should have been more committed.

Most paints are made up of pigments, binders and solvents. Pigments give the colour, which is held in the solution by the solvent, and the binder sticks the paint to the wall. Other ingredients help with properties such as flow, consistency and preservation.

Synthetic paints are made with petrochemicals, use huge amounts of energy and create toxic wastes, yet working out the best alternative is enough to give you a headache. There are natural paints, whose priority is to use 'natural' renewable ingredients. Then there are paints whose focus is on removing the smelly fumes that are bad for your health. And there are quite a few shades in between.

Napoleon was apparently killed by the 'natural' arsenic in his wallpaper, so using natural ingredients isn't always better for your health! Some 'natural' paints, for example, use citrus peel instead of white spirit as a solvent, but this still has some quite powerful unhealthy fumes. These come from volatile organic compounds (VOCs) (see glossary) which, when released, are called 'off-gassing'. Paints labelled as 'low VOC' or 'odour-free' generally use water as the solvent but with a different binder. And gloss paints use more solvents than emulsions.

Alternative paints do cost more. But when you consider the entire cost of painting and decorating, the extra expense is relatively small. Think how much it would cost to use wallpaper instead …

Not whiter than white

In Victorian times paints contained a number of toxic ingredients, including lead, arsenic and mercury. Modern paints have largely replaced these with titanium dioxide (TiO_2). This white substance is used in a multitude of products, including detergents and paper, but its biggest application is as a paint pigment. Titanium dioxide is responsible for the most significant environmental impact from paints, using lots of energy in production and processing, as well as causing pollution from mining. Another problem is that there's a global shortage of the raw materials for TiO_2, which leads to intense pressure to open up new mines in areas that are unique habitats for plants and animals.

TiO_2 is used not only as a whitener but also to make paint cover a surface effectively. This is an important environmental consideration because it may make the difference between applying one coat or several. Even 'natural' paints use TiO_2, but paint companies should ask their suppliers about their environmental performance and make sure they're not destroying precious habitats.

Getting rid of it

The best way of disposing of paint is to reuse it, and Community Repaint helps you do that. It keeps a list of existing paint reuse schemes and encourages people to set up more. You shouldn't put paint in your normal household waste – I'm afraid it's yet another thing to take to your local authority hazardous waste point. But some natural paints can actually be composted.

NATURAL and ECO-PAINT WEBLINKS

Auro Natural Paints Extensive range of paint products made with mostly natural ingredients. A thorough approach to minimising environmental impact although they do use VOC solvents.
My Rating 6/10

www.auro.co.uk

Biofa Extensive range of paints and wood treatment products, without VOC solvents.
My Rating 7/10

www.villanatura.co.uk

Ecos Paints Odourless solvent-free paints, although they do use acrylic binders (petrochemical). Their marketing seems a little over the top for what they offer.
My Rating 3/10

www.ecospaints.com

Georgina Barrow – Natural Paints Claim to be natural paints, but do use VOC solvents and some artificial pigments. *My Rating 2/10*

www.naturalpaints.org.uk

Green Paints All their paints use water-borne solvents, but they do use a synthetic binder. Good-quality paints with an extensive colour range. *My Rating 8/10*

www.greenpaints.net

Livos Natural Paints German brand of natural paint, with an emphasis on health. Good environmental credentials, including challenging TiO2 manufacturers on their environmental policy. But their paint may darken with age and takes a long time to dry.
My Rating 8/10

www.ecomerchant.co.uk

Natural Building Technologies UK company producing water-based paints with good environmental and health credentials. The only paint I found with reduced TiO2, achieved without compromising performance. Cheaper than other eco-paints but with limited colour range.
My Rating 9/10

www.natural-building.co.uk

Nutshell Paints Thorough approach to environmental and health issues. Still use citrus peel oil solvent in some products, although not their emulsions.
My Rating 8/10

www.nutshellpaints.com

Community Repaint Helps find community initiatives that can use waste paint.

www.communityrepaint.org.uk

Eco Artisan Decorating company that offers advice on and uses eco-paints.

www.ecoartisan.org

Eco Paints Sells Auro paints.

www.ecopaints.co.uk

Green Building Store – Natural Paint Collection Sells Biofa and other paints.

www.greenbuildingstore.co.uk

Green Shop Sells a wide range of the paints listed above and runs Auro UK.

www.greenshop.co.uk

Good Woods
Another life

Apart from being bright red, my kitchen cupboards don't look unusual – as it happens they could be the greenest part of my eco-renovation. When I realised a friend was ripping out her perfectly serviceable units I asked if I could have them. With a bit of wizardry from my carpenter, they fitted my kitchen layout – at a fraction of the price.

You may not have a friend conveniently chucking out old fittings, but salvage companies often have supplies of doors, wood frames and floorboards. There are also schemes which recycle old furniture and shelving. And make sure your waste wood is recycled too Most local authorities will have wood recycling facilities or can recommend wood reuse projects.

Save the forest

Style and price are likely to be your top concerns when buying cupboards and shelving. But you should also be thinking about your impact on rainforests and other woodland areas. The UK still imports wood that's been illegally logged – in fact less than 1 per cent of tropical timber harvested for the international market comes from well-managed sources.

The Forest Stewardship Council (FSC) has set up a well-recognised international certification scheme for wood. By tracking it from the forests right through to the end consumer, they're able to verify whether it comes from well-managed sources. The FSC also has criteria for recycled wood.

Demand for better-known woods, like mahogany and teak, results in more forests being destroyed. Unknown species that have already been chopped down might be just as good for the job. Greenpeace have produced an excellent *Good Wood Guide* to tell you which wood is suitable for which purpose.

EXOTIC WOODS

Avoid exotic woods from ancient forests, such as Abachi, Iroko, mahogany and teak. Iroko is a substitute for teak, but none of it comes from sustainable forests. Much better is a South American wood called Tatachuba, which has FSC certification.

Most people are now aware of 'food miles', but what about 'material miles'? Although more than two-thirds of wood used in the UK is imported, it's far better to use local wood, which can still get FSC-certification.

Is MDF good or bad?

Contrary to expectations, medium density fibreboard (MDF) could be a good environmental choice. Made from mixed chipped wood with resin, MDF can also contain waste wood and forest trimmings and therefore use materials that would otherwise go to waste. But recycling waste MDF is not common – it's still at an experimental stage which is a pity because 1 million tonnes of it is thrown away every year.

Concern over MDF comes from its use of formaldehyde, which is carcinogenic and an irritant to the eyes, nose and throat. The chief issue is dust particles in the air, so wearing a mask is essential, even if you are using low-formaldehyde MDF. Formaldehyde-free MDF is also available.

If you're buying wood, here's your priority list:
1. **Repair something you already have.**
2. **Use reclaimed wood.**
3. **Buy FSC-certified wood.**
4. **Look for locally sourced wood.**
5. **Consider alternative species.**

WOOD WEBLINKS

Association for Environment Conscious Building
www.aecb.net

Benchmark Furniture All furniture comes from certified, sustainably managed forests.
www.benchmark-furniture.com

Forest Stewardship Council (FSC) The main certification body for sustainably sourced timber. Call their information service if you want further help: 01686 413916.
www.fsc-uk.org

Friends of the Earth (FoE) FoE's Good Wood Guide advises on the best choices when buying or using wood for DIY or self-build.
www.foe.co.uk

Furniture Reuse Network Promotes the reuse of unwanted furniture and links to local organisations.
www.frn.org.uk

Greenpeace Campaigning to save ancient forests with its SaveorDelete campaign. It also produces a Good Wood Guide which gives examples of commonly used tree species and recommends alternatives.
www.greenpeace.org.uk

The PEFC Council (Programme for the Endorsement of Forest Certification Schemes) Another sustainable wood certification scheme, sometimes used instead of FSC.
www.pefc.org

RecycleWood Finds your nearest wood recycler, and products made from recycled wood.
www.recyclewood.org.uk

Salvo Lists architectural salvage organisations.
www.salvo.co.uk

Timber Recycling Information Centre Information on everything to do with timber recycling. www.recycle-it.org

Waste Resources Action Plan (WRAP) Free interactive resource that helps find recycling and collection services for wood waste.
www.wrap.org.uk

Carpets and Flooring

Carpeting over

You either like carpets or you don't. Those of us who are carpet fans point out that apart from being cosy, they stop heat escaping, reduce noise, and you're less likely to slip on them. But opponents complain that they collect dust mites, contain some rather nasty chemicals, use lots of resources and produce tonnes of waste.

I have to agree about the waste. When I moved to my current house every room had old patterned carpets from wall to wall – even the kitchen. I ripped them all out and was rather disappointed to discover that there was no carpet recycling scheme I could take them to. One of my workmen said he would remove them for me, but I then discovered his intention was to burn them. That's not a great idea – it's not even legal. So they went to landfill, some after a brief interlude of suppressing weeds in my garden.

You can now get recyclable carpet tiles. The idea is to lease the tiles for their usable life and then return them for recycling into more carpet tiles, backing materials or other products (see Heuga Home Flooring in Flooring Weblinks). One advantage to tiles is that you can replace a single tile if it gets damaged, rather than recarpeting the whole room. This carpet revolution may take a while to catch on, and however appealing, I think home owners might be slow to embrace carpet tiles in their bedrooms. But we have to hope that this new approach will be a success – a staggering 2 per cent of landfill waste is carpeting.

A good lay

You might spend a lot of time thinking about which carpet to buy, but don't forget about what goes underneath. Carpet retailers are often only too aware of this, slashing the price of carpets whilst marking up the cost of underlay. More importantly, a good underlay will help prolong the life of a carpet.

There are three main sorts of underlay: jute felt, wool and rubber. Jute felt is made by weaving the jute with other similar materials into a sort of web. Wool underlay is usually recycled from the offcuts of carpet factories. Rubber underlay is more often made from synthetic rubber – no natural rubber underlay is sold in the UK – however, some companies use recycled car tyres, which is a really excellent use for them.

Most carpets have a backing material, such as hessian (jute) or polypropylene, which is stuck on with glue. Synthetic latex is often used as the adhesive and it's this that gives new carpets their powerful smell – it lets off VOCs. You can get natural latex glues as an alternative, although they're not common (see Flooring Weblinks). Woven carpets have an integral backing material, which means they use only a small amount of adhesive – again, usually synthetic latex – but they're more expensive.

Wood, stone, tiles and more

Linoleum is back in fashion, and it has good environmental credentials too. It's available in bright colours, which suited me – I laid orange lino in the bathroom. Chiefly made from plants such as linseed, jute and pine, lino is long-lasting but can be used as an energy source at the end of its useful life, as well as to make carpet underlay.

If you like the idea of wood flooring, it's best to reuse old floorboards. Failing that, check that it's FSC-certified. One downside to wood is that it needs more maintenance than lino or PVC. Laminate wood floors can be made using recycled waste wood from the lumber industry, which is good – it's worth checking with the manufacturer what proportion of recycled materials they've used. In general they're laid without using any adhesives.

Cork gets my vote as the best natural flooring. Cork bark can go on being harvested for over 200 years without damaging the tree that produces it. And cork forests are rich in wildlife and plants. Unfortunately, they're being threatened by other forms of agriculture, and by wine producers moving to plastic corks. More cork flooring won't solve this problem, but it

might help a little. Soft under foot, durable, fire-resistant and a good insulator, cork is also a practical solution. Give it a go.

I can't recommend PVC flooring. Apart from concerns about its manufacture and disposal, there are worries about toxic chemicals being added. PVC is cheap, but is it worth it? Lino, cork and PVC flooring all need adhesives. Low-VOC and non-VOC adhesives are widely available, so look out for these.

CARPET TYPES

It's not just whether or not to have carpets, it's what type of carpet to choose. Here's a brief summary of their environmental credentials:

Wool *My Rating 7/10*
Comes from a renewable resource and has excellent insulation properties. But washing and treating wool requires energy and huge quantities of water.

Sea grass *My Rating 7/10*
Sea grass beds are breeding grounds for marine life and protect against coastal erosion. Harvesting the crop encourages local people to value and protect this vulnerable eco-system, although cropping it reduces its value as a fish nursery. Sea grass is apparently impossible to clean, which means it's useable life will be shortened.

Recycled plastic (PET) *My Rating 6/10*
Aside from replacing virgin materials, these carpets have the added benefit of better stain resistance and less indoor air pollution – solvents aren't released. But so far not many have been made.

Coir *My Rating 4/10*
Coir is made from coconut husks, which are soaked in natural ponds to soften them. There's some concern that this may be damaging to pond wildlife.

Sisal *My Rating 2/10*
The waste, pollution and poor farming practices in the sisal industry are threatening its existence. Only 4 per cent of the sisal leaf is used for flooring; the rest of the plant is wasted. Small-scale innovative projects
exist to make more use of the plant, but they're in their infancy.

Synthetic fibres *My Rating 0/10*
Most carpets are made from nylon, polyester or polypropylene. They're not only made from oil but use lots of energy in their manufacture and are therefore a major source of greenhouse gases, acid rain and toxins. Nylon is the worst, but synthetic carpets containing recycled fibres are not so bad.

FLOORING WEBLINKS

Alternative Flooring Offers natural floor coverings.

www.alternativeflooring.com

Concept Carpet British-made carpet in natural colours using no dyes or chemicals, with hessian backing and natural latex glue.

www.concept-carpet.co.uk

Construction Resources Sells Geysira wool carpets made from 100 per cent untreated Icelandic wool, washed in natural steam from local geysers. Uses natural backing material, natural latex glues and natural stain protector.

www.constructionresources.com

Forbo World leader in linoleum – their brand is Marmoleum.

www.forbo.com

Healthy Flooring Network Offers advice on flooring, particularly for people with allergies and asthma.

www.healthyflooring.org

Heuga Home Flooring Sells easy-to-use carpet tiles with a commitment to recycle them at the end of their useful life.

www.heuga.com

Pergo Produces laminate flooring using recycled materials.

www.europe.pergo.com

Siesta Cork Tile Advice on all sorts of cork flooring, and sells by mail order.

www.siestacorktile.com

Treadmore Makes underlay from recycled car tyres, as well as jute, wool and lino waste. Its Duralay company has set up a recycling plant using 45,000 waste car tyres a week, thus stopping them going to landfill.

www.interfloor.com/Treadmore

GREEN BUILDINGS and ECO-LIVING WEBSITES

Association for Environment Conscious Building A sustainable building association.
www.aecb.net

Building Research Establishment (BRE) Offers a huge range of building-related information and services.
www.bre.co.uk

Construction Resources An ecological building centre.
www.constructionresources.com

Global Action Plan Promotes environmentally sustainable lifestyles through individual action.
www.globalactionplan.org.uk

Green Moves Sells homes that are more energy-efficient than conventional homes.
www.greenmoves.com

Greenspec Informative website comparing a whole range of building products, from flooring to paints.
www.greenspec.co.uk

Low Impact Living Initiative Demonstrates how to reduce human impact and improve quality of life.
www.lowimpact.org

Ecos (formerly the Somerset Trust for Sustainable Development) Campaigns to make sustainable building the norm (I'm a trustee!).
www.ecostrust.org.uk

South West Eco Homes Eco-homes developer.
www.swecohomes.co.uk

Tip the Planet Encourages discussion of ideas for helping the planet.
www.tiptheplanet.com

What do I do with this Sells surplus building material, recycled by builders or end of the line building stock.
www.whatdoidowiththis.com

HEAT AND POWER

One-third of all energy is used at home, and over 80 per cent of that is used for heating – saving it is probably the most important thing we can do to help the environment. It doesn't matter what sort of house or flat you live in, there are lots of things you can do. So here's a hierarchy to help you prioritise your actions:

1. Insulate as much as possible to prevent heat escaping
2. Reduce the amount of fossil fuels you use by being energy efficient.
3. Use renewable energy, such as solar or wind, wherever practical.

In this section I look at the choice of insulation materials, which green electricity supplier to sign up to, which renewable energy technology might work for you, and how to reduce your energy impacts in other ways.

Insulation
Snug as a bug
In Scandinavia they're far better at insulating buildings than we are in the UK. Insulation makes an enormous difference to the cost of heating and should be top of your list of energy-saving measures. If you live in a flat you should check with your landlord about the building's insulation, if it's not obvious.

Once you've decided to insulate you need to think about which material to use. Understanding the technical issues can be tricky. For example, the environmental performance of a material might be good, but will it be suitable for where you want to use it? And it's also important to consider ventilation – buildings need to breathe. Any material is better than none, and each has its pros and cons.

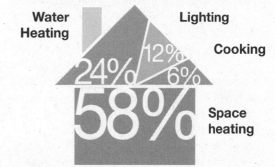

Water Heating 24%
Lighting 12%
Cooking 6%
Space heating 58%

FAKE SNOW
Fake snow used in the Harry Potter films was made from recycled newspapers – also used in insulation.

INSULATING MATERIALS

Recycled newspapers *My Rating 9/10*
Recycling newspapers and telephone directories for insulation is an excellent use of waste. It is an effective insulator and is particularly good at getting into all the nooks and crannies. It also has excellent sound-proofing qualities, and in terms of cost is competitive with synthetic materials. The powder has to be sprayed by a professional installer, isn't suitable for cavity walls and doesn't perform at all well if it gets wet.

Sheep's wool *My Rating 8/10*
Sheep's wool has excellent insulating qualities, is safe, easy to install and isn't badly affected by moisture. It takes the least amount of energy to produce of all insulation materials, but is also the most expensive, costing about four times more than glass fibre. It has to be chemically treated for pest- and fire-resistance; the same chemicals can also be used in sheep dipping.

Glass fibre *My Rating 4/10*
Glass fibre is made from melted-down glass, which can come from recycled materials. It's widely available and cheap, but it takes a lot of energy to make, releases solvent emissions or VOCs, and doesn't biodegrade when disposed of. There are also health concerns about installing it because fine particles are released, so it's vital to wear a mask. It doesn't work so well if it gets wet or if its fibres flatten, which they may do over time.

Mineral wool *My Rating 3/10*
Mineral wool is made from melted-down volcanic rocks and steel slag, and sometimes from 100 per cent recycled materials. It's fireproof, cheap and widely available, but like glass fibre it takes a lot of energy to make, releases fine particles when being installed (remember the mask), and its performance may be reduced by the fibres flattening over time or getting wet.

Polystyrene – Expanded and Extruded
My Rating 2/10
These foams can be made with recycled materials, are long-lasting and have good resistance to moisture, air movement, rot and compression. Extruded polystyrene requires more processing than expanded and therefore double the amount of energy to make – three times more than mineral wool. They're made with petrochemicals, release solvent emissions and produce toxic fumes when burnt. Performance apparently deteriorates over time as gases are released.

Polyurethane/Polyisocyanurate Board and Foam *My Rating 1/10*
Foam and board are excellent insulators and can fit into narrow spaces where other materials would be less effective. They're particularly suitable for cavity wall insulation, but not so good for fitting snugly between rafters. The trouble is that they're the most energy-intensive insulating materials to make and they use chemicals that are powerful greenhouse gases. Ironically, these HFCs were introduced as a replacement to ozone-depleting CFCs in the 1990s. Like other foams, they produce toxic fumes when burnt.

Other natural fibres

Cork
Cork board is ideal for flat roofing and has good environmental credentials. It comes from sustainably managed cork farms that may be threatened by reduced demand for natural wine corks.

Hemp
Hemp is a traditional crop, a good insulator and about half the price of sheep's wool

Cotton
The heavy use of chemical pesticides for growing cotton (page 208) makes it a poor environmental choice for insulation. But using recycled cotton fibres is an excellent use of waste textiles and clothing.

Straw
Straw bale houses offer excellent thermal efficiency. Straw boards can replace timber for internal partitioning.

Insulating scandal

Recognising that my uninsulated attic was sucking huge amounts of heat from the rest of the house, I decided to do something about it. I was attracted by the idea of sheep's wool but put off by the cost, so I decided to go for recycled newspaper insulation.

The next step was to see if I could get a grant; I called the Energy Efficiency Hotline to see if I was eligible. Apparently I was, although not for a full grant, which would have been due if I had been on benefits or a pensioner. Then came the trouble. It appeared that I couldn't get a grant – or discounted insulation – if I wanted to use 'environmentally friendly' materials. I wondered if this could be right. Why would choosing an energy-efficient material rule me out?

I tracked down the main players in the chain, which wasn't easy. It starts with DEFRA, the Government department charged with reducing carbon emissions. Their scheme forces power companies to promote energy efficiency, in part by offering discounts on insulation. It appears that they do this by offering the cheapest material possible, on which they can get bulk discounts – generally mineral wool or glass fibre but not recycled newspaper.

Scottish Power, the company in question, is not alone. When I contacted British Gas and London Energy the response was the same: discounted insulation was only available if you used the material of their choice. Another problem with the system is that companies run out of grant money before the year end, so apply in April if you want to beat others chasing discounts.

DEFRA say they're improving the system, but industry insiders say it's likely to get worse before it gets better. It's a muddle that needs sorting out. The grants system should be simple, available to all who apply, and it should certainly not discriminate against 'environmentally friendly' materials.

INSULATION WEBLINKS

British Gas Insulation Line	0845 971 7731
Construction Resources Supplies energy efficient plant cellulose insulation.	www.constructionresources.com
Ecological Building Systems Sells hemp, wood fibre and other natural insulation products.	www.ecologicalbuildingsystems.com
Energy Efficiency Advice Centre Advises on grants and energy efficiency measures.	0800 512 012
London Energy Insulation Line	0800 085 1439
OFGEM Government regulator for electricity and gas.	www.ofgem.gov.uk/ofgem
Pen Y Coed Construction and Insulation Ltd Installs Warmcel recycled newspaper insulation.	www.penycoed-warmcel.com
Plant Fibre Technology Ltd Produces hemp and other plant fibre insulation products.	www.plantfibretechnology.com
Recovery Insulation Insulation made from recycled textiles.	www.recovery-insulation.co.uk
Scottish Power For cavity wall and loft insulation grants.	0845 601 7836
Thermafleece – Second Nature Main manufacturer of sheep's wool insulation.	www.secondnatureuk.com
Warmcel – Excel Manufacturer of Warmcel recycled newspaper insulation.	www.excelfibre.com

Electricity
Electricity suppliers

Changing electricity supplier is something that everyone can do; it need only take a few minutes if you do it online. Some of the green electricity suppliers charge a little more than the standard suppliers, but not all of them – you will need to check tariffs because they fluctuate.

The best reason for changing your supplier is to give greater support for renewable energy generation. But if you have wind turbines, solar panels or a CHP boiler (page 110), you'll also want to check out how much you'll be paid for electricity fed back into the grid.

The Government has set minimum targets for the amount of renewable energy electricity companies must provide. But what we want is to support companies exceeding these targets, rather than just meeting their legal obligations. Below is a summary of the greener electricity schemes on offer to help you choose which one is for you.

GREEN ELECTRICITY SUPPLIERS

Eco Energy – Northern Ireland Electricity
My Rating 6/10
www.nieenergy.co.uk
Just 2 per cent of NIE's 750,000 customers – 15,000 in total – have signed up to the Eco Energy scheme, which contributes to renewable energy generation over and above Government requirements. With links to organisations such as the Wildfowl and Wetlands Trust and the Woodland Trust, the Eco Energy scheme promotes new technologies, such as CHP, and supports tree-planting. They give higher rates for home solar energy than for other renewables because it is generated at peak times.

Ecotricity *My Rating 9/10*
www.ecotricity.co.uk
Ecotricity offers two green electricity packages. The Old Energy Scheme, as it is known, charges a premium for supplying 100 per cent of its electricity from renewable sources, but there are no profits to be invested in renewable energy. Most of Ecotricity's 15,000 customers, however, have signed up to their New Energy Scheme. This buys 75 per cent of its electricity from mainstream generators and only 25 per cent from renewable suppliers. This is profitable and so they are able to invest in renewable energy – chiefly wind. Ecotricity is supported by WWF and the Soil Association. They have a tree-planting scheme and pay a good rate for renewable energy produced at home.

EDF Energy *My Rating 5/10*
www.edfenergy.com
Customers pay more to join EDF's Green Energy Fund, and the money, along with a matching contribution from EDF, is invested in renewable energy projects. Only a small percentage of the power you buy comes from renewables.

10 DOWNING STREET
According to Juice, they offered to pay for sheep's wool insulation at 10 Downing Street, but were declined for 'security reasons'.

EDF has recently set up another scheme called Climate Balance, which enables customers to carbon offset their energy use.

Good Energy *My Rating 9/10*
www.good-energy.co.uk
All electricity supplied to Good Energy's 18,000 customers is renewable. Good Energy is simply a supply company and does not generate any electricity itself – it buys it from others. The company pays a good rate for renewable energy produced at home, and has set up a scheme called Smartgen in partnership with HSBC bank to encourage farmers and landowners to generate renewable energy.

Green Energy *My Rating 7/10*
www.greenenergy.uk.com
Green Energy Plus 10 is the most popular of its two green energy schemes. It commits to supplying 10 per cent more renewable energy than the Government requires it to do. Green Energy Plus 100 costs nearly 10 per cent more, but all of it comes from renewable sources. Green Energy supports small-scale hydro power schemes and offers a variable rate on home-produced renewable energy.

Juice *My Rating 7/10*
www.npower.com
Npower is one of the largest UK power companies, and its Juice scheme, launched in partnership with Greenpeace, has over 50,000 customers. All the electricity initially came from one off-shore wind farm, but others are coming on stream. Tariffs are the same as for other Npower customers, the company has an energy-efficiency

advice service, is a big supporter of heat pumps, and pays a good rate for home-produced renewable energy. Although it's an excellent scheme, I do have one eco-criticism. Npower includes the renewable energy bought by Juice customers as part of what it's legally required to produce by Government dictat, rather than buying extra.

RSPB Energy *My Rating 6/10*
www.rspbenergy.co.uk
Scottish and Southern Energy Group, which runs RSPB Energy, claims to be the largest generator of renewable energy in the country, most of which comes from large-scale hydro power. Ninety per cent of the electricity for RSPB energy comes from hydro and 10 per cent from other renewables and CHP, and money is donated to the organisation. This is used to buy wetlands and endangered bird habitats. Wind is part of the mix, but the RSPB campaign to make sure turbines are not in areas where they disturb birds.

Scottish and Southern Energy Group – Power 2 *My Rating 5/10*
All of the energy supplied to Power 2 customers comes from large-scale hydro power. Money raised is used to sponsor the Tree Council's Walk in the Woods Campaign (www.treecouncil.org.uk). Scottish and Southern also supports large-scale tree-planting.

For up-to-date comparisons of green electricity schemes, see the Green Electricity Marketplace at www.greenelectricity.org. This also provides a link to a site giving details of the proportion of energy sourced from various fuel types for all UK electricity providers.

Intelligent Meters

Have you ever heard of intelligent houses that open and close windows, turn on heating and even cook your dinner, all at the touch of a remote control button? Intelligent metering – the next stage on from the devices mentioned above – will be a key part of any thinking house. They'll not only measure the amount of electricity, water and gas you use, but even call out the boiler repair man (or woman) to keep your system working at peak efficiency. These devices will know when you come home, when you use your kettle or wash your hair – they'll not only monitor how much you use but when you use it. In fact the time of day will be important too because charges will vary – you'll pay more at peak times and less at low times.

So what's that got to do with being green? Well, reducing carbon emissions from electricity generation is not only about decreasing the amount of electricity used, it's also about cutting electricity demand at peak times, when power stations are working full tilt and falling back on their dirtiest fuels. The all-knowing intelligent meter will be coming your way soon – it should be in widespread use within a couple of years. Welcome it with open arms.

ENERGY-SAVING GIZMO

I bought a brilliant electricity-saving device called Electrisave. Essentially it's a meter that tells you how many kilos of greenhouse gases your house is consuming per hour and also works out the cost. It's so simple to set up that once you've had a go you can lend it to others. I'm a brilliant sales person for the device because everyone who comes to my house goes away saying they're going to get one.

So what's so good about it? Well, it doesn't look very exciting – there's an attachment to fix onto the wire coming from your electricity meter, and a hand-held screen a little bigger than a pocket notebook.

But once I had set it up, a friend and I ran around the house turning everything off to get the reading down to nought. We thought we'd found every possible electrical device, but still there was something on the screen. Then Eureka!, we switched off a CD player in one of my sons' bedrooms and we had a 'zero energy house'.

As we gradually switched on the fridge, freezer and telephones, we discovered how much electricity they were using. I've now taken a number of energy-saving measures, such as plugging all the TV-related appliances onto a panel of sockets so they can all be switched off at the same time. The meter is also a great advertisement for energy-efficient lighting (page 104-108) – they barely register on the screen, whereas ordinary bulbs have quite an impact.

An Electrisave metre isn't cheap at about £80 but it claims you can save up to 25% of your electricity bill – and I saved considerably more than that, easily covering the cost of the device in six months! You can get a cheaper version that costs around £30, which will measure how much electricity one appliance is using. I don't think it's nearly so good.

SAVAPLUG

A type of plug that's promoted as saving electricity on domestic fridges and freezers. They may be worthwhile on old equipment but even then will take about seven years to pay back the cost of purchase. My fridge man says they can actually be damaging to new fridges.

METER WEBLINKS

Electrisave Markets and sells Electrisave, which can also be found in some small electrical shops as well as on the internet.

www.electrisave.co.uk

Greenshop Sells both the adapter-type meter and Electrisave.

www.greenshop.co.uk

Lighting

Top of my list of things to do in my new house was to replace all the light bulbs with energy-efficient ones. They're called compact fluorescents (CFLs) and are available in bulb shape as well as the rather unattractive loopy ones. Both fit into ordinary light sockets. One thing to be aware of is that CFLs take a little while to warm up when you turn them on – they're not actually any dimmer.

However, switching over hasn't been as easy as I expected. Even at Ikea, which was promoting CFLs, there weren't any bathroom or kitchen lights that actually worked with CFLs – or maybe there were, but I couldn't find anything or anyone to tell me about it, even when I phoned its helpline. I think it's scandalous that halogen bulbs are so hard to avoid. I didn't succumb, but neither did I find a light fitting for my bathroom sink that took CFLs.

Most modern kitchens are lighting disasters from an energy-saving point of view. We all have far more lights than 40 years ago, and I'm no exception, but I've made sure I use energy-efficient spotlight bulbs. At first I put in bulbs that used 23 watts rather than 100, but they stuck out of the fittings like bulbous eyes and the light colour was too white and sterile, even though they were marketed as 'warm white'.

Being rather determined about these things, I rang the lighting manufacturer to discuss the problem. They suggested I replace the existing bulbs with smaller 11-watt bulbs. This was an improvement – they didn't stick out so much and the light quality was better. If I'm honest, I don't think the light is as nice as the energy-guzzling alternatives, but my lights now use 10 per cent of the electricity they would have and they'll last me more than twice as long. I think it's worth the aesthetic compromise.

! A CALL FOR ACTION

All new light fittings should be designed to work with energy-efficient bulbs, and information about this should be available in shops.

In most homes lighting accounts for about 15 per cent of the electricity bill, so there are real savings to be made. If you're designing a new room, make the most of the natural light from the windows; don't be tempted by halogen bulbs; see if you can reduce the number of bulbs you use; and make sure there's a light switch at the door so you're not tempted to leave the lights on.

I don't always admit it but I've started counting how many bulbs people have in their kitchens. I found one with 22 60-watt bulbs in the ceiling alone, more up-lighters in the floor and yet more under the cupboards. Most of us aren't as bad as that, but if you're installing a new kitchen, see if you can limit the number of light fittings. Dimmers do save electricity and prolong the life of the bulb, but you need to get specially adapted ones to work with CFLs.

Ban the Bulb

www.banthebulb.org is a campaigning organisation pushing to:

- **Increase the use of energy-efficient bulbs.**
- **Encourage the taxing and phasing out of incandescent light bulbs.**
- **Introduce a time limit for light fittings that take incandescent bulbs.**
- **Include environmental costs in the prices consumers pay for bulbs.**

LIGHTS OUT

I've often heard people say that you shouldn't turn the lights out because it uses more energy to turn them on again. This isn't true – it's always worth turning off lights when you don't need them.

WHY MOST LIGHT BULBS SHOULD BE BANNED

- If homes in the UK replaced just one traditional 100-watt light bulb with an energy-saving alternative, we'd be able to do without the energy produced by Sizewell B nuclear power station or equivalent.

- Energy-efficient light bulbs can last around 8–12 times longer than ordinary bulbs.

- At least 90 per cent of energy consumed by ordinary bulbs (incandescents) is given off as heat.

- Each energy-efficient bulb can reduce your electricity bill by around £7 per year. The extra cost of the bulb is paid off after just seven months.

LIGHTING YOUR LIFE

There are four main types of lighting readily available today. Here's a summary of their environmental credentials.

Incandescent
My Rating 1/10
These are the most commonly used light bulbs in the house – but they shouldn't be. They waste energy by turning it into heat, and they're short-lived.

Fluorescent
My Rating 8/10
Most energy-efficient bulbs use fluorescent technology. An electric current passes through gas in a tube, which makes the coating glow brightly without getting hot. They do contain mercury, however, which is not ideal. They should be used as much as possible, wherever their light quality is not a problem.

Compact fluorescent lights (CFLs)
My Rating 7/10
Fluorescent technology has been adapted to fit into bulbs. These bulbs are generally a little bigger than incandescent ones, but they last a lot longer and use 4–5 times less energy. They will work only with specially adapted dimmers and should be used wherever possible.

Halogen
My Rating 0/10
Halogen lights use the same filament technology as incandescent bulbs, but they're placed in a quartz capsule containing halogen. The bulbs get extremely hot and don't last very long. Halogen floor lamps typically use 300 watts and get so hot they can give you serious burns.

Light-emitting diodes (LEDs)
My Rating 9/10
LEDs last 40 times as long as an ordinary bulb and could cut the cost of lighting homes and offices in half. One expert claims that 90 per cent of our lighting could come from LEDs by 2020. This would save the world billions of pounds in energy costs – 100 billion dollars in the USA alone, which is the equivalent output of 133 power stations.

Stand-by lights on televisions and videos, exit signs and other speciality applications have been using coloured LED lights for a while. But the white lights are only just being developed and marketed, as garden and Christmas lights for example. They're particularly suited for the outdoors because they can be solar-powered.

The really staggering thing about LEDs is their life expectancy. It's estimated that they could last more than ten years. This makes them ideal for places where it's difficult to reach. The bulbs don't actually burn out, they just get dimmer over time, and unlike fluorescent bulbs they don't contain any hazardous materials.

If you're about to rush down to the shop to get some LEDs, hold your horses. They're not yet suitable as a direct replacement for everyday household bulbs, and they're expensive, even compared to CFLs. But this is a fast-changing technology. Between 2002 and 2004 the price per lumen came down from $250 to $50, and further dramatic improvements mean that it won't be long before everyone will be swapping their CFLs for LEDs.

DID YOU KNOW?

Traffic lights are beginning to use LEDs. They save 80 per cent of the electricity used by the old bulbs – enough to power around 40,000 households in the UK – and only have to be changed every ten years rather than every six months.

LED RIGHT NOW

I went to stay with my brother and was interested to see that he had **LED** spotlight bulbs in his newly installed kitchen. They were 'warm white' in colour and seemed to work well, using 2 watts of electricity each.

If you want to do the same, here's some tips:

- LEDs are not yet up to the level of replacing 60-watt bulbs. It's best to use LEDs if you are installing new lighting.
- Current LEDs can replace a 20-watt halogen bulb. You'll need triple the amount of LED fittings to get equivalent light.
- LEDs are excellent for mood lighting.
- LEDs don't get hot, so they can be used near insulation materials or in confined spaces without being a fire hazard.

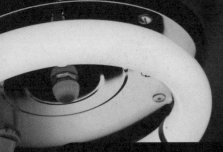

Lighting waste

I was rather surprised to find out that I shouldn't be throwing my CFL bulbs in the bin. Each one apparently contains 5mg of mercury, which can be recycled and used to make more light bulbs. A standard 6ft fluorescent tube contains three times as much mercury. The government has been slow to compel local authorities to set up and promote collection and recycling facilities for this hazardous waste, and the growing market for CFL bulbs means that more mercury is ending up in landfill sites – or even worse, being burnt.

It may be tedious, but you should contact your local authority to ask them about recycling fluorescent tubes and CFL bulbs. If they don't have facilities – and mine doesn't – it's worth badgering them because they should. The lighting industry worries that raising awareness over mercury in CFLs will put people off buying them. They rightly point out that using an energy-efficient lamp reduces mercury pollution from power stations by more than the amount in a bulb. It's not just the mercury in a light bulb that's recycled. Every year light bulb waste in the UK could produce 12,000 tonnes of glass, 670 tonnes of metal, 350 tonnes of plastic, 100 tonnes of phosphor and half a tonne of mercury.

LIGHTING WEBLINKS

Ban the Bulb Campaigns to increase the use of energy-efficient lighting and phase out incandescents.	www.banthebulb.org
Efficient Light Sells energy-efficient lighting and offers advice on suitable household applications.	www.efficientlight.co.uk
Energy Saving World Sells energy-efficient lighting and other energy-saving products.	www.energysavingworld.co.uk
LED Light Bulbs Stocks an extensive range of LED bulbs.	www.led-lightbulbs.co.uk
Solar GB Designs and sells high-quality LED lighting.	www.solargb.co.uk

Radiators and Boilers

Radiators

The radiators in my new home were old, rusty and numerous. However, I discovered that instead of having two in each room, I could have just one energy-efficient one. Each radiator has its own thermostat so you can turn off individual ones in rooms that aren't being used.

Another discovery was the value of radiator panels. You put these behind the radiator so they reflect the heat back into the room rather than it being absorbed by the wall behind – they can reduce your heating bill by as much as 10–15 per cent.

There are two different sorts of radiator panel: flat and slatted. I found to my cost that the flat ones aren't as good. When my radiators were being installed I was in a rush to get the panels. So instead of ordering them from the Energy Saving World website, where I had found them, I got some from B&Q that looked like padded foil. All is not lost – I can apparently retro-fit the slatted ones quite easily. This is a simple, low-cost change that most people can make to their radiators.

How hot?

Men's bodies are apparently warmer than women's, which can lead to fights over what temperature to set the thermostat at – men are often happier to turn it down. Even a drop of one degree Celsius could save as much as 10 per cent of your fuel bill. So if you're young and healthy, try putting on an extra jumper. You'll find you quickly get used to having a cooler house.

For people with well-insulated houses, it can make sense to have the heating on all the time, rather than in surges at the beginning and end of the day. I have to point out that this is definitely not the case with my Victorian house – there are still too many draughty areas. One of these used to be my cat flap; despite having rubber seals around the flap, itwaved in the wind and let in a lot of cold air. I've now replaced it with a 'draught-proof' cat flap with brushes around the edges and it's much better.

Heating controls are also becoming more sophisticated. You can now programme them with the time you want to be warm, rather than when you want them to come on. This should improve on efficiency because the heating won't be on for longer than necessary.

FAKE FIRES

Gas log and coal fires may be visually appealing but they're incredibly inefficient and wasteful. Gas log fires are the worst because they generally produce a higher flame and therefore use more gas.

Boilers

My boiler is over ten years old, but my boiler repair man told me it's surprisingly efficient now he's serviced it. Yet replacing an old boiler with a more efficient condensing one will often save as much as one-third off your heating bill. Since 2005, the higher standards of efficiency required by law for new boilers can only be met by condensing boilers, which reuse the heat from the exhaust gases to pre-heat the water in the boiler system.

DOMESTIC CHP

Domestic combined heat and power (CHP) boilers are just becoming available. Like condensing boilers, they're also efficient at reusing heat, with the added benefit of making electricity too. Up to now CHP boilers have been used for community heating schemes, where the heat is diverted from other sources or made from wood chip.

I can't understand why our Government has been so slow in getting more of these schemes going. In Finland virtually all heating comes from CHP schemes, but in the UK they provide a very small proportion of what we use, with about 1,300 sites around the country.

If you're thinking about installing a domestic CHP system, you need to be on mains gas. That rules me out. The boilers are as efficient as condensing boilers; the difference is that about 12–15 per cent of what is produced is generating electricity – enough to supply about one-third of an average house.

From an environmental point of view, the main advantage of CHP is that it replaces inefficient and dirty electricity from power stations with locally produced power. It also works well with solar technology because CHP makes electricity when the heating is on, whereas solar makes more when it's sunny outside. An average house using CHP should reduce carbon emissions by around 1.6 tonnes and nitrous oxide emissions by 40 per cent.

But you may be more interested in whether you can save any money. The extra cost of a CHP boiler compared to a condensing one should be paid off in about three to five years, although higher electricity prices mean it could be less.

Here's my assessment of the three CHP domestic boilers:

Baxi Senertec *My Rating 8/10*
www.baxitech.co.uk
Baxi is one of the biggest boiler manufacturers in the UK. To date it has made CHP boilers for multi-residential buildings such as schools and care homes, and is now planning a mass-market replacement for ordinary boilers, using a similar technology to fridges.

BG Group Microgen *My Rating 9/10*
www.microgen.com
Launched in 2007, the Microgen CHP has been developed and distributed by the companies that took over from British Gas. It's designed as a mass market replacement for ordinary boilers and is able to use existing boiler connections, which will reduce installation costs. Large energy users will benefit most because more electricity is generated if more heat is used.

Whispertech *My Rating 7/10*
www.whispergen.com
The Whispergen CHP has been imported from New Zealand, and in 2006 was first to market in the UK. It's primarily sold and promoted to new housing developments, so they can benefit from the economies of scale, with their own trained installers. The size and shape of a dishwasher, the first model is aimed at well-insulated, low-energy three-bedroomed houses, but other larger-scale versions will follow.

BOILER JACKET

Putting an insulating jacket on your boiler prevents about 150kg of carbon dioxide going into the atmosphere.

CHP fuel cells on the way

Some experts believe that fuel cells powered by hydrogen will be the key to solving the world's energy crisis. They work with CHP systems and offer the same benefit of producing local electricity. The differences are that they're much more efficient and could provide *all* your heating, electricity, and even air conditioning too.

Now for the technical bit. I've been told it's simple but I'm not convinced. Low-temperature fuel cells produce energy through an electro-chemical reaction rather than through burning. The fuel used is hydrogen and only water comes out – no CO_2, NOx (nitrous oxide) or soot. But the key issue is how the hydrogen is produced. If it were made from solar energy or wind power, for example, it would be a really clean option. However most hydrogen will be made from natural gas, which still produces CO_2 emissions. I'm not sure this will be the greenest domestic heat and power system possible, but it will be an improvement on what we have today. And

it's predicted that by 2015 fuel cells will be cost effective and widely used. They're also being developed for cars and portable gadgets such as mobile phones and electronic organisers.

CHP IN LONDON?

London has the greatest potential to use CHP in new and existing homes. For example, residents of the Thames Gateway development should be able to benefit from free heat sourced from neighbouring Barking power station. The London Energy Partnership is looking at sustainable energy options for London.

Home Renewable Energy

Before you even think about installing renewable energy systems in your home you should make sure you've done all you can on insulation, energy efficiency and boiler systems. That is, unless you're undertaking a major renovation or building a house from scratch. You also have to be aware that cost savings are likely to be made over quite a number of years, so this isn't generally something that's worth doing solely on financial grounds.

Here comes the sun

I love the idea of tapping into free energy from the sun. In fact I was so keen that I was nearly

hoodwinked by a rogue company with some rather underhand sales techniques. They sent me a flyer telling me that my house had been selected as ideal for solar panels and they'd like to use it 'in their promotions'. When the salesman came round to tell me more I realised that it was a classic hard sell. The 'specially selected' bit was just to get their foot in the door, and when I researched further it appeared the product they were selling was fine but the price was astronomical.

Solar panels on your roof can be used for producing hot water or electricity. Either way, they use the sun's heat and therefore should be placed in the sunniest position possible; bad installation can reduce efficiency dramatically. There are two main types of panel: flat plates or evacuated tubes. Flat plates are less efficient and so need more space, but they are cheaper.

Solar hot water

Solar thermal, as these systems are known, uses the sun to heat water passing through a panel. This water is then fed into the hot water tank, reducing the heat needed from the boiler. Hot water will account for about one-fifth of your energy bill, and a well-designed solar thermal system should provide between 50 per cent and 70 per cent of that. If you're thinking of buying a solar thermal system it's important to know that this won't generally mean solar central heating – just hot water. Some companies don't make this clear in their sales pitch. Solar heating is much more difficult to do.

Solar electricity

Photovoltaic systems – as solar electricity is known – use cells to convert radiation from the sun into electricity. You can do this with solar panels or, for new roofs, use tiles with solar technology built in, which is less expensive than paying for a roof and solar system separately.

Solar electricity has a longer pay-back period than solar thermal – either way it'll take several decades. Unless you are a pioneering green – and we do need some of those – this may not be for you. If you're going to take the plunge, check the costs, including all the equipment you need to make it work, get a competitive quote and find out if you are eligible for a grant (page 117).

Household wind turbines

A wind turbine appeals to me even more than solar power. And I live in an ideal location on a hill – it's so windy that our trampoline blew over several times until we battened it down. If you're also tempted, here are some things to consider:

- **Electricity generated:** experts say that most wind turbine companies exaggerate the amount of electricity a wind turbine can produce. A reasonable guide is that you can save between 20–30 per cent on an average electricity bill, depending on your location, size of turbine and efficiency of the system.

- **Energy to grid:** when your wind turbine is producing more electricity than you're using, it can be fed back to the grid.

- **Rural location:** wind turbines don't work well in urban areas because the wind flow is interrupted by other buildings.

- **Siting:** Putting a wind turbine on your roof will substantially reduce its efficiency – ideally it should be at least 10 metres above any obstruction within 150 metres.

- **Structure:** if you do put a turbine on your roof, make sure the building is sturdy enough to support it and check out your buildings insurance.

- **Noise:** wind turbines are much less noisy than they were, but you can still hear the blades going through the air.

- **Wind:** clearly, if you are in a windy spot you'll get more electricity. But it's worth checking that the installation is not vulnerable to storm damage when there's too much wind.

- **Planning:** planning permission is required, but at the time of going to press this was subject to review. I think wind turbines should be treated the same as TV satellite dishes, where no permission is needed.

- **Neighbours:** avoid ferocious battles over your turbine – get your neighbours onside.

- **Installation:** check what other equipment will be needed to make your wind turbine work. For example, an inverter makes the electricity generated usable in the house.

- **Testing:** there are no independent comparative trials of wind turbines being carried out, and their efficiency is very much dependent on their location. This makes it hard to choose which is the right one for your site.

- **Grants:** grants are available for wind turbines, but you need to check that the company you are buying from is eligible.

- **Costs:** in the last couple of years domestic wind turbines have become more affordable, particularly with the grants available. But you do need to check what's included in the price quoted.

DOMESTIC WIND TURBINES IN THE UK

The main accredited domestic wind turbine companies in the UK are:

Iskra Wind Turbines	**www.iskrawind.com**
Proven Wind Turbines	**www.provenenergy.com**
Renewable Devices Swift Turbines	**www.renewabledevices.com**
Windsave	**www.windsave.com**

B&Q WIND TURBINES

B&Q's wind turbines are apparently flying off the shelves. It's great that they've brought the price down and made them more available, but they're still expensive relative to the energy they save. So my advice is do your research before investing and make sure you've done the less exciting energy-saving measures first!

Wood heating

Wood fuel heating isn't just another name for the log fire. You can get wood-fuelled boilers that are up to 90 per cent efficient, compared to 65 per cent efficiency for a log-burning stove. And one of the big advantages is that it's a lot cheaper than oil.

I think the environmental benefits of using wood for fuel can be over-played. Sure, it's natural and renewable, but it still releases CO_2 when burnt. You also have to consider the impacts of transporting wood. Currently there's a shortage in the UK and much of it comes from Scandinavia; for its green credentials to stack up, the wood has to be locally grown or recycled.

If you think it might be for you, here are the main wood fuel options for boilers:

- **Logs:** you need a lot of storage space, because even with an extra-large system it's necessary to refuel once a day.
- **Pellets:** made from recycled, compressed sawdust, less storage space is needed. But boilers still need refuelling every one to three days.
- **Wood chips:** they can be more automated, but are only cost-effective for large houses with extensive storage facilities and a regular supply of chips.

Heat pumps

Heat pumps are an extremely good renewable energy option and have real environmental benefits. The idea is to take heat from air, water or the ground and use it for both heating and hot water.

A well-designed ground-source heat pump in an insulated house will give you roughly 3–4 units of heat for one unit of electrical input. Ground-source heat pumps draw most of their heat from the earth – pipes are laid underground, or, where space is limited, in a borehole (although this is more expensive). Unfortunately, they're not suitable for many houses, and it's far easier installing them when you're building a new house or doing a major renovation.

Air-source heat pumps are commonly used in both America and Japan, and there's renewed interest in them in the UK. The main advantages of these systems are that they're about half the price of ground-source heat pumps, use less space and are easy to install in existing buildings. The downsides are that a back-up system may be needed, domestic electricity systems limit their size, and they're noisy – they sound like air-conditioning systems.

So is this something for you? Here are some issues to consider:

Cost: there's little point installing a heat pump system if you have mains gas supplied to your house. Even if gas prices rise, the savings will be offset by higher electricity charges. For people currently using oil, the long-term savings are considerable.

Air or ground source: as a rule of thumb, new-build properties and those with land should go for ground-source heat pumps; air-source heat pumps will be more suitable for existing properties.

Current heating system: heat pumps work better with under-floor heating than with radiators.

Installation: make sure you find a reliable installer who can advise on the optimum solution for you. A good-quality system will last for at least 15 years and require virtually zero maintenance; however, cowboy contractors have been known to install systems that fail after a few months.

Planting trees: it's not advisable to plant trees on land where ground-source heat pumps have been installed – flowers and vegetables are fine.

Live by the sea?: air-source heat pumps are not advisable if you live near the sea – the salt corrodes the heat exchangers.

Blowing hot and cold
Heat pumps work for cooling as well as for warming, and they're widely used for air-conditioning. Like fridges and other air-conditioning systems, they use gases as coolants. Ozone-destroying CFCs have been replaced by ozone-friendly HFCs, but these are 1,400 times worse than CO_2 in their impact on global warming. The real scandal is that there's only one company in the UK supplying heat pumps that don't use HFCs: Earthcare Products.

It doesn't stop there. B&Q are selling thousands of household air-conditioning units containing HFCs. Given our temperate climate, I'm not convinced we need to cool our homes in this way, and it's adding insult to injury that the systems we're using contain a powerful greenhouse gas – thus warming the planet – when a far less damaging alternative is both technically feasible and cheaper.

Grants and Action
Getting started is often the hardest part, but what should come first? Most people would benefit from getting someone in to do an energy audit. That means having a look at your house and seeing where energy is being wasted, what improvements could be made and, if you're interested, whether there are any renewable energy technologies that would work in your home. If you're planning to do any major work, it's certainly worth the relatively modest charge.

There's also free advice available. The first port of call should be your local Energy Efficiency Advice Centre. They'll tell you what grants you might be eligible for and how to apply. The main grants body for renewable energy is the Low Carbon Buildings Programme, which was launched by the Government in 2006 and is run by the Energy Savings Trust.

A few companies such as Encraft offer technical support and advice on home energy, including grants, energy efficiency measures, insulation and renewable energies. Charges will vary.

A CALL FOR ACTION
All new buildings should be required to install renewable energy technologies, harvest rainwater, and be super-energy-efficient.

HOME ENERGY GENERATION SUMMARY

Here's a summary of the main renewable energy options that are available for home power. I have included my own rating score for each of them, but I should point out that the sustainability and environmental benefits will vary enormously deoending on your situation.

Ground-source heat pumps My Rating 8/10
Pros: long-term, reliable use of renewable energy; relatively short pay-back period.
Cons: high installation costs; land space needed; requires electricity input.

Wood boilers My Rating 7/10
Pros: cheap plant-derived fuel source.
Cons: transport impacts if not locally sourced; needs storage space for fuel and regular supplies.

Combined Heat and Power (CHP)
My Rating 7/10
Pros: supplies home-produced electricity from gas, which reduces CO_2 emissions.
Cons: still uses fossil fuels; provides electricity only in conjunction with heat.

Air-source heat pumps My Rating 7/10
Pros: inexpensive technology that uses readily available air.
Cons: noisy; not as reliable as ground-source heat pumps; will need back-up system for long cold spells.

Fuel-cell heat and power My Rating 7/10
Pros: flexible, high-tech clean power using energy that could be sourced from renewable technologies and stored.
Cons: hydrogen still has to be made, initially from gas, and the technology is some way off becoming mass market; difficult to match the energy mix of each household in terms of heat and electricity with the energy produced by the fuel cell; main benefits will only be realised if the hydrogen is made using wind power or solar energy.

Household wind turbine My Rating 6/10
Pros: uses renewable energy from wind; becoming affordable.
Cons: unsuitable for urban dwellings; requires maintenance; at best will provide only 30 per cent of your electricity needs.

Solar thermal (hot water) My Rating 6/10
Pros: gets energy from the sun; the most widely used renewable technology to date.
Cons: high initial investment; long pay-back period.

Condensing boiler My Rating 4/10
Pros: high-efficiency mass market boiler that fits current legal requirements.
Cons: uses fossil fuels.

Solar electricity (Photovoltaics)
My Rating 4/10
Pros: uses renewable energy from the sun; low maintenance costs.
Cons: unlikely to be cost-effective within the next ten years; a lot of money for relatively little power.

Solar thermal (Heating) My Rating 3/10
Pros: uses renewable energy from the sun.
Cons: technology more complicated than for solar hot water; not as well established.

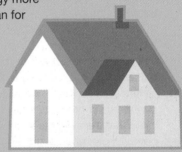

HEAT and POWER WEBLINKS

British Photovoltaic Association Information on solar photovoltaics (PVs) and list of accredited suppliers and installers.

www.greenenergy.org.uk/pvuk2/

Earthcare Products The only supplier of climate-change-friendly heat pumps.

www.earthcareproducts.co.uk

Encraft Offers home energy audits.

www.encraft.co.uk

Energy Efficiency Advice Centre Advice on home energy efficiency and grants.

0800 512 012

Energy for Good Charity offering advice on renewable energy and energy-efficient installations. Not available nationwide so you need to check whether it covers your area.

www.nef.org.uk/services/ energyforgood.htm?

Energy Saving Trust Provides useful information on energy efficiency and renewable energy.

www.est.org.uk

Energy Saving World Sells energy-efficient products, including slatted radiator panels, heating controls and light bulbs.

www.energysavingworld.co.uk

Geoscience Reliable company that installs ground-source heat pumps.

www.geoscience.co.uk

Ground-Source Heat Pump Club Good source of information on heat pumps.

www.nef.org.uk/gshp

Low Carbon Buildings Programme Provides an accredited list of renewable-energy installers and offers grants.

www.lowcarbonbuildings.org.uk/home Helpline: 0800 915 7722

National Energy Foundation Promotes renewable energy and sustainable development to a wide audience.

www.nef.org.uk

Off-Grid Promotes home-produced energy and water systems.

www.off-grid.net

Pet-Mate Sells cat flaps with brushes to stop draught coming through.

www.pet-mate.com

Powergen Offers a free energy survey of your home after you complete an online questionnaire.

www.energyefficiency.powergen.co.uk

Solar Century Leading solar PV company in the UK offering an accredited list of installers

www.solarcentury.co.uk

UK Heat Pump Network Good source of information on heat pumps.

www.nef.org.uk/gshp/gshp

KEVIN McCLOUD GREEN GRAND DESIGNS

Kevin McCloud and his family live in a seventeenth-century Somerset farmhouse. As the presenter of Channel 4's Grand Designs, you might have expected something a little more modern. The kitchen is actually quite high-tech and open-plan, but, Kevin says, 'without compromising the integrity of the building'. This is clearly something he feels strongly about.

Making eco-improvements to old buildings, he points out, may really destroy their character. One man who came on the programme had obliterated all the historic features in his house by re-lining it. Kevin was horrified. He says that living somewhere with a bit of history can be quite restrictive in terms of what green measures you can take beyond insulating your loft, fitting secondary glazing – not double-glazing – and putting in radiator panels. Oh, and installing shutters, which along with thick curtains are at least as effective as double-glazing, and nice to look at too.

If, on the other hand, you're building something new, remember you're creating the old of tomorrow. For buildings to last, he thinks designers have to make them flexible so they can be used in lots of different ways.

Apart from anything else, it's so wasteful to knock down an old building, rip out its fittings and build something new. English Heritage, he points out, estimates that it takes the energy equivalent of a gallon of petrol to make six bricks. So the embodied energy (the amount of energy it took to make a building in the first place) in the bricks of a typical Victorian house would be enough to drive a car more than ten times around the world.

Over the time that Kevin has presented *Grand Designs*, there's been an explosion of interest in eco-building. At the beginning, he remembers, about one in 50 participants were 'eco-warriors' wanting to build their green dream. Now almost half the house builders have some degree of interest in being eco-friendly. But Kevin says he sometimes feels that the enthusiasm is little more than tokenism. For example, if someone builds an enormous property with vast sheet-glass windows and eight bedrooms, introducing a few 'green features' can seem trivial. Why not, he suggests, build a smaller house in the first place?

He also notices that not everyone gets the full eco-benefits of the products they use because they don't follow the instructions properly. When insulation boards were being installed at his house, it was the first time he'd seen them taped together to stop air escaping. This was clearly recommended on the instruction sheet and would significantly improve the insulating performance.

Even with the extra insulation, Kevin's house and farm get through a lot of oil. He's decided to install a biomass boiler, which will, within five years, be fed entirely from wood grown on site. The estimated savings are £4–£5,000 per year. He's chosen the only dual-fuel boiler on the market, which takes both wood chips and pellets.

But it's not just at home that Kevin is involved in eco-initiatives. He set up an ethical furniture company and has become involved in a pioneering community housing project in Somerset.

ww.channel4.com/4homes/ontv/ grand-designs

GARDENING

A friend of mine accused me of being a 'slob' gardener because I told her my solution to bindweed was to 'not worry about it'. I do think too many gardeners worry excessively about having to get rid of every single weed and pest for ever. This is why gardeners apparently use more chemicals per acre than farmers. And well-kept lawns are the equivalent of deserts in the natural world, in terms of their lack of diversity. Below are some ideas on what can be done about the five big issues for gardeners.

SAVE WATER

Water saving is already a high priority, particularly for people living in the South East of England. And with the effects of climate change intensifying, the rest of the country may well become parched too. Sprinklers and hosepipes can use 1,000 litres of water per hour, so it's easy to splash out in the garden. Here are some water-saving tips:

Water butts: buy a water butt to collect rainwater. These large drums come in many different shapes and sizes and are widely available. You need to set them up to catch water running off your roof – and cover them to avoid green slime.

Reuse water: reuse household water for watering plants (page 74), but avoid using it on edible crops and throw earth on the top after watering.

Hosepipes: if you need to use a hosepipe, get a trigger-type nozzle that doesn't let the water out when it's not being squeezed. Use a bucket or watering can for washing your car.

Keep moisture in: put 2–3 inches of mulch on your plants, particularly on root areas. Straw can also help retain moisture.

Watering time: don't water in the full heat of the day because more will evaporate; early mornings and evenings are ideal.

Use a hoe: hoeing removes weeds before they've had a chance to take hold, and so reduces the amount of water and nutrients they take up. It also stimulates plant growth.

Choose plants wisely: consider the water needs of your garden. For example, large-leaf varieties and bedding plants need more water than most. Plants with grey and silver foliage, such as lavenders, thymes and sages, don't need much water.

No pots: potted plants are generally thirsty. If you must have them, choose glazed or galvanised pots, because unlike terracotta pots they keep the water in. Water gel mixed with compost is a water saver for hanging baskets. And decorative stones also stop water evaporating.

MINIMISE LAWNS

There's nothing very green about a lawn. Maintaining this unnatural carpet of one or two plant species often means using vast amounts of chemicals, energy for mowing, and even water when it's dry. For those who want to keep their lawns, here are some tips on how to minimise its impact:

Weeds: avoid using chemicals on your lawn, and follow organic guidelines.

Clover: encourage clover because it's good for the grass.

Mowing: don't cut the grass too short because the longer blades shade each other, preserving moisture. Scalping the grass weakens it and encourages moss.

Feeding lawn: leave grass clippings on your lawn during the spring and summer, but not at the beginning and end of the seasons; when they rot they release nutrients. Municipal compost is good for feeding your lawn, but beware of over-feeding because this can lead to disease.

Wild flowers: consider planting a wild flower lawn. There are lots of companies offering seed mixes and advice on how to get started. Just remember that most wild flowers like poor soil fertility.

TOO MUCH MOWING

There are 3 million people in Britain who mow up to 270 million miles a year. But litre for litre most mowers will be producing far more greenhouse gases than cars. This is because a lot more attention has been put into cleaning car emissions. New mowers are more energy efficient than old ones – some even have catalytic converters (see glossary). So if you're buying a new one, ask about its emissions.

When buying a mower, the options, from worst to best, are:
1. Old petrol sit-on mower
2. Old petrol push mower
3. Electric mower
4. New petrol sit-on mower
5. New petrol push mower
6. Mechanical push mower
7. Scythe.

You may not want to switch to a human-powered contraption, or even a scythe, but one thing to consider is a slightly wilder lawn. It doesn't need to be a close-cropped carpet. Personally I like lawns that have moss, wild flowers, daisies and buttercups – and not a chemical in sight.

REDUCE CHEMICALS

Organic gardening doesn't completely eliminate chemicals, but it does reduce them to a minimum. Here are some ideas on how to make your garden a chemical-free zone.

Do you need it?: before using any chemical in your garden, ask yourself whether you really need to control the weed or pest concerned.

No overdoses: if you do use garden chemicals, take care to follow the instructions. Using more than you need can damage the plants you're trying to protect.

Weed prevention: it looks rather hideous, but laying down old carpets or plastic film during the winter keeps weeds at bay.

Companion planting: apart from using garden space efficiently, companion planting can prevent pest problems. Some pests, for example, don't like the smell of onions. And some plants lure pests from more desirable plants or attract beneficial insect predators.

Predators: a good way of getting rid of some garden pests is to introduce predators. If you don't have enough ladybirds to eat your aphids, for example, you can actually buy them (see Green Gardeners weblink).

Disease resistance: choose plant varieties that are disease-resistant. Often this means species that are local; for example, some apple and strawberry varieties are more vulnerable to pests than others.

Chemical disposal: never pour garden chemicals down the drain. If you want to dispose of these chemicals before they are empty, you should take them to your local council disposal site.

A friend of mine rang to invite me to supper. By way of an aside she said that she and her husband had managed to stop using chemicals on their terrace because they'd bought a flame-thrower – one that burns the weeds. She asked if I'd like to borrow it. I have to admit I think it would be rather fun, however burning fossil fuels to kill your weeds is probably not going to give you many eco-credits!

BEATING SLUGS

I've tried lots of methods to combat slugs – for example 'slug pubs', using half a grapefruit filled with beer, and scattering egg shells. But I think the most effective method is slug hunts. As darkness descends, head out to your cabbage patch, or other vulnerable area, and catch the slimy plant-guzzlers. I recommend carrying a container of water to put them in. I once found one crawling up my dress! Another good idea is encouraging slug predators such as frogs and hedgehogs.

Slug pellets may leave chemical residues in food and they can kill birds that eat contaminated slugs.

USE WASTE

BEST OFFER EVER!

I was waiting at a bus stop in the London suburbs when an advertisement caught my eye:

Bring your garden waste to the council between the 3rd and the 6th of the month and you might win 2 free biodegradable rubbish bags'.

If they want to encourage people to recycle, I think they need to come up with something a little more rewarding than that!

Compost is a gardener's delight. It's easy to make, excellent for plants and gives you some green brownie points too. Even people without gardens can make compost, and there's real value in removing heavy, wet kitchen waste from rubbish collections, not least in saving energy. Here are some of the options.

Gardener's compost heap

The perfect compost heap is almost an art form. Pile up straw, animal manure, garden and household waste, add water and turn the steaming pile regularly. There's lots of advice on the perfect ingredients. You can still get good results with a more haphazard approach, but you'll have to wait a bit longer for the material to break down.

Compost bins

There are lots of different types of compost bin to choose from. Many councils offer discounts on them because it means they have to collect less waste. If you go for a plastic one, make sure it's made from recycled plastic. Be sure to check instructions before you buy because some types need to be half buried in the garden.

Wormeries

You may be surprised to know that wormeries can be kept in your kitchen. My worms arrived in the post. They then went into a specially designed bin with a sealed lid to help my kitchen waste decompose. I loved them, and was always thinking about how happy they would be when I gave them a juicy load of vegetable cuttings. Unfortunately, I found that my kitchen waste was a bit too juicy – and they drowned. I realise that the little tap at the bottom of the wormery needs to be on most of the time, with a container below to catch the liquid waste. If the wormery is working well, the liquid won't be too smelly and is a brilliant plant fertiliser. The worms don't have any trouble with meat waste and most cooked foods, but they're apparently not very keen on onions, orange peel or too many banana skins. For people without much space a wormery is an ideal compost solution. Every 6–12 months you get a really excellent soil conditioner – and the worms will start again with a fresh batch.

Bonfires

They might be fun to make, but garden bonfires are polluting. The only excuse for making one is to get rid of diseased plants.

FOR PEAT'S SAKE

'Digging it up is like ripping out ancient hedgerows just to make sawdust' **Monty Don**

Most people don't realise that destroying peat bogs is like destroying rainforests, except that it's happening right on our doorsteps. Amazingly, the carbon stored in this decomposing vegetable matter is greater than in all the world's forests – and equal to the amount in the atmosphere. Peat bogs are also home to many rare plants and animals, some of which can't live anywhere else.

In Britain we have lost 94 per cent of raised peat bog since the 1950s. And horticulture is the main culprit. Despite vigorous campaigning, the peat industry has not given up its claim to these rich and biodiverse habitats. Why not?

By all accounts peat is an ideal growing medium for particular types of plants. It's also mixed with compost and other substances to make soil conditioner. And peat is a mainstay for mushroom growers (page 139). But research has shown that there are good-quality, competitively priced alternatives to peat for most applications – although this is easier for soil conditioners.

A friend of mine gave me some tomato plants, which I neatly planted against a wall to bear delicious autumn fruit. But they came potted in peat. There are still lots of people who have no idea how serious this problem is. The issue needs overwhelming consumer awareness and support to stop more peat bogs being destroyed.

What needs to happen:

• Consumers should boycott companies producing products containing peat, and avoid the few plants such as camellias and azaleas for which peat is considered to be essential for healthy seedlings.

• Garden centres and shops shouldn't sell any peat products, and should provide information on peat alternatives as well as putting clear labels on soil conditioners and plant-growing mediums.

• All councils, public gardens and flower shows should introduce a peat-free policy.

• Supermarkets should ban the use of peat in horticulture for products they sell.

• The Government should impose heavy penalties on companies which don't meet the targets they have set for 90 per cent of growing media to be peat-free by 2010.

Stopping the use of peat shouldn't be so difficult, with few potential losers and a significant gain. Use your consumer power to save our last remaining peat bogs.

PEAT WEBLINKS

English Nature Promotes peat alternatives and conservation of peat bogs.

www.englishnature.org.uk

Friends of the Earth (FoE) Their campaign encourages boycotts of companies producing and selling peat-based products.

www.foe.co.uk

National Trust Supports studies into peat alternatives and has a peat-free policy in all 200 of its gardens, except 'where there is no alternative' to maintain particular plants.

www.nationaltrust.org.uk

Peatering Out Free plant-finder service. Will direct you to the nearest garden centre selling peat-free plant varieties of your choice.

www.peateringout.com

Plantlife Campaigns for an end to peat-digging in the UK.

www.plantlife.org.uk

Royal Horticultural Society Supports studies into peat alternatives and does not allow peat 'for staging purposes' at their flower shows, including the Chelsea Flower Show. They have produced an excellent leaflet entitled 'Peat and the Gardener'.

www.rhs.org.uk

Royal Society for the Protection of Birds (RSPB) Campaigns on peat and offers peat-free bedding plants.

www.rspb.org.uk

Waste Resources Action Plan (WRAP) Produces a buyers' guide showing what peat-free products are available.

www.wrap.org.uk

OUTSIDE LIVING

I'm not really anti-barbecues; in fact I love charcoal-cooked foods and the sheer fun of eating outside. I particularly enjoy barbecues on the beach with a group of friends. But barbecuing is not such a good thing for the planet. Without being a complete killjoy, here are some ideas on how to minimise your impacts.

Gas

Gas is cleaner than charcoal for barbecuing.

Charcoal

The process of making charcoal wastes heat, and burning it produces dirty smoke that adds to air pollution. Self-lighting charcoal is even worse because it's pre-soaked in chemicals that contribute to ozone pollution. If you are still determined to use it, make sure it's locally sourced and FSC-certified, because imported charcoal may come from illegally logged forests. Briquettes that contain sawdust – recycled waste wood – are recommended.

Disposable barbecues

I really dislike disposable barbecues – they're so wasteful. After only one use the large foil tray and grid are just chucked away – often as litter on the beach.

Patio heaters

Patio heaters are another environmental horror story. In 2004 there were over 750,000 patio heaters in use in the UK, producing enough CO_2 to fill over 2 million double-decker buses. I wonder what useful product could be made from recycled patio heaters. Actually, I'd like to recycle the people that buy them!

Garden furniture

It's still possible to buy garden furniture that comes from destroyed rainforests. To avoid this you should first check that it's FSC-certified. Greenpeace is running a campaign to highlight this issue, and has an updated list of garden furniture, retailers and brands with details of their wood-sourcing policies.

GREENPEACE GARDEN FURNITURE GUIDE

In 2006 Greenpeace identified those major UK retailers still selling furniture that comes from 'illegal or destructively logged sources OR forests that have not been certified as well managed'. The following companies had some products that were included in this category:

Argos, Co-op, Dobbies, Focus, Habitat, Homebase, John Lewis, Morrisons, Robert Dyas and Woolworths.

All garden furniture sold by the following companies was either certified by the FSC to say it came from environmentally responsible sources, forests working towards FSC, or other forest certification schemes:

Asda, B&Q, M&S, Tesco, Wyevale Garden Centre

Please check the Greenpeace website for the most up-to-date information on this.

GARDENING WEBLINKS

BBC Gardening A good source of garden information, including advice on organic lawn care.

www.bbc.co.uk/gardening

Beth Chatto Large experimental dry garden and nursery in Essex, with drought-resistant plants.

www.bethchatto.co.uk

Centre for Alternative Technology Information on composting and water butts.

www.cat.org.uk

Compost Guide

www.compostguide.com

Compost Information

www.compostinfo.com

Dorset Charcoal Company Produces sustainable British charcoal.

www.barrel-barbecue.co.uk/charcoal.htm

Garden Organic Also known as the Henry Doubleday Research Association (HDRA), this is the primary organic gardening organisation in the country.

www.gardenorganic.org.uk

Graig Farm Organics Produces sustainable British charcoal.

www.graigfarm.co.uk/charcoal.htm

Green Cone Sells a special bin designed for disposing of food waste.

www.greencone.com

Green Gardener Offers advice and sells green gardening products such as wormeries and pest predators.

www.greengardener.co.uk

Greenpeace Garden Furniture Guide An excellent guide to the rainforest impact of companies making and selling garden furniture.

www.greenpeace.org.uk/
Products/GFG/home.html

Pesticide Action Network (PAN) Campaigns on pesticide issues.

www.pan-uk.org

3 Food and Drink

As a great food enthusiast I welcome the revival of local, good-quality produce, with farmers' markets, delivery schemes and organic food moving into the mainstream. But I'm also aware that there's a huge divide between those who eat a healthy diet with lots of fresh fruit and vegetables, and those who survive on junk food and TV dinners.

I like to point out that if you make a machine with poor-quality parts, you'll get a shoddy machine. It's the same with people. If you give babies and children poor-quality food it should come as no surprise that you won't be making healthy bodies. Obesity and poor diets aside, this chapter looks at the environmental impacts of food, from climate change to pesticides and from animal feed to fish farming, as well as what supermarkets are up to.

Supermarket Survey

A Power For Good?

The sheer popularity of supermarkets is a testament to their convenience, but should 'green' consumers feel guilty about using them? It's tempting to think that the most environmentally friendly shoppers give them a miss. Is that really the case?

Certainly supermarkets have transformed the way we shop and the communities in which we live. In many cases they've obliterated small local retailers – butchers, bakers and grocery stores – and often they're situated in huge out-of-town shopping centres that can only be reached by car – perhaps on land that was once an orchard, a water meadow or lush grassland.

It's also true that these retail giants have become immensely powerful. Farmers and other suppliers can't afford to ignore their requirements, and often have little leeway to negotiate a fair price.

And we as customers are stuck with whatever it is we find on the shelves – a vast array of products – most of which are mass-market goods with little room for regional variation or quirkiness.

Conversely, the might of the supermarkets can actually be a significant force for good. When they start saving energy, cutting waste or specifying environmental improvements, it really has an impact, not only because of the sheer volume of their purchases, but because of the influence they have on suppliers.

Green competition between supermarkets is fuelled by customers, and I believe it's a good thing. So if you're a supermarket shopper, don't feel guilty, make a difference. Use your power as a consumer to encourage them to improve their environmental performance and discourage them when they don't.

My Questionnaire

In 2006 I sent a questionnaire to eight of the main supermarkets: **Asda**, **Co-op**, **M&S**, **Morrisons**, **Sainsbury's**, **Somerfield**, **Tesco** and **Waitrose**. All except **Somerfield** replied. Throughout the book I've included summaries of how these supermarkets compare on a range of issues, and I've given them a rating out of 10 (10 is good; 1 is bad). The rating is entirely based on my own view from the responses to my questionnaire and my knowledge of the companies concerned. This is a fast-moving sector with things changing all the time – you should chiefly look at what I've written to give you an idea of the important issues and then check for updated information where you can. The main issues covered are:

• Energy and climate change
• Packaging and waste
• Pesticide residues and organics
• Food miles and seasonality
• Meat and poultry
• Fish

MY SUPERMARKET RATINGS

	Asda	Co-op	M&S	Morrisons	Sainsbury's	Tesco	Waitrose
Energy and climate change	6	7	8	1	8	6	8
Packaging and waste	9	6	8	6	8	7	7
Pesticide residues and organics	6	8	9	6	7	6	8
Food miles and seasonality	8	7	8	7	8	5	8
Meat and poultry	5	8	9	3	8	6	9
Fish	7	5	9	3	8	7	9
TOTALS	41	41	51	26	47	37	49

Supermarket Watch

Energy and Climate Change

Co-op claims to be one of the largest purchasers of 'green' electricity in the world, with 98 per cent of what it uses coming from renewable sources. Whilst **Asda** has made a long-term commitment to follow suit, 40 per cent of energy for **Waitrose** stores comes from 'green' sources, and **M&S** aims to generate half of its energy like this by 2010. **Sainsbury's** has wind turbines on three of its stores and solar panels at one of its filling stations. I expect it won't be long before many individual stores will be generating power.

Tesco has recently received a lot of attention for investing heavily in energy-saving initiatives, including cutting the energy used per square foot of floor space in half between 2000 and 2010. This is to be welcomed, but it should be noted that it's coming from behind.

Waitrose is also making a significant investment in energy efficiency. To date, **M&S** seems to have made the most dramatic cuts, even whilst expanding the number of stores it runs, but **Sainsbury's** is the most energy-efficient supermarket when measured per square foot of floor space.

Supermarket Watch

Packaging and Waste
Carrier bags

In 2005 **Tesco** gave out close to 4 billion plastic bags – which is equivalent in weight to about 220 jumbo jets. Of course, as the biggest supermarket, it does have huge sales, but distributing bags on this scale is sheer wastefulness. On one single **Tesco** delivery my shopping came in no less than 23 plastic bags, some containing just one box of cereal. **Tesco** now says it's aiming to reduce the number of bags by a quarter (that's nearly 1 billion bags), and one of the ways it's doing this is by awarding customers Clubcard points for reusing bags.

All the supermarkets have reusable bags – many refer to them as 'Bags for Life'.

These have already saved thousands of tonnes of plastic heading for landfill. **Asda** is considering stopping any single-trip carrier bags by 2010 and is calling on other retailers to do the same.

Some supermarkets have adopted degradable bags (page 35), which are oil-based and break down chemically. **Co-op** has used these bags since 2002, and **Tesco** has just introduced them on a large scale. **M&S**, **Sainsbury's** and **Waitrose**, on the other hand, are not convinced of the eco-benefits of this sort of bag – and I agree with them.

Packaging
All the supermarkets surveyed are working to redesign packaging in order to minimise waste. Even

relatively small changes can result in huge savings. For example, **Co-op** points out that by removing the outer cardboard layer of its tomato purée it's saved 8.5 tonnes of cardboard a year; **M&S** is using 5,000 tonnes of recycled cardboard to make sleeves for the equivalent of 200 million ready meals; and at **Tesco**, packaging reduction on drinks bottles, pizza and potatoes saved 11,000 tonnes of waste last year.

Biodegradable packaging for food products has been or will be introduced by **Asda**, **Co-op**, **M&S** and **Sainsbury's**. This is made from plant matter and should break down even in your household compost bin. The biodegradability benefits will be lost, however, if it's discarded with general household waste. The eco-merits will depend on good labelling and councils having systems in place to collect compostable materials.

M&S is the only major retailer to have removed PVC (see glossary) from all its packaging, but **Sainsbury's** and **Waitrose** are also phasing it out.

Waste

Tesco has apparently invested in 100 extraordinary-sounding recycling contraptions, which have inbuilt cameras to identify and sort the different types of waste. What intrigued me about them were the high-speed knives that work at over 60km an hour shredding plastic and aluminium. That, along with the crushed glass, means these techno recycling banks can hold up to four times more than their low-tech counterparts.

Currently, most of the waste from supermarkets ends up in landfill sites. This is changing. **Sainsbury's** already diverts well over half its waste from landfill, **Asda** has announced that by 2010 all waste from stores will be reused, recycled or composted, while **M&S**, **Tesco** and **Waitrose** have set targets for reduction.

What really interests me is the potential for the huge volumes of food waste to be composted – and even made into a usable fuel. This fuel, or 'biogas', could either be used to heat and power the store, or even as fuel for vehicles (page 183).

FRUIT and VEGETABLES, CEREALS and PULSES

There can't be many people who aren't aware that fruit and vegetables are an important part of a healthy, balanced diet. The Government campaign promoting five portions every day has been effective at raising awareness and improving nutrition, but there are other issues with fruit and vegetables, as well as with cereals and grains, that are not so widely understood. In fact sometimes there's an awful lot of confusion: how good for you is an apple that's been sprayed 16 times before being harvested? Should we be eating beans imported from Kenya? And why are strawberries crunchier than they used to be?

? DID YOU KNOW? ?

43 per cent of all fruit and vegetables tested by the Government contain detectable levels of pesticides.

Pesticide Action

I don't find it very reassuring to be told that by peeling an apple or washing grapes I'm reducing my exposure to pesticide residues. Apart from anything else, the skin of fruit and vegetables is often the most nutritious bit.

But without pesticides it's estimated that almost a third of the world's crops would be lost before they've been harvested. By killing bugs, preventing diseases and preserving food, chemicals do enable us to have a far greater range of produce on our tables, including exotic fruits like mangoes and bananas. But are we paying too high a price? Here are some of the questions we're asking:

Is testing for pesticide residues good enough?

Although Government guidelines on the amount of residues permitted in food err on the side of caution, it's not unusual for legal limits to be breached. Furthermore, they test only a minuscule amount of produce compared to what we eat.

Are some imported fruit and vegetables grown with chemicals banned in this country?

The simple answer to this is 'yes'. Sometimes even chemicals regarded as dangerous are used on imported produce. And testing procedures may well not pick up the problem.

Are children being exposed to dangerous levels of chemicals?

There are concerns that children may have a greater exposure to pesticide residues per pound of body weight because they're smaller. They're also more vulnerable to the effects because of their developing immune systems.

HOW TO MINIMISE RESIDUES

1. **Grow your own produce**
2. **Buy organic**
3. **Buy local, seasonal produce**
4. **Avoid imported fruits**
5. **Peel or wash fruit**

Do we know enough about the 'cocktail effect' of multiple chemical residues?

Whilst one individual chemical may not be harmful, the impact of multiple chemicals in our bodies may be lethal – but far more difficult to gauge.

Are farm workers safe from the pesticides they use?

There have been some horrendous instances of workers on banana plantations, for example, who have suffered severe health problems as a result of the pesticides used.

How much are we paying to clean up pollution from pesticides?

One of the hidden costs of 'cheap' food is the amount we pay to clean up soil and waterways from pollution caused by the use of agricultural chemicals.

What effect are pesticides having on wildlife?

In the past, many birds and other wildlife were directly poisoned by pesticides. Nowadays, the biggest issue is the indirect impact of pesticides: they kill plants and insects that may be essential food for other wildlife.

TOP 10 WORST OFFENDERS FOR PESTICIDE RESIDUES

The Pesticide Action Network looked at Government tests for pesticide residues over a five-year period and identified the Top 10 foods from which our exposure to residues was greatest:

- Apples
- Beans
- Bread
- Cucumbers
- Flour
- Grapes
- Pears
- Potatoes
- Strawberries
- Tomatoes

They found that some varieties of apples and pears were more vulnerable to pests than others, which made them more likely to contain residues – Cox's apples, for example – although in general more pears had residues than apples. Part of the challenge for organic growers is to select more disease-resistant varieties.

Over two-thirds of strawberries and over half the grapes tested had measurable residues and quite often multiple residues. A large proportion of speciality beans (such as kidney beans) also contained residues, with a staggering 45 per cent of samples having at least one chemical over the legal limit. Green beans (such as French beans) weren't nearly so bad and wouldn't be included on the list.

Perhaps the most surprising thing to emerge was that residues in wholemeal and brown flours and breads were considerably worse than for white flour and bread.

SUPERMARKET WATCH

Pesticide Residues and Organics

Whilst **M&S** used to top the list for having the highest levels of residues in its produce, it now – along with **Co-op** – tops the list of supermarkets doing something about it. It requires its suppliers to move away from the most harmful pesticides and has been proactive in making information available to customers on the levels of residues in products. The really positive thing is that consumer pressure has led all the major supermarkets to review and limit the amount of pesticides used on crops.

Consumer pressure has also been partly responsible for the surge of enthusiasm for organics. **Asda, M&S, Morrisons, Sainsbury's, Tesco** and **Waitrose** all reported a huge rise in their sales of organic produce over the past year and are now promoting it much more widely. **Tesco**, for example, has said that integrating its organic range alongside conventional produce has led to a dramatic rise in sales. **Waitrose** seems to be leading the field in terms of the most organic products available (over 1,500).

Your supermarket should be:
- setting targets and timescales for zero chemical residues
- working with suppliers to minimise pesticide use
- publishing data about chemical residues on its website
- avoiding fruit and vegetable varieties that require high levels of pesticides
- relaxing standards on the cosmetic appearance of products and explaining this to customers
- increasing the amount of organic produce they sell.

Food Miles
Jet-Set Produce

If you look at the travel section in your newspaper you expect to see details of exotic holiday locations. Nowadays we can get the same thrill by looking at the packaging on supermarket produce: mangoes from Pakistan, tomatoes from Spain and cherries from Chile. Even when there are apples falling off our trees in seasonal abundance, it's easy to find their foreign friends that have travelled all the way from China.

Concern about this has led to someone coining the term 'food miles', the idea being to illustrate how far our food has travelled. And the key worry is that the energy consumed – and therefore the climate change impact – is horrendous. For example, it has been worked out that it takes 127 times more energy to fly a lettuce from the US to the UK than it provides, and 66 times more energy for a carrot from South Africa.

The answer to this concern is more complicated than you might think. Stopping imports would certainly reduce food miles dramatically. But this leads to worries that it would also cause serious hardship for many poor people in developing countries, whose livelihoods depend on selling abroad. It would also result in a drastic change in our lifestyles if we learnt to live without even the foods that are shipped into the country, such as coffee, tea, bananas and oranges.

So what about eliminating imports of produce we can grow here? Surely we could rely on our own apples, strawberries, tomatoes and carrots? Even that's not as easy as it sounds. It would mean being prepared to restrict your purchases to seasonal produce, which in some months – March and April, for example - would be extremely limiting. What's even more complicated is the fact that there may be fewer carbon emissions caused by importing beans from Kenya in December than growing them in greenhouses in the UK.

DID YOU KNOW?

The energy impacts of importing just one 250g pack of Kenyan beans by air is the equivalent to working on a large laptop computer every weekday for a month.

BEWARE OF AIR!

Sending goods by air is 100 times more polluting than sending them by train, and 200 times more polluting than sending them by boat.

Top air-freight products:
Asparagus (non-European)
Figs
Lycees
Mangoes
Papaya
Passion fruit
African imports of beans, mange tout, sugar peas, baby corn and herbs

Products that may well have arrived by plane include:
1. Avocados
2. Blackcurrants
3. Blueberries
4. Cherries
5. Cut flowers
6. Exotic vegetables
7. Grapes
8. Peaches and nectarines
9. Pineapples
10. Strawberries and raspberries

Only 1.5 per cent of fruit and vegetables come by air, but this accounts for over one-third of their overall transport-related greenhouse gases.

I think supermarkets should put a sticker of an aeroplane on all products that have been air-freighted into the country. And they should include facts and figures about their use of air freight on their website and in their annual reports.

If there's only one thing you do to reduce food miles: avoid air-freighted produce.

How Local?

The advice generally follows that you should buy local and seasonal produce whenever you can. But you have to consider what this actually means.

Locally produced food should, by definition, have come from within 30 miles of where it's sold. If you're buying from a supermarket, this may not actually make sense in terms of cutting food miles. Supermarkets have large-scale distribution systems with thousands of different product lines coming to their stores, so sending out lots of vehicles to pick up from small-scale suppliers could actually increase the amount of energy used.

For supermarkets, the best option is to sell regional foods that are specialities in the area: Cornish cream, Kent strawberries or

Scottish beef, for example. This may also overcome the problem of supermarkets directly competing with local retailers, farmers' markets or organic box schemes.

In the last decade these sorts of initiatives have flourished. When I first came back to Somerset over ten years ago, it was almost impossible to find good-quality local produce, let alone anything organic. Now I'm spoilt for choice. And I buy almost all my food – and some other groceries – from a local organic delivery service. I was surprised to find that they're price-competitive with **Tesco**, and on some lines they're actually cheaper.

SUPERMARKET WATCH

Food Miles and Seasonality

All the supermarkets say they're doing something to reduce food miles. Most commonly, they're trying to increase the amount of food grown in the UK, when it's in season. This also applies to meat and dairy products, although they all sell New Zealand lamb when British lamb is not available. **M&S** and **Waitrose** seem to be narrowly ahead of **Sainsbury's** in terms of the proportion of British fresh meat, poultry and eggs available across the range.

It's difficult to choose between **Asda** and **Waitrose** in terms of the greatest range of regional and local food available. **Asda** says that all its stores have at least one locally sourced product, and half of them have more than 40, while **Waitrose** says that over half its stores sell regional fruit and vegetables, which have labels promoting seasonality. Along with **M&S**, **Sainsbury's** and **Tesco**, **Asda** and **Waitrose** are working with small suppliers to make it easier to sell to their stores.

Sainsbury's launched the first supermarket organic box scheme, starting in the Fens. On the positive side this should increase demand for organic and seasonal products – nothing will be imported. Not so good is that it could be serious competition for smaller, local box schemes. And it may not be great from a food miles point of view either, because products can be sourced from anywhere in the country and are distributed from one depot, albeit local to customers. **Tesco**'s box scheme is even worse for food miles because they have one depot that sells all over the South East.

Bizarrely, all the supermarkets claim to be reducing the amount of food imported by air, yet air-freighted food is increasing. The only significant measures taken on this front have been by **M&S** and **Waitrose**, who are cutting back on importing fish by air – more now comes by sea.

REDUCING FOOD MILES

If you want to reduce your food miles impact, don't forget to include your travel to and from the shops. Clearly, if you can combine your shopping with other trips, such as dropping your children off at school or going to work, that makes a difference. Equally, walking to the shops cuts food miles. And having your food delivered is a good idea, particularly if it actually reduces your shopping trips.

Here are some ideas for reducing your food miles. But remember that it'll be different for everyone, depending on where you live and what you do.

- Grow your own produce.
- Have all your food delivered weekly.
- Support local box schemes.
- Go to farmers' markets.
- Walk or cycle to shops where possible.
- Buy seasonal products whenever you can.
- Look out for regional produce at supermarkets.
- Avoid anything that might have been imported by air.

FRUIT AND VEG STALL

Going Bananas
Bananas are big business. And the British are big banana lovers: each of us eats an average of 13kg a year.

But how many people think about how bananas are produced? In comparison to all other crops except cotton, bananas grown for export are the biggest chemical users. By all accounts we're far more interested in what they look like than how they taste – and making sure they're blemish-free is one of the reasons for all the chemicals.

Dozens of different chemicals may be applied to produce the perfect-looking yellow fruit on sale in our shops.

Another reason is that 97 per cent of the world's banana trade focuses on just one variety. Huge single-crop banana plantations are more susceptible to pests, fungi and disease than if they were mixed with a number of different varieties – there are over 300 to choose from. The intensity of banana production can also leave the soil infertile. And the fact that bananas thrive in the same areas as coastal rainforests means that expanding plantations can threaten these precious habitats.

If you've ever been to a banana plantation you'll find the most striking thing is that the

large bunches of fruit are frequently wrapped in plastic bags treated with toxic insecticides. One problem with this is that these bags are not always properly disposed of. It's been calculated that for every tonne of bananas, there's a tonne of waste left behind. Another problem is that there's very rarely sufficient protection for plantation workers – many still suffer the ill-effects of the chemicals used.

If you're concerned about all this, the answer is to buy organic bananas, which are chemical-free. But if you want to guarantee good conditions for plantation workers, they need to be fair trade too. Demand for fair trade, organic bananas often outstrips supply. Let's hope the supermarkets use their buying power to help growers produce more of what we want.

CHOOSE CARIBBEAN BANANAS

Most banana producers in the Windward Islands are small family farms. They tend to use fewer chemicals, and have better environmental standards than their large-scale 'dollar' banana competitors. And so many of them are registered fair trade that there are plans for the entire islands' production to go this route. If you see bananas from the Windward Islands, give them a try.

Mushroom Mania

The really big environmental issue regarding mushrooms is the use of peat (page 124). Apparently it's a vital ingredient in the top layer of soil used by commercial growers. However one company has now produced a casing material that reduces the amount of peat used by two-thirds. They do this by replacing the peat with fibre from peat extraction and a mining product – both of which normally go to waste. What's more, the mushrooms produced are less watery and have more flavour. I wondered why the supermarkets weren't falling over themselves to use both this product and the super-reduced peat that is following on its heels.

Not surprisingly, it all comes down to price. Mushroom growing is a fiercely competitive business, and switching to this material might increase the price of mushrooms by 2 per cent. That's not much considering the importance of the issue. So what about organic mushroom growers? Not many of them are using reduced peat either – they're certainly not required to do so.

Supermarket Watch

Mushrooms and Peat

Supermarkets should be specifying reduced peat for the mushrooms they sell and labelling the products to tell us what they're doing. All the supermarkets in my survey claimed to be looking at alternatives and/or trying to reduce the amount of peat used, but none has yet specified reduced peat casing for all mushrooms sold in their stores. It will be interesting to see who does it first. **M&S** has a long-term goal to phase out the use of peat for the whole of its business.

Rice

A staggering 10–15 per cent of global methane comes from rice fields, which makes them a significant contributor to climate change. Equally mind-boggling is that it takes about 5,000 litres of water to produce just one kilogram of rice. Some rice growers are using new systems that can save up to two-thirds of the water previously used, so there are innovations being introduced. Less positive is that the trend towards a single rice variety has the knock-on effect of increasing the use of pesticides.

My advice is to stick to locally grown potatoes as your staple starch.

Soya

Do you remember the *Monty Python* sketch asking customers if they would like 'spam, spam or spam'? Today it's a bit like that with soya, except that its proliferation is less obvious. Soya is in more than 60 per cent of processed foods in some shape or form, as well as being a key ingredient in animal feed (page 145). It's lurking in foods such as ice-cream, crisps, sausages, pastries, noodles, cereals, soups and vegetable oils, and it's become a vital ingredient in vegetarian diets.

Although soya is often promoted as a healthy food, there are serious doubts about whether this is actually the case. On the environmental front, there's also the concern about soya crops leading to the clearing of vast areas of forest (page 48). And then there's GM soya (page 42), which was sneaked into our food before we were given the opportunity to debate whether this was desirable or even acceptable.

Strawberries

If you talk about food miles and seasonality, a lot of people will ask 'Why are strawberries, that don't even taste very nice, on sale at Christmas time?' The answer is that it would take a very brave supermarket to be the first to stop selling year-round strawberries – the fear is that customers would go elsewhere.

On the positive side, the growing season in Britain is now around six months, from May to October, and only a very small proportion of these are grown in greenhouses. In addition, supermarkets have apparently started paying more attention to the taste of strawberries, as well as selecting varieties that are long-lasting, although Spanish imports are sometimes picked under-ripe, which makes them less sweet.

Another issue with strawberries is that the industry has managed to make them exempt from legislation designed to protect the ozone layer. Strawberry growers have been the main users of methyl bromide, an ozone-destroying chemical used to treat the soil, which was banned for most uses in 2005 – but not for strawberries. Given that few growers still use it, one has to wonder why an exemption was thought necessary.

Try to limit yourself to British strawberries when they're in season; buy something else during the winter months.

- -

Tomatoes

The eco-credentials of tomatoes are difficult to fathom. The most critical issue seems to be whether they are British or imported, for example from Spain.

British tomatoes are almost exclusively grown in heated greenhouses, which makes them energy intensive to produce. The tomato industry, however, says it's managed to reduce its energy use by a quarter in the last two years, and it's highly likely there'll be even greater reductions as more tomato growers make use of Combined Heat and Power (CHP) (page 110) – making use of waste heat from electricity generation.

Spanish imports may actually use less energy in their transport than is used in UK greenhouses. But the energy implications of the Spanish using five times more land for their produce have not been calculated. Nor have any studies looked at the impact of the huge volumes of plastic used in poly tunnels, which have to be replaced every three years.

Another tricky issue is the use of pesticides. British tomato growers use natural predators to get rid of pests, and bees to pollinate their crops. The controlled conditions in greenhouses mean they have less of a problem with disease than Spanish growers. One Dutch study found that

Spanish tomatoes used 19 times more pesticides per kilo than tomatoes grown in Holland – and British tomato growers say they use less than the Dutch!

Tomatoes are the fourth most popular fruit in the UK, after bananas, apples and oranges. Whatever their energy impacts, we're not going to stop eating them – they're also good for you.
My recommendation is to buy British, but use your buying power to push the tomato industry to do more – apparently lots of tomato growers have the potential to use CHP but aren't yet doing so.
If supermarkets and other retailers had to let us see how much energy was used per kilo of tomatoes, I'm sure they'd save a lot more than they have to date.

TRADITIONAL TOMATOES
Traditional varieties of tomatoes are less disease-resistant than modern ones, so they're more likely to have chemical residues.

HUGH FEARNLEY-WHITTINGSTALL

Supermarket Horrors

Anyone who's watched Hugh Fearnley-Whittingstall's *River Cottage* programmes will not be surprised to hear that he's not a supermarket fan. Hugh says that he only visits these mega stores for research – essentially to check out what he dislikes so much.

Ready meals particularly disgust him. The packaging makes the food look quite enticing, but when you lift the lid and look inside it's another matter. He points out that it's also extremely expensive – a real money-spinner for food companies.

Neither is Hugh impressed with the supermarkets' new interest in being 'green'. Why go to a supermarket for an organic box? What's the point of **Tesco** staging Local Food Fairs? He recommends farmers' markets, particularly those where the people selling the food are those who've produced it.

But Hugh doesn't object to supermarkets selling organic produce. He thinks the environmental benefits of organic farming mean we should convert as much land as possible. And with supermarket shoppers adding to demand, he believes that over the next ten years 20–30 per cent of UK farming could be organic.

Wild Food

On the home front, Hugh's diet is a little unusual: pigeons, rooks, snails and squirrels (less gamey than rabbit) often feature on his household's menu. I asked him whether he ate woodlice too – I remembered them from one of his programmes. He says that woodlice fritters were worth trying, but that these 'land shrimp' had rather too much crunch (the shells) to be very tasty.

The point about wild food – and that includes nettles and blackberries – is that for those living in the country they're free, abundant, local, nutritious, and their eco-credentials are excellent. For a start, there's no packaging or food miles.

What about pheasant? Pheasant chicks are often bred intensively, reared free-range and later released into the wild. So at least in the beginning many of the issues are the same as for chickens, he says. Hugh likes shooting, but not when huge numbers of birds are 'bagged' in a day. And he's truly horrified that in the past some shoots would bury the pheasants rather than making sure they were eaten.

One of the main benefits of shooting as a sport, Hugh points out, is that it leads to conservation of coppices and woodland. Even some intensive farmers keep tree cover for birds, which might otherwise be ploughed up like the other fields they own.

River Cottage Fish

It's not just wild birds that Hugh likes but wild fish too! In fact when I interviewed him he was working on the *River Cottage Fish Book* with Nick Fisher. He says that fish is one of the most difficult areas for consumers to get their head around. Cod, for example, is generally high on the list of fish not to eat on sustainability grounds, yet Icelandic cod stocks are in a better state than those of many other fish that aren't blacklisted. There's also the long-standing obsession we have in Britain for a small number of high-profile fish such as cod, haddock and flat fish like sole and plaice. At River Cottage HQ they use lots of pollack – Hugh says it's just as good as cod but has a bad reputation because of the way it's been caught and stored. Pollack is usually caught by anglers who don't pay as much attention to fish preservation at sea as commercial fishing fleets.

The simplest solution for the ethical fish shopper, Hugh says, is to look for the MSC label (page 153). But if you want to engage a bit more – and particularly if you live near the coast – you should check out your local fish shop or market to find out which is the fish of the day. Small-scale local fishing boats are far less harmful than big factory ships, so what you buy from them will be seasonal, fresh and perhaps something a little more unusual. Freshly caught gurnard, he says, is far tastier than haddock that's been stored on ice for ten days at sea.

The Real Point

Hugh's passionate about what he does – promoting a better understanding of food and nature and encouraging people to reduce their environmental impact. He says that getting involved is what counts, even if our good green intentions are misplaced. Should we give up? Absolutely not. It's more important, he thinks, for people to engage and show they care. Ultimately, he's trying to help all of us to make a difference.

MEAT and DAIRY

It may surprise you to learn that after cars and home heating, our meat-eating habit is probably the most destructive thing we do. In the second half of the twentieth century, world meat production increased around five fold, and there are now 22 billion farm animals on the planet.

The high volume of meat eaten by people living in industrial countries is a significant factor in the surge in levels of obesity – and the amount of meat we eat is *rising*. And it's rising even faster in developing countries, where people currently eat only a third as much as Westerners. This increasing demand also applies to milk.

Eating and Excreting
Land take
It's estimated that livestock in Europe require an area of vegetation seven times the size of the EU to meet their feed requirements. In the UK roughly 70 per cent of agricultural land is used for farm animals, and it's the same in most other industrialised countries. There's simply not enough land to support so much meat eating.

The problem is that it takes a lot more protein to produce meat than you get back. Simply in terms of feed you need about 2kg of feed to produce 1kg of chicken, 4kg for pork and at least 7kg for beef. In energy terms, for every calorie of protein it takes an estimated two calories of fuel to produce soya beans, three calories for wheat or corn and a massive 54 calories for beef.

But it's not just feed that animals consume – water is a huge issue. Estimates of the amount of water needed to produce 1kg of beef vary from about 50,000 litres to 100,000

litres. Whichever estimate you take, it's a staggering figure. For chickens it's apparently 3,500 litres per kilo. This includes water used for irrigation of feed crops, as well as in production – slaughterhouses in Brazil, for example, use 14 litres of water to process a single chicken. At the same time about a quarter of Brazilians don't have access to safe drinking water.

Munching forests
One of the most worrying aspects of modern farming practices is the amount of soya used in feed. It's ideally suited to provide essential protein in animal diets, and it's fed to chickens, pigs and cows on a massive scale. In the last 20 years, worldwide soya production has doubled and 85 per cent of it is used in animal feed.

Much of this soya comes from land that has been cleared of forests or other precious habitats. In Brazil the agri-industry is clearing swathes of the Amazon forest for soya production, in large part to meet demands from Europe. Apparently 90 per cent of the rainforest soya from Brazil is grown in Mato Grosso, and half of that is exported to Europe. Apart from the rainforest destruction, this expansion is also causing chemical pollution. In the last ten years, pesticide sales in Brazil have tripled and a quarter of these chemicals are used on soya.

Another contentious issue is the use of GM technology on soya beans. By far the largest part of the 100 million acres of agriculture that have been given over to GM production has been devoted to soya beans and maize, almost exclusively for animal feed. Worryingly, the demand for GM-free soya may actually be causing *further* destruction. It's almost impossible to source GM-free soya from America, which has meant increased demand on Brazil.

Rainforests are threatened too by what's been dubbed 'hamburgerisation' – fattening cattle for the hamburger trade. Forests are cleared to rear cattle, which are sold on to fast-food outlets all over the world.

Supermarket Watch

Animal Feed

Asda, M&S, Sainsbury's, Tesco and **Waitrose** all say that they are working with Greenpeace to call for a suspension of soya produced on rainforest land. **Co-op** and **Morrisons** also claim to be concerned about this.

All the major supermarkets recognise that most of their customers don't want any GM ingredients in the products they buy, and this extends to buying meat or dairy products from animals fed on a GM diet. **M&S** has the most comprehensive policy on this – it says that no GM is used in animal feed for its meat, fish or dairy products. Much of **Co-op** and **Sainsbury's** meat and fish are fed a non-GM diet, and all the other supermarkets have some non-GM lines.

Chicken and fish

Like us, chickens and pigs are omnivores – they eat both meat and vegetables. But if you talk to chicken producers you'll discover there's a move to make them vegetarian.

10 REASONS TO EAT LESS MEAT

1. It can make you fat.
2. Meat production takes up too much land.
3. It's an inefficient source of protein.
4. Over-grazing can lead to land becoming desert.
5. A massive amount of water is used in raising, transporting and processing animals.
6. Soya production (for animal feed) is leading to destruction of rainforests.
7. Lots of GM soya and maize is grown for animal feed.
8. The use of fish meal in animal feed contributes to over-fishing.
9. Some animal farming methods can be cruel.
10. Animals reared in over-crowded conditions are more vulnerable to some diseases.

As most people know, the BSE crisis in the 1980s was generally thought to be caused by feeding ground-up meat and bone to cows (and sheep), even though they're herbivores. So what's that got to do with chickens and pigs? Well, concern over this practice led to a complete revision of animal feed practices. Waste meat and bone had to be 'safely disposed of' and other protein sources found.

Many chicken and pig producers have managed to find enough protein from plant sources to get by, although it's not ideal for all their growing needs. However, others feed their hungry pigs or laying birds with fish. Like farmed fish, the fish in feed comes in the form of fish meal and fish oil, and many of the fish used to make it are industrially caught – almost hoovered out of the sea. This is a big issue for organic producers because they're not allowed to use a synthetic alternative. Their criteria are continually being updated and there are plans to disallow fish meal completely.

I like the idea of looking back at the natural diets of chickens. They scratch around in the dirt and love eating grubs and insects, so why isn't anyone producing worms, maggots and wood lice for chicken feed? This would save fish, reduce demand for soya, and almost certainly be a lot healthier for the chickens too.

More muck than brass
One dairy cow produces an average of 57 litres of excreta every day, and liquid from dairy farms is apparently 100 times more polluting than human sewage. Pig manure is even more powerful; in fact it was considered to be such a problem in the Netherlands that the Government demanded a 25 per cent reduction in the number of pigs. And in North Carolina, where they have 6.5 million people and 7 million pigs, the porkers produce four times more waste than the humans.

Apart from polluting ground water and soil, animal waste is a major contributor to global warming. Worldwide, livestock are responsible for 15–20 per cent of methane emissions, 7 per cent of nitrous oxides and 10 per cent of all greenhouse gases.

Bizarrely, it's animal manure that makes farm animals an essential part of sustainable agriculture practices. Organic systems, for example, require mixing livestock and arable

CHICKEN McNUGGETS
Greenpeace's 2006 report highlighting McDonald's use of rainforest soya in chicken feed was successful. The fast food giant decided to work with Greenpeace campaigners and major supermarkets to encourage more 'rainforest-friendly' feed. The campaign then switched to Kentucky Fried Chicken and Burger King, who at the time of writing were maintaining a stony silence on the issue.

farming, primarily so that manure can be used rather than energy-intensive fertilisers – the problem comes when animals are reared intensively in large numbers.

Factory Farms
Fast growth
With the world's appetite for meat, milk and eggs growing faster than its population, the sheer quantity of animals needed leads to some pretty unattractive 'farming' practices. A shed containing 25,000 chickens may not be what springs to mind when you think about the countryside, yet sadly that's the reality of modern animal husbandry.

Chickens grow so speedily that they reach slaughter age at less than 40 days – twice as fast as they did in the 1960s. And egg-laying hens produce an average of nearly one egg a day all year round; when they slow down they're killed off.

Pigs in the UK apparently get a better life than those living in most other parts of the world. Here we have banned stalls for breeding sows that are so narrow they can't even turn around or lie down comfortably, but elsewhere conditions like this are commonplace for these intelligent farm animals. Piglets are weaned after just a few weeks, so the sow can go on to produce as many as five litters in two years – inevitably this makes them cheaper.

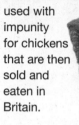

Dairy cows get a pretty raw deal too. They're bred to produce enormous quantities of milk – the amount from each cow has doubled over the last 50 years. And they too have early weaning of their offspring so they can get back to milk production as fast as possible.

All this speed and efficiency takes its toll. Up to 6 per cent of intensively produced chickens die before they're ready for eating. Many also find that the fast weight gain means their legs can't hold the weight of their bodies, so they collapse in their own excrement. Pigs also show signs of stress, as they bite their cage bars and roll their heads. And mastitis – an infection of the udder – occurs in around a third of dairy cows.

Treatments and trade

Most of us are aware that stress makes us more vulnerable to illness – this is something we share with other animals. And over-crowded conditions compound problems of disease because infection can spread quickly from one animal to another. Some producers respond by giving antibiotics to all animals to *prevent* disease rather than cure it. This practice has now been banned in the EU because of concerns that it will lead to

antibiotic resistance – for human diseases too.

Another practice that's banned on health grounds in the whole of Europe is the use of growth-promoting hormones; however, they're commonly used in America. This has led to trade wars as the Americans react to the European ban by contesting our right to place restrictions on their meat imports.

There are other medicines permitted overseas that are not allowed in the UK. For example, chickens reared in Brazil and exported to Britain may well contain drug residues that would not be permitted if they were home-grown.

Perhaps we should be asking why so much of our meat – particularly chickens – is imported. Do countries like Thailand, Brazil and China have special chicken-rearing expertise? Maybe their climate is more suited to rearing happy chickens? Actually, that's not the case. The fact is that chicken production is carried out overseas because they can do it cheaper than we can here – even taking account of the fact the chicken meat has to be transported thousands of miles. In some of these countries, intensive chicken production is carried out to high standards. But sometimes the demand for cheap 'protein' means that corners are cut, and systems that wouldn't meet even minimum standards here are used with impunity for chickens that are then sold and eaten in Britain.

De-stress

One organic dairy farmer was advised by an animal welfare expert that his cows were sexually dissatisfied. He may have thought the advice was a little crazy, but a bull was duly found to 'service' the cows whenever they felt inclined. The bull was firing blanks, but amazingly the fertility of the herd improved. The conclusion was that the cows were more receptive to the artificially inseminated sperm because they had previously been sexually aroused – perhaps they were more relaxed too!

Reducing stress and rearing 'happy' animals has been shown to be effective at preventing illness and boosting immune systems. In part this is done by giving animals more space. All organic animals, for example, are free-range.

But other ideas include roosting perches for chickens and giving toys to pigs. This has given rise to a debate about what sort of 'toys' the pigs actually enjoy – the RSPCA are concerned that EU law on this is inadequate. Instead of rooting materials for pigs to chew on, the animals may be given inert toys that don't satisfy their natural behavioural habits.

Practices that consider animal welfare issues produce not only happier animals but healthier ones too. That's something we should all be signing up to.

FREEDOM FOOD

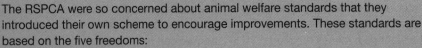

The RSPCA were so concerned about animal welfare standards that they introduced their own scheme to encourage improvements. These standards are based on the five freedoms:
1. Freedom from hunger and thirst
2. Freedom from discomfort
3. Freedom from pain, injury or disease
4. Freedom to express normal behaviour
5. Freedom from fear and distress.

Freedom Food-labelled products are widely available. They have been assessed as meeting RSPCA welfare standards during rearing, transport and slaughter.

Meat Less

You might assume that the only answer to the problems caused by producing meat is to become vegetarian – apparently 5 per cent of people in Britain have taken this route. A much smaller number are vegan and therefore not eating any animal products. But I'm not convinced that everyone should become a vegetarian – I'm not.

As mentioned in relation to animal wastes, manure is actually an important part of sustainable farming systems, providing vital nutrients for growing crops, which otherwise would come from artificial fertilisers. In India it's thought that the whole economy would collapse if cow dung were to be removed from the system – they also use it for fuel.

Animals are also important for grazing so-called marginal land, where it would be impossible to grow crops. For example, hill farmers rearing sheep or goats in remote mountain areas wouldn't be able to replace their stock with fields of barley, oats or even cabbages.

Of course, we couldn't produce all the meat we eat – or plan to eat – in local, non-intensive systems. It may sound a bit draconian – perhaps even elitist – but shouldn't we challenge a food system that manages to sell a chicken for only a couple of pounds? The answer has to be to eat less and pay more. Meat should be a luxury.

MEAT ADVICE
- **Eat less meat**
- **Choose chicken or pork rather than beef**
- **Buy locally produced meat**
- **Include offal in your diet**
- **Make sure the meat you buy is from a known source**
- **Buy free-range or organic**
- **Be prepared to pay more**
- **Make the most of what you do eat, for example by making soup from bones**

BUTCHERS SHOP

Pork
If you want to buy pork that comes from pigs reared outside for the whole of their life, it's not easy. Unlike chickens there are no clear rules about how much time 'outdoor-bred' pigs need actually be outdoors in order to be labelled as such. They could have been born in a field and spent the rest of their time in a barn.

Organic pigs are allowed inside for a maximum of one-fifth of their life. And like other farm animals you're also required to give them organic feed. This means no kitchen scraps, even for home-grown pigs. These scraps are now banned for all commercial pigs because it's thought they may have been the original source of foot-and-mouth disease. It's a pity because feeding pigs has been a great way of reusing waste food.

Lamb
From an environmental point of view a big issue with sheep is controlling pests – blowflies are one of the worst. For years farmers have been doing this by dipping sheep in organophosphate chemicals, which are highly toxic to humans. An alternative dip was adopted by the organic movement – and more widely – but has since been banned because it proved to be highly toxic to fish and other water life. Organic criteria now allow injections for sheep scab and a pour-on liquid to prevent flies. However, most farmers are sticking with organophosphates, albeit with stricter safety standards so they're not made ill by them.

I'm concerned about the continuing use of organophosphates: we should be encouraging farmers to adopt the organic approach to pest control.

Beef

Controls on British beef are far more stringent than prior to the BSE crisis: all animals are coded so they can be traced back to where they were raised.

However, larger slaughterhouses still tend to operate on the basis of cattle going in and beef coming out, rather than following each individual cow through the system. Keeping track of animals is easier for smaller slaughterhouses, but many of these operations have gone out of business, or are under threat, as they face controls and systems designed for their bigger counterparts. Often this means animals travelling much further for slaughter, which increases both animal suffering and their food miles.

As consumers, many of us want to know more about what we're buying, such as the breed of animal and how it has been reared. Ask your butcher or supermarket to tell you more.

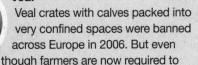

Veal

Veal crates with calves packed into very confined spaces were banned across Europe in 2006. But even though farmers are now required to keep calves in groups and give them more space, animal welfare on the Continent still falls some way short of what's practised in the UK. Here veal calves are generally able to have more exercise, eat more fibrous material and have straw bedding. The meat is sold as 'rose veal' because the more developed muscles mean the flesh loses its traditional white colour.

In my view, eating veal is to be recommended. Most of it comes as a by-product of the dairy industry – male calves that are no good for milking can be reared for veal. Shooting them the moment they're born seems criminally wasteful.

? DID YOU KNOW? ?

43 per cent of greenhouse gas emissions in New Zealand come from flatulent sheep.

Milk

Modern milking herds are generally selected, fed and reared to be extraordinarily productive – some individual cows can produce nearly 10,000 litres of milk a year, which is double what would have been normal only a few decades ago.

In America they've taken this a step further. Many of their dairy herds are injected with bovine somatatrophin (BST), a hormone designed to boost milk production. The hormone manufacturers say it helps make better use of feed, and therefore reduces the amount of methane going into the atmosphere. What they don't say, however, is that the use of BST may weaken the cow's immune system and make it more vulnerable to mastitis. This in turn can lead to more animal suffering, as well as greater use of antibiotics and therefore antibiotic resistance. The BST hormone is not permitted for use in Europe.

Animal health is a key factor in organic standards. Tighter limits have been imposed on both the use of antibiotics and the time before milk from treated cows can be sold. Their criteria also stipulate that cows eat more grass and less concentrated feed, which means they produce less milk.

There's some debate over the health benefits of organic milk, but studies indicate that it generally contains higher levels of beneficial nutrients and vitamins than milk from non-organic cows. My view is that it's worth the premium charged because you're getting a good-quality product, and at the same time you're supporting happier, healthier animals and a better environment.

Eggs

In the UK we eat over 10 billion eggs a year – that's 172 each. Nearly two-thirds come from laying cage systems, which is a highly mechanised process with cages stacked on top of each other and automated systems for supplying food and water as well as for collecting droppings and eggs.

Barn systems are less intensive than cages – the birds are given nest boxes, perches and even dust-bathing facilities. But it's still far removed from five-star chicken accommodation, because it's pretty cramped – new houses are allowed no more than nine hens per square metre, but it used to be 25. Try having a dust bath in those conditions!

Nearly one-third of hens are free-range, which means they must not only have access to the outdoors but be encouraged to make use of it. All organic chickens are free-range, but other criteria vary depending on the organic certification body they conform to. Soil Association standards are apparently too strict for many large-scale producers: they recommend no more than 500 hens in a flock and will permit no more than 2,000. Other certifying bodies, such as Organic Farmers and Growers and the Organic Food Federation, will allow up to 12,000 hens in a flock.

You may have noticed that most eggs you buy come stamped with a little string of numbers. The first number tells you what system the hens were kept in: 0 = organic; 1 = free-range; 2 = barn; 3 = cage. Then it tells you which country the egg comes from, and lastly it gives a farm ID number. I have to admit that I have found this to be rather useful. Close to where I live I discovered a lovely looking farm selling duck and chicken eggs – there were lots of birds pecking about in the farmyard. However I was put off when I discovered that the egg stamp showed they'd been produced in a barn system. I haven't been back since.

EGG HIERARCHY

Eggs from home-reared hens
↓
Organic eggs
↓
Free-range eggs
↓
Barn eggs
↓
Cage eggs

SUPERMARKET WATCH

Eggs

M&S was the first supermarket to sell only free-range eggs, even in its ingredients. **Waitrose** now does the same for its own-brand products, and one-third of its fresh eggs are organic. All **Co-op** brand eggs are now free-range, whilst over half of **Sainsbury's** and **Tesco**'s eggs are free-range. **Asda** says it has recently released half a million laying hens from battery cages to open barns, which means it sells 140 million fewer battery eggs each year.

FISH

Health Equation

Eating fish is good for you – particularly oily fish. At least it used to be. Oily fish, such as tuna, mackerel and swordfish, have high levels of Omega 3, which is excellent for brain development, a healthy heart, relieving depression and a whole raft of other things, including dyslexia. Yet today we face a rather complex equation when deciding how much oily fish to eat and how often to eat it.

The reason is that pollutants such as polychlorinated biphenyls (PCBs) and mercury are widespread in our oceans and build up in animal fat, including that of fish. Pregnant women and young children are particularly vulnerable; however, they're also the group that has the most to gain from Omega 3.

The Food Standards Agency recommends no more than one or two servings of fish per week for pre-menopausal women and children. The pollutants will still be building up in the body, but apparently not to dangerous levels. It's also worth noting that Omega 3 is found in non-animal sources, such as flax, seaweed and walnuts, although the fats aren't quite as good as those from fish.

You may remember there was a huge furore about toxic pollutants being found in farmed salmon. The concern was that any PCBs and dioxins consumed by the salmon would build up in their flesh. A further complexity is that North Sea fish are more contaminated than those from the Pacific, caught, for example, off the coast of Chile. However, bear in mind that the Government imposes strict limits on levels of contaminants.

There's no simple advice. The reality is that environmental pollutants have compromised one of the healthiest foods on the planet.

MOSHI MOSHI

Japanese sushi bar Moshi Moshi was so concerned about the plight of bluefin tuna that it stopped selling them. That was a bold move for a sushi bar. It now has an environmental policy covering all the fish and other produce it sells and is leading the way in terms of responsible sourcing of its fish. Ask other restaurants what they're doing.

Good Fish, Bad Fish

As discussed in Seas and Oceans in Chapter 1, there are many fish species on the brink of extinction and others whose numbers are severely depleted by over-fishing. I sometimes wish I knew a bit less about which fish to buy – and which not to buy! The sad fact is that many delicious fish, such as monkfish, skate and cod, should largely be avoided. But rather than ignore the problem, enthusiastic fish eaters like me need to find out more about which fish we *can* eat with a clean conscience.

Yes fish

If you're buying fish in supermarkets look out for a Marine Stewardship Council (MSC) label. The MSC has developed standards for sustainable well-managed fisheries, so consumers can support good practices. Unfortunately it's not yet that widespread and not all well-managed fisheries are convinced it's worth applying for. My view is that for those of us who aren't dedicated fish experts, it's a big help in choosing 'good' fish.

Another organisation with a confusingly similar name, The Marine Conservation Society (MCS), does give us another option – but it's more time-consuming. It publishes *The Good Fish Guide*, which explains which fish to buy and which to avoid on sustainability grounds. It also provides this information on a website called Fish Online and publishes an annual *Pocket Good Fish Guide* to use when you're shopping.

One easy piece of advice: if you buy fish that has been caught locally off our coasts, you're more likely to be in the clear. It also means you won't be contributing to too many food miles – or in this case 'fish miles'. One thing many of us forget is that an awful lot of fish are flown huge distances, and yet more 'swim' the oceans in refrigerated ships. Our fish-eating habits are not very climate-change friendly.

FISH TO BUY

It's not easy listing sustainable fish species because their status will depend on where and how they have been fished. Go for the following when you're at the fish counter:

✓ Fish caught locally, from day boats – this will generally have been caught with more sustainable fishing methods and won't have clocked up lots of fish miles
✓ Shellfish such as cockles, mussels, whelks, crabs, lobsters and cold-water prawns
✓ Mackerel, line-caught sea bass, flounder
✓ MSC-certified fish
✓ White fish alternatives to cod and haddock, such as pollack and whiting.

Check with Fish Online (www.fishonline.org) for up-to-date information.

No fish

One of the most valid reasons for avoiding particular types of fish is slow breeding. Orange roughy, for example, don't breed until they're 25 years old, so if they're over-fished before maturity, stocks may never be able to recover. Other slow-breeding fish include skate, monkfish, grey mullet, plaice and Chilean sea bass – it's quite likely that if you're offered one of those, it will have been illegally caught.

There are other fish that are simply too popular for their own good. Even now it would be hard to find a fish and chip shop that didn't sell cod, yet cod has become one of the most expensive fish on the market. It's been so over-fished in most places that it's widely predicted there'll be hardly any cod left in 20 years' time. Other fish in this group include Atlantic halibut, Atlantic salmon, European hake and some haddock.

Consumer habits die hard though. One fish and chip shop got its customers to taste pollack as an alternative to cod. Half of them said they didn't like it. But a blind tasting revealed that customers couldn't tell which fish they were eating! Unilever also tried to shift their customers from traditional Birds Eye 'cod fish fingers' to ones made from hoki, an MSC-certified fish from New Zealand. It didn't work.

SHARK-FIN SOUP

To make this Chinese favourite they cut the fins off sharks, often whilst the fish are still alive, and throw the finless corpses back to sea. Sharks are also killed by fishing trawlers – sometimes as by-catch – and many species have declined by between 60 and 80 per cent. They have a slow rate of reproduction, which means that even without shark-fin soup enthusiasts they'll take a long time to recover.

FLYING FISH!?

'Environmentally friendly' fish flown live from Australia to America – I wondered if I was reading the advertisement properly! The idea seemed to be to fly Australian Barramundi fish to America so they could be reared in state-of-the-art indoor fish farms. I'm afraid that as soon as those fish booked their seats, their eco-credentials went out of the window!

There are some fish species that simply shouldn't be sold because they're nearly extinct or impossible to fish sustainably. But for many species it's a question of where and how they are fished – sometimes stocks that were depleted will have recovered. Here are some tips on what to avoid:

✗ All bigeye and bluefin tuna, most albacore and some yellowfin
✗ Slow-breeding fish like the orange roughy, Patagonian toothfish, monkfish, skate and most rays
✗ Shark, marlin and swordfish
✗ Common white fish such as cod, haddock and plaice from some areas
✗ Tropical prawns – wild-caught prawns are generally best avoided (page 156); and if you buy farmed prawns, try to ensure they have been managed to high standards
✗ Atlantic salmon, Atlantic halibut, European hake and blue ling
✗ Sea bream, trawl-caught sea bass, North Sea turbot
✗ Squid below a certain size.

Check with Fish Online (www.fishonline.org) for up-to-date information.

FISHMONGER

Tuna

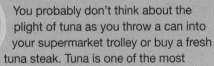

You probably don't think about the plight of tuna as you throw a can into your supermarket trolley or buy a fresh tuna steak. Tuna is one of the most popular fish in the world and demand is increasing all the time, despite concerns over mercury contamination. The problem is that almost all commercially fished tuna species are under pressure, except skipjack, which is commonly used for tinned tuna.

You may have seen labels on tins of tuna saying they are 'dolphin-friendly' or 'dolphin-safe'. This is because some tuna fishing practices result in large-scale killing of dolphins and other marine mammals. Yellowfin tuna in particular often swim alongside dolphins, and so both species are caught in fishing nets. Unfortunately the labels have no legal status and so are pretty meaningless. In some cases companies will have taken measures to reduce dolphin catch, but the different fishing methods used can mean more sea birds and other wildlife getting caught instead.

At $60,000 or more for one fish, the southern bluefin tuna is highly prized, and not surprisingly it's also on the verge of extinction. Fishermen using spotter planes may take as long as two weeks to track down a single fish, and then the exorbitantly priced flesh is sold for sashimi in Japan.

Even northern bluefins are endangered. And this is made worse by tuna ranching or penning, in which tuna are rounded up from the wild and herded into ocean pens – although many die along the way. Once in the pens they're fattened: it takes 20kg of bait to produce just 1kg of tuna. The tuna collected for ranching don't need to be officially declared for quotas, and many of them are breeding females, which further decreases their numbers in the wild.

And watch out, bigeye tuna! Apparently they're being seen as a possible replacement for bluefins. My advice is to avoid all tuna except line-caught skipjack.

Prawns

There are two main types of prawn – or shrimp, as the Americans like to call them – cold-water and warm-water. It's the warm-water or tropical prawn that is the biggest cause of concern to environmentalists.

Wild prawns are caught in nets dragged behind trawlers. The chief problem with this is that, in warm-water areas, the by-catch is huge – far bigger than for most other fish types. What's more, the non-prawn catch includes thousands of turtles. For the turtles, at least, there's a way around the problem – turtle-extruder devices can be fitted to the nets, allowing them to escape whilst still trapping the prawns. Unfortunately not all fishing boats use them.

Prawn farming in the tropics has become big business, but in many areas it has been extremely destructive. Coastal mangroves are the marine equivalent of tropical rainforests. They're also fertile breeding grounds for fish and are surprisingly effective at cleaning dirty water, even from urban areas. Apparently, prawn farmers in countries like Thailand, Bangladesh, Vietnam, Honduras and Ecuador have cleared large tracts of these wetland trees to make space for their enterprises.

Organic prawn farmers have to use local prawns and feed, as well as avoid overcrowding and the use of antibiotics and other chemicals.

A major problem is that once a prawn farm has been set up, it actually requires some skill to keep it going. Without careful management, the water can become contaminated and the prawns killed off by disease. Some farmers resort to high doses of chemicals and antibiotics, which don't always help. When prawn farms are abandoned there's little else that can be done with the land because it will have become salty and infertile. And often the prawn farmers will just move on and destroy another mangrove.

Consumers may be the answer to the prawn problem. If we want to continue to eat this luxury product we need to be sure they have been produced responsibly – shops and restaurants should be able to guarantee this. Cold-water prawns are almost always the better option.

Shellfish

The good news is that most shellfish can be eaten with a clean, green conscience. And a lot of it comes from British waters. Actually, rather surprisingly, much of the shellfish eaten in France, Spain and Italy also comes from around our shores – 80 per cent of what we produce is exported.

Crabs, lobsters, mussels, clams, oysters and whelks are filter feeders. That means they get their food by straining particles out of the water, which makes them particularly sensitive to water quality. As a result, the shellfish industry is a vigorous campaigner for clean water controls.

The water quality of breeding sites is categorised from A for the cleanest to D for the dirtiest. There's a strict code of practice which stipulates how shellfish have to be purged (cleaned of impurities) before being put on the market. Suppliers can't sell any that have been produced in D-grade water, but in reality most supermarkets won't accept anything below grade A.

Still on the health front, shellfish are high in Omega 3 – the healthy ingredient in fish oil – but unlike oily fish, they don't store PCBs and dioxins in body fat. So you get the up side without the down. Pregnant women should still take note of advice about not eating shellfish for fear of other contaminants.

LOBSTER HATCHERY

At the moment there's no shortage of lobsters, but as their popularity increases this might not always be the case. The Lobster Hatchery in Padstow, Cornwall, is working on a lobster restocking programme. They take pregnant female lobsters from the wild, nurture their offspring in captivity, away from predators, and release them into the wild. You can go and have a look at what they're doing if you like – they're open to the public.

Another advantage of shellfish is that any under-size ones can be put back without causing them any harm. However, scallop dredging is not so good. A weighted metal-edged basket is dragged along the sea floor, scooping up not only scallops but other fish too, whilst pulverising rock and coral along the way. Some scallop fisheries have now introduced less harmful practices.

The MSC has labelled relatively few shellfish, and as yet there's no other label to help us. Wherever you buy them, ask about fishing practices and size restrictions, so that fish suppliers know more information is wanted.

Salmon

The lochs of Scotland are erupting with fish like never before – farmed salmon is big business, with worldwide exports. It's certainly been good for the Scottish economy, but not quite so good for water quality in the lochs – or for the wild salmon that migrate there.

It's sometimes suggested that fish farming is a good alternative to over-fishing, but that argument doesn't really stack up. Salmon are carnivorous and need a high-protein diet, which is mainly composed of fish meal and fish oil. So a lot of smaller fish have to be scooped out of the ocean to sustain our appetite for salmon. Only a small proportion of feed comes from fish-factory waste – this is the source of all feed for organic farmed fish. Some of the feed, along with faecal matter, falls to the bottom of the loch, below the moored cages. Unless it's properly dealt with, the surrounding seabed is stripped bare. On the West Coast of Scotland, wild salmon populations have been decimated. One of the main reasons is thought to be the vast numbers of their farmed relatives that escape.

Many then breed with their wild cousins and contaminate the gene pool. This is no small problem – in a single year over 400,000 fish were reported to have broken free, excluding the unreported ones. To make matters worse, the escapees can exacerbate the transfer of sea lice to wild salmon. This is a gory parasite, which starts by eating the slime coating of a fish and then more or less eats it alive. One of the challenges for fish farmers is how to prevent this disease or treat it when it does occur – either way, there are some pretty nasty chemicals involved.

That's the bad news about salmon farms. But there's some good news too. The salmon farming industry has been under pressure from campaigners and has made considerable improvements over the past decade. And you can buy organic farmed fish, which amongst other things are given more space, thereby reducing sea lice problems.

Cod farming

It's the new fish on the block – farmed cod. In a few years' time it could well be as popular as farmed salmon, but will it do better in terms of its eco-credentials?

Johnson Seafarms are at the forefront of this new industry. They plan to produce literally thousands of tonnes of organically farmed cod. And I can't criticise them for being unimaginative. One of their first innovations is to provide toys for the cod, in the form of ropes for them to gnaw on – apparently, cod like chewing. And the more expensive nets they use mean they've managed to avoid killing scores of sea birds that prey on stocks. But the most important questions about farming any fish have to be whether it's actually going to help relieve pressure on wild stocks, and whether it's sustainable. In part this comes down to the amount of other fish they eat. Being carnivorous, cod require a similar amount of fish feed to salmon. For both fish, research is going on to find out how well they might respond to a more vegetarian diet, which would have less impact on other fish stocks.

Unlike salmon, farmed cod is unlikely to boost demand for this already popular fish. Apart from anything else, the organic production methods make it 20–30 per cent more expensive than wild cod.

I have to admit that I was initially rather hostile to the idea of farmed cod. Now I think it's no worse than farmed salmon – in fact it might actually have some eco-advantages over its pink-fleshed fellow carnivore. But these advantages will only be apparent if cod is farmed to the highest environmental standards. Johnson Seafarms may be doing this; let's hope that other cod farmers will follow their lead.

LOCH DUART

Loch Duart fish are not organic, but they have been reared with superior sustainability standards. They use sea urchins to eat up feed that isn't consumed by the salmon and cultivate seaweed that also helps clean the water. Both the urchins and the seaweed are then sold on for sushi.

The big salmon farmers may not be able to introduce the same measures, but we have to hope they're learning some lessons from the eco-pioneers in their industry.

SUPERMARKET WATCH

Fish

Fish is certainly an issue that the supermarkets are taking seriously. **M&S** and **Waitrose** are leading the way in promoting more sustainable fishing practices, staff training, and not selling blacklisted fish. They're closely followed by **Sainsbury's,** which has assessed all its seafood against sustainability criteria and has an interesting initiative promoting locally caught fish in the South West. **Asda** was trailing the field until its dramatic turnaround in 2006 – all wild fish sold by **Asda** will be MSC-certified within three to five years.
Co-op has focused its attention on fish-farming practices, with particularly stringent standards on fish welfare. Although they won't buy fish whose origin and method of catch is unknown at the time of writing they were still selling wild-caught, warm-water prawns, which feature on the **MCS** fish-to-avoid list. They said they were working with suppliers to find an alternative. Check with **MCS** to see if any supermarkets are still selling their blacklisted fish.

Both **M&S** and **Waitrose** set high standards for fish farming, pushing the industry towards innovative and continuing improvements. But **Asda**, **Sainsbury's** and **Tesco** have also developed sustainability standards for their fish farm suppliers. Only **Waitrose** indicated that they were doing anything to reduce their 'fish miles'.

All supermarkets should:
- only buy fish from fully traceable sources
- specify sustainable fishing practices
- blacklist fish from unsustainable stocks
- promote the best seasonal, local and sustainable fish
- label fish origin, details of how it was caught, and how it was transported
- support research into sustainable fish solutions
- campaign for marine conservation
- set stringent requirements for farmed fish.

FISH WEBLINKS

Fish Online Run by the Marine Conservation Society, this site gives information on which fish to avoid and which to eat based on the sustainability of stocks. It also helps with questions to ask fish retailers and provides a league table for fishing methods.

www.fishonline.org

Greenpeace Major campaigns on defending the ocean and protecting the Mediterranean.

www.greenpeace.org.uk

Johnson Seafarms Produce organically farmed cod.

www.johnsonseafarms.com

Loch Duart Pioneering innovative best-practice measures for fish farming in Scotland.

www.lochduart.com

Marine Conservation Society (MCS) Charity campaigning to protect the marine environment and its wildlife. Produced *The Good Fish Guide* and runs the Fish Online website.

www.mcsuk.org

Marine Stewardship Council (MSC) Encourages sustainable fishing practices through accreditation and labelling of fish.

www.msc.org

Moshi Moshi Chain of sushi bars practising responsible fish-sourcing policies.

www.moshimoshi.co.uk

National Lobster Hatchery Lobster-breeding centre open to the public; based in Padstow, Cornwall.	www.nationallobsterhatchery.co.uk
Organic Food Federation Main body for organic standards in farmed salmon and cod.	www.orgfoodfed.com
Shell Fish Association of Great Britain Trade association for shellfish producers.	www.shellfish.org.uk
Soil Association Organic standards body that has developed criteria for organic farmed fish.	www.soilassociation.org
World Wide Fund for Nature (WWF) Campaigns to prevent over-fishing and protect ocean habitats.	www.wwf.org.uk

MOSTLY DRINKS

Hard and Soft
Drinking climate

Whatever your favourite tipple you probably haven't given much thought to its impact on global warming. So you may be surprised to learn that at least 1.5 per cent of greenhouse gases produced in the UK come from the alcohol consumed here. That's quite significant – and it doesn't even include soft drinks and water.

WHISKY MADNESS
In 2005 over 5 million litres of Scottish whisky was imported back into the UK. Globetrotting whisky doesn't make eco-sense.

ECO-FRIENDLY DRINKING HABITS
- Drink draught beer rather than bottled beer or cans.
- Buy cans rather than bottles, where possible.
- Choose UK-produced alcohol to reduce transport.
- Select European wines rather than New World brands.
- Choose drinks that don't need cooling.
- Never buy duty-free alcohol before or during a flight.

A key element of this is the packaging – single-use glass bottles are the worst, even if they're recycled. Cans are better, but as part of the shift towards more portable drinking habits they're actually increasing the global warming impact of booze. It's better to drink

161

draught beer at a pub – depending, of course, how far you've travelled and how you got there.

What's even trickier in weighing up the climate change impacts of drink is how much to attribute to what's called 'the hospitality industry' – pubs, clubs and restaurants. However it's measured, this industry is tremendously wasteful.

Have you ever been to a pub with energy-efficient lighting? I haven't. But I have noticed that a new restaurant near where I live has so many halogen light bulbs in every available space that it could light the whole village!

Probably our worst drinking habit has to be buying duty-free alcohol at airports. Doesn't it seem completely mad for a bottle of whisky to be transported thousands of miles abroad, only to be sold to someone who carries it onto a plane and brings it back to where it was made in the first place? Luckily, this is something that's already been reduced by a change in duty-free law – although not for eco-reasons, I'm certain. And it's still cheaper to buy booze abroad.

Organic Drinking

Do you think organic alcohol is not much different to organic cigarettes – a bit of a paradox? One major brewer I spoke to said that people bought organic chiefly for health reasons, so there wasn't much point making organic beer. I'm not convinced – what about the reduced eco-impacts of organic farming?

Interestingly, there may actually be health benefits in drinking organic wine. The organic standards not only reduce the level of pesticides used on grapes, but restrict the amount of sulphur in wine-making. It's thought this could reduce the hangover potential – it's certainly worth a try, especially if you think you

might be sensitive to sulphur. But don't use it as an excuse to drink more!

Apart from the supermarkets, the biggest organic wine seller is Vintage Roots. And its closest competitor is Vinceremos. Both also sell organic spirits such as Juniper Green Organic Gin, Utkins Organic Vodka and Highlands Harvest Whisky. There are also quite a number of small brewers producing organic beer (see Food and Drink Weblinks).

WORST WATER
Water from the artisans of Fiji (Fiji Water) or Canadian glaciers (Iceberg Water) may be pure but it's not good for the planet. It makes me shudder to think of the climate change impacts of transporting this water thousands of miles across the world.

Drinking Water

Shipping or trucking huge quantities of bottled water around the planet is absurd when there's a plentiful supply piped direct to our houses. Bottled water is 10,000 times more expensive than tap water – and often costs even more than car fuel. Yet people get all steamed up about the price of fuel and happily pay through the nose for water.

In Britain we consume a staggering 2 billion litres of bottled water every year – and our annual consumption is forecast to grow by 9 per cent in the next five years. Luckily most water is sold in plastic bottles rather than glass (page 34), but a quarter of what we drink is imported from abroad.

Many people say they prefer the taste of bottled water, yet this isn't borne out by the taste tests – tap water often comes out on top. And if you filter this water and cool it in your fridge, any concerns about the taste are likely to evaporate along with the chlorine. Although you can't get fizzy or carbonated water direct from the tap, using a carbonated drinks maker such as Sodastream is better than buying bottles.

I'm afraid the health argument is not going to wash either. There are apparently tighter controls on tap water than on bottled water – there's certainly no guarantee that you're buying a healthier option when you splash out the extra cost.

A real bug-bear of mine is going to an office that has bottles of water on the table for meetings. If there's one really simple thing you can do it's invest in jugs and fill them from the tap. And for the rest of us, remember to take a water bottle whenever we're travelling.

KEEPING COOL

If you're buying cool drinks, don't forget about the fridge coolants (page 71). It's not difficult for companies to switch to cooling fluids that are neither ozone-destroying nor a big problem for climate change.

BELU MAY BE BEST

If you're really stuck and have to buy bottled water, buy Belu. They give away all their profits to clean water projects around the world, collect bottles for recycling and generally try to reduce their environmental impact. Not so brilliant is the fact that they make a big deal about using biodegradable plastic (page 35) – made from corn – for their bottles. However, I still think Belu may be best.

Fizzy or Juicy

There are worse things in life than fizzy drinks –
but there's also not much that's good about
them. Loaded with sugar and sugar
substitutes, they're neither good for your
health nor for your teeth. I'm not so anti-juices
– they're better for you, although still
not very tooth-friendly. Look out for some of
the organic brands like Grove Fresh and
James White.

Not organic but still pushing the boundaries
on the environmental front are Innocent
Drinks. They tell you where all their ingredients
come from, never use air freight, donate
money to innovative overseas projects and,
most impressively, are leading the way in
using recycled material in their packaging. The
obstacles to this are chiefly technical, which
makes one ask: 'How come the bigger
companies are being beaten to it by a drinks
minnow?'

Fair dos

Café Direct introduced the world to the idea
of 'fair trade', and this approach has now
spread to many other products – over 1,500 to
date. But nowhere have the changes been
more marked than for tea and coffee
producers, who have been spearheading the
introduction of fairer working practices in
developing countries.

The Fairtrade mark is awarded to products that
comply with strict standards relating not only to
working conditions but also to sustainability
and fair terms of trade for farmers. It's not
primarily an environmental award, although the
eco-impacts of fair trade products are generally
better for mainstream products. And it works
the other way too – organic producers will
generally have better fair trade practices.

- **Fair trade coffee:** more
  money goes to producers
  and communities in coffee-
  growing areas.

- **Rainforest coffee:** certified by the
  Rainforest Alliance, which has
  detailed criteria on coffee
  production that minimises impacts
  on rainforests and supports coffee
  production workers.

- **Shade coffee:** Coffee would
  naturally grow in shady areas –
  shade coffee is grown amongst
  trees rather than in full sunlight.

- **Organic coffee:** Organic criteria
  (page 44) are applied to coffee
  growing although there are different
  standards for coffee sold to Japan,
  America and Europe.

Tea's up!

When you're drinking your
morning cuppa I bet you're not
thinking about the number of
worms on tea plantations. Well
maybe you should, because a
lack of worms is a sign of poor
soil quality and leads to high
chemical inputs. It may surprise you to know
that some non-organic teas have high levels of
pesticide residues. Fair trade teas do tend to
use fewer chemicals because it's better for
worker health.

Another key issue in tea production is the
clearing of forests and other wildlife-rich land
for new plantations. Some companies, such
as Clipper Teas, will only buy from established
plantations for this reason. Then there's the
threat to forests caused by the large volume of

wood used for drying tea. In Sri Lanka it's been estimated that it takes between 1.5 and 2.5kg of wood to dry 1kg of tea; the tea industry is therefore the biggest industrial user of fuel wood in the country.

Coffee time

Throughout the life of one little coffee bean its eco-impacts are considerable – from land clearance and pesticides in growing, to the energy used in roasting, and most significant of all, boiling the water for drinking.

Coffee used to be grown under the leafy canopy of rainforest trees, but now most bushes are planted in dense, military-style rows. Although this means lots more beans being produced, the transformation in coffee growing has been achieved by using heavy doses of agrochemicals, polluting waterways and clearing forests. Concern over forest clearing for coffee growing has led to the introduction of 'shade coffee' or 'rainforest coffee'. If that's not confusing enough, you can also get organic coffee, fair trade coffee, and some brands that are a mixture of any or all of these – coffee ethics are actually quite complicated.

What's more, there are a number of big coffee buyers who've developed their own standards. Starbucks, for example, have developed quality, social and environmental criteria that are specific to them – and they pay more for it. Nestlé, who produce Nescafé, have also set up sustainable coffee initiatives.

Satisfying our craving for coffee is big business – in fact it's the second most traded commodity in the world, eclipsed only by oil. The social dimension of coffee beans is pretty important too, as 24 million people in the tropics depend on it.

When fair trade coffee was first introduced some people weren't impressed with the taste. Now there's far more choice, so you should be able to find something you like. Don't forget that the eco-credentials of what you're drinking aren't worth much if the final product is poured down the drain.

BRING A MUG
Starbucks in the US runs a scheme to encourage customers to bring their own mug to the store - in one year it saved 13.5 million disposable paper cups weighting 586,000lb. I hope this initiative spreads to the UK.

FOOD AND DRINK WEBLINKS

Banana Link Campaigns for a fair and sustainable banana trade.

www.bananalink.org.uk

Belu All profits from this bottled water go to clean water projects.

www.belu.org

Café Direct The first coffee brand to carry the fairtrade mark in the UK, it now has fair trade sales of nearly £25m.

www.cafedirect.co.uk

Clipper Teas Sells organic and fair trade tea, coffee and cocoa.

www.clipper-teas.com

Commonground Champions the local, especially orchards

www.commonground.org.uk

Compassion in World Farming Campaigning organisation that regularly compares supermarket performance on animal welfare issues. Its 2005–2006 survey was led by Waitrose, followed by M&S, Co-op, Tesco, Sainsbury's, Somerfield and Asda – in that order.

www.ciwf.org.uk

Fairtrade Foundation Promotes and licences fair trade products.

www.fairtrade.org.uk

Food Commission Campaigns on food and health issues and publishes *The Food Magazine* quarterly.

www.foodcomm.org.uk

Friends of the Earth (FoE) Publishes a regular survey on supermarket performance on pesticide residues: Pesticides in Supermarket Food.

www.foe.co.uk

Grove Fresh Produces organic fruit and vegetable juices.

www.grovefresh.co.uk

Innocent Drinks Produce smoothies and other fruit drinks.

www.innocentdrinks.co.uk

James White Produces fruit and vegetable juices, including an organic range.

www.jameswhite.co.uk

National Consumer's Council Campaigns on consumer issues, including sustainable consumption. Produced a report on Greening Supermarkets.

www.ncc.org.uk

Organic Farmers and Growers Organic certification body.

www.organicfarmers.uk.com

Out of this World Small supermarket chain selling ethical, local and organic produce.

www.outofthisworld.coop

Pesticide Action Network UK (PAN) Working to eliminate the dangers of toxic pesticides.

www.pan-uk.org

Soil Association The main organic standards body.

www.soilassociation.org

Somerset Local Food Direct Excellent local food delivery service that sells everything from meat and fish to coffee, fruit juices and yoghurt – I'm a regular customer.

www.sfmdirect.co.uk

Sustain Promotes better food and farming practices.

www.sustainweb.org

Vinceremos Organic wine specialist.

www.vinceremos.co.uk

Vintage Roots Leading supplier of organic wines, beers and spirits.

www.vintageroots.co.uk

Transport

There aren't many people in the Western world who haven't been stuck in a nose-to-tail traffic jam. Sadly, congestion has become an unavoidable part of our lives. We sit at the wheel agonising over being late, dealing with children squabbling in the back, or listening to loud music and traffic updates on the radio. Air passengers suffer from congestion too. Have you ever been on a flight that has had to circle the airport several times before it finds a landing slot?

All these jams are not merely because there are more of us. We're travelling more and travelling further; our lifestyles are built around our ability to jump into a car or onto a plane whenever we like.

Since I was born in 1961 there's been a 10-fold increase in car traffic and a 20-fold increase in air traffic. Yet all this travelling comes at a cost: about a quarter of CO_2 emissions come from transport and it's predicted this could increase to a third by 2010.

Private cars create half of all transport emissions. Our enthusiasm for them is partly fuelled by the fact they're relatively cheap to run. Whilst the costs of rail and bus fares have grown by around a third since 1980, the overall cost of motoring has actually decreased.

Our obsession with cars and planes can't continue unabated. The crunch point is going to come when there's no longer affordable fuel to put into the tank. Motor and aircraft manufacturers are tinkering around the edges, making fairly minor improvements to fuel efficiency, and governments are extraordinarily timid about introducing measures that restrict motorists. But our motoring profligacy hasn't got many more years to run.

We all need to travel less and walk and cycle more. For longer journeys we should use public transport – buses, coaches and trains. But if we travel by car, we need to know what sort of car to buy, what fuel to put in it and how to minimise the environmental impacts of our driving. This section answers questions such as why low-cost airlines are an environmental horror story.

TRANSPORT MATTERS

Car-less

If you're thinking about your transport needs, your first priority should be to travel less. This may mean redesigning your life by living closer to your children's school, your work or leisure activities, for example. It might also mean changing your shopping habits – perhaps buying in bulk – so you don't have to go into town or to the supermarket so often. Another alternative to regular shopping could be to get your food delivered. I use a good local food delivery service, and as a result I go to the shops just once every few weeks.

The Ebay phenomenon has not only been good for recycling, it has also reduced the number of shopping trips people make. When I wanted some brass curtain poles for my sitting room, I put the details on Ebay and waited until the right ones came up for sale. Even though the delivery van had to come to my door, it meant far less fuel was used than if I'd been on a number of shopping expeditions to find what I wanted.

LIFTSHARE
It's the largest national lift-share organisation in the UK, with a rapidly expanding membership. Sign up for regular lifts such as school runs, commuting or shopping, or for one-off trips to festivals, events or visiting friends. It saves you money and means there are fewer cars on the road.
www.liftshare.org

? DID YOU KNOW? ?

Car ownership in Beijing doubled between 2000 and 2005, whilst in India they're making three times the number of cars they did eight years ago.

Sharing lifts

Another way to reduce car travel is to car share. Only a decade ago this would have been a logistical nightmare; now there are lots of organisations to help you along the way.

There are two main types of car sharing. The first is sharing lifts, for example to work. In the UK we call this 'car sharing' or 'lift sharing'; in the US they call it 'car pooling'.

Did you know that up to 80 per cent of cars travelling to work in the rush hour have only one person in them? Just sharing a lift with one other person would halve the number of cars on the road. If you travel anywhere regularly or go on long journeys, it's worth checking out these schemes. Remember that you don't have to share a lift with the same person all the time – there's lots of flexibility now that the schemes are more popular.

The second sort of car sharing is what we call 'car clubs'. Confusingly, the US and the rest of Europe call it 'car sharing'. Becoming a member of a car club entitles you to use a vehicle from a pool of cars whenever you want. Generally you pay a membership fee and then a set amount per hour of use. For people who don't drive all the time it can be a lot cheaper and more convenient than owning a car because all the bills and maintenance are paid for.

On a more informal basis some groups of friends or neighbours have formed car clubs. This could mean five or so households joining together to buy one or two cars, which would be enough for all of them.

Bus rides

It goes without saying that travelling by bus or coach is far greener than going by car or plane. Leave your car at home and climb aboard.

And buses are getting cleaner. EU regulations on exhaust pipe emissions have become increasingly strict over the past decade – London buses are leading the way. In his commitment to make London greener, Mayor Ken Livingstone fitted particulate filters to diesel buses and has pioneered a number of cleaner technologies, such as hydrogen fuel cells and diesel hybrids. Surprisingly, he hasn't yet caught on to the joys of biomethane. Perhaps that's in the pipeline. Read more about these fuels later in this section.

Have you ever noticed that coaches have a horrible habit of sitting in car parks with their engines whirring? Apparently, one of the main reasons for this is that their air conditioning systems don't work unless the engine is turned on. Why not? I haven't worked out how much CO_2 and other pollutants are emitted from buses and coaches, keeping their drivers cool (or warm) or waiting for their customers to return, but it must be a lot. In some areas drivers can be given an on the spot fine for leaving their engines on – and members of the public can report them to the local council.

Trains are us

If you travel from London to Edinburgh by train you'll be producing about six times less CO_2 than travelling by car, and eight to nine times less than going by plane. That's assuming one and a half people per car, so if there's only one of you it will be even worse. And you won't be surprised to hear that trains are a lot safer than cars – apparently nine times safer per passenger mile.

The problem is that demand for trains exceeds supply. Passenger numbers have reached a billion a year and they're forecast to go on rising over the next 20 years. This is almost certain to mean more of us squashed into overcrowded trains and fare increases way beyond the rate of inflation, yet expanding train services to meet demand simply doesn't seem to be on the Government's agenda.

If people become disenchanted with rail travel, they'll go back to the roads. That means more congestion, more pollution and more destruction of the countryside. We should be investing in railways, opening more stations, reducing fares and generally encouraging rail travel, both as an alternative to road and to short-haul air travel.

On your bike

Cyclists are not universally popular with motorists, but they get lots of eco-points for zero-emission travel. And cycling is getting easier – in the UK over half of us live within a mile of the National Cycle Network, a system of cycle routes that have been set up all over the country. Rather less people commute by bike, but there are lots of advantages for those that do. For a start it saves money; it means you can tell how long your journey is going to take; it helps keep you fit; and for

some there's also the benefit of arriving at work with their brain already in gear. More companies are now providing parking facilities for bikes, and showers in case you need to freshen up after your journey.

Only around 2 per cent of all trips are by bike, but this is no longer declining, in part because cycling in London has dramatically increased

in the last few years. There are organisations promoting cycling to work, to school and for pleasure. Also look out for fold-up bikes – they're great for commuting and easy to take on the train. There's even an electric folding bike on the market (see Transport Weblinks).

BIKE AWARE

Given that cyclists are amongst the most eco-virtuous of all planet dwellers, we should be supporting them in every way we can. Avoid being part of the anti-cyclist brigade by:

• Never erecting notices banning cycle parking (e.g. on fences)
• Encouraging cycle routes wherever possible
• Driving with consideration for cyclists

In return, cyclists should be careful not to give their cycling friends a bad reputation by

making sure they use lights at night, wear visible clothing, don't ride on pavements and generally behave with respect. In other words, don't provide fuel for the anti-cycling brigade!

BUYING A CAR

More Miles Per Gallon

I've recently had to replace my rainbow-painted VW Golf because it failed its MOT, and was amazed to discover that second-hand diesel cars can be almost twice as expensive as their petrol equivalent. The mechanics I spoke to said they thought this was because they are more fuel efficient. I still didn't find it easy working out which car models I should be looking for to get the most miles to the gallon. Clearly there needs to be better information for budget car buyers with a conscience.

For new car buyers help is at hand. You may have noticed eco-labels on the windscreens of new cars. They're the same style of label as is used for electrical appliances, using an A–G rating system, with A being the most efficient.

The Department of Transport, which set up this scheme, also has a website which details the fuel efficiency of cars (see the Vehicle Certification Agency in Transport Weblinks). It will tell you how many grams of CO_2 will be emitted per kilometre of travel, as well as the car's tax band and miles per gallon for urban driving and combined city and country – urban driving is generally less fuel efficient.

The most gas-guzzling mass-market cars emit close to 300 grams of CO2 per kilometre, and the most fuel efficient close to 100 grams. There are plans to extend this site to cover all cars made since 2001, so second-hand car buyers will soon be catered for.

To give you an idea of the sort of cars to look for here are the least polluting cars at the time of writing. For up to date information look at The Green Car Guide (see weblinks)

LEAST POLLUTING HYBRID CARS
The first hybrid cars on the market were the Toyota Prius and Honda Civic Hybrid, both of which are impressive in terms of their fuel efficiency.

LEAST POLLUTING DIESEL CARS
Toyota Aygo ♥ Citroën C1, C2, C3, ♥ Peugeot 206 ♥ Fiat New Panda ♥ Vauxhall Corsa ♥ Ford Fiesta ♥ Renault Clio ♥ Ford Fusion

LEAST POLLUTING PETROL CARS
Peugeot 107 ♥ Toyota Aygo and Yaris ♥ Citroen C1 ♥ Mitsubishi Colt ♥ Smart for two Coupe and Cabrio ♥ Daihatsu Charade and Sirion ♥ Vauxhall Corsa

? DID YOU KNOW? ?

Americans own 30 per cent of the world's cars but account for half of all greenhouse gases emitted from them.

FORD'S BILLION

In 2006 Ford announced that it planned to spend £1 billion on developing greener cars. The key focus was to produce lighter vehicles made from aluminium rather than steel. They're anticipating that a standard Ford Focus will be able to go 70 miles to the gallon and emit less than 100 grams of CO_2 per kilometre.

FUEL EFFICIENCY TIPS

- **Choose the smallest type of car for your needs.**
- **Check car labels for the most fuel-efficient vehicles in that category.**
- **Choose a hybrid only if that's the most fuel-efficient.**
- **Choose diesel rather than petrol, particularly if you're driving long distances or live in the country.**
- **Don't go for air conditioning.**
- **Lighter cars will generally use less fuel.**
- **Automatics generally use more fuel**
- **Reduce drag by removing roof boxes, bikes, and even St George flags!**

Check out The Green Car Guide (see Transport Weblinks) for up-to-date information on fuel efficiency.

Small is beautiful

As a rule of thumb, the bigger and heavier your car, the more fuel it will use. So 4x4 off-road vehicles are pretty thirsty. Worryingly, these giant gas-guzzlers have become fashionable, and are no longer used only by farmers and hunters to pull horseboxes or cross muddy fields; they're often the vehicle of choice for taking children to school, shopping or visiting friends, even in built-up areas.

In fact they've become such a feature of city travelling that a campaigning organisation has been set up to oppose them. The Alliance Against Urban 4x4s points out that these vehicles are heavy, dangerous for other road users, and that there are better alternatives offering the same sort of space inside whilst using less fuel. There are also some council-led initiatives to charge gas-guzzlers more for parking – let's hope they become less fashionable as a result.

The nine worst offenders, at the time of writing, all have petrol engines. For city driving they average no more than between 12mpg and 15mpg, which is truly horrendous. Starting with the worst, they are:

- **Range Rover • Land Rover Discovery •**
- **Porsche Cayenne • Toyota Landcruiser •**
- **Isuzu Trooper • Mercedes ML500 •**
- **VW Touareg • Audi All Road Quattro •**
- **Mitsubishi Shogun**

But just for the record, don't forget that most 'high performance' cars are even worse than 4X4s in gas-guzzling terms. The very worst include models from Ferrari, Dodge, Bentley, Aston Martin, Maserati and Mercedes Benz. Some of them are not far off 500 grams of CO_2 per kilometre.

Air Conditioning and Mod Cons

By 2050 air conditioning in vehicles could be contributing as much to climate change as the tailpipe emissions of all the private cars in the world. But as the summers get hotter, it's going to be harder to convince people that they don't need it. Also, all new cars are fitted with these systems, so they're hard to avoid.

So why is car air conditioning such a problem? First, it's because they use HFCs (page 41), which you may remember are around 1,400 times more powerful greenhouse gases than CO_2. They use as much as 2–3kg per car, and what's worse is that they have an extremely high leakage rate – between one-quarter and one-third every year. This means that when your car is serviced, they'll be topping up the HFC coolant at the same time.

Some car models use CO_2 air-conditioning systems, which are less of a climate change problem, but these are not yet for sale in the UK.

Using your car air conditioning also drains power from the engine – there's a 5 to 15 per cent reduction in fuel efficiency. You might also be concerned to know that by using air conditioning you may be at greater risk of catching germs. Apparently they circulate within the system and are particularly bad if you don't change the filters.

It's not just air conditioning that reduces car fuel efficiency: CD players, satellite navigation systems, electric windows and luggage carriers all add to the weight of a vehicle and therefore make it more thirsty. Even an electric sunroof has to have a motor and wires to connect it. So rather than getting lighter, cars are actually getting heavier as more and more gadgets are fitted as standard.

DO WITHOUT AIR CONDITIONING

- **Open the windows!**
- **Choose tinted windows.**
- **Buy a light coloured vehicle.**
- **Use sunshades or car covers if you leave your car in the sun.**
- **Leave windows open when parked, if you can.**
- **On hot days, flush the heat from the car by opening the doors for a few minutes before getting in.**

MOTORBIKES

Surprisingly, although motor-bikes emit more than six times less CO_2 than the average car, they can be far worse for other pollutants. For example, the 1997 124cc Piaggio Vespa emits 36 times more carbon monoxide (CO) per km, 141 times more hydrocarbons, and 1.7 times more NOx.

ON and OFF THE ROAD

Driving

Now you've got a car, here are some tips on eco-driving and keeping your car working at its best.

Speed: driving slowly uses less fuel. If you drive at 50mph you use 30 per cent less fuel than at 70mph.

Smoothly: drive smoothly without accelerating and braking too much. Pulling away from another vehicle at speed can use up to 60 per cent more fuel than when you are cruising. So aggressive drivers are fuel guzzlers.

Gears: get into a high gear as soon as you can – this can reduce fuel consumption by 15 per cent.

Cold start: don't leave the engine on to warm up when it's cold. It'll cause rapid engine wear and wastes fuel.

Planning: where possible, avoid rush hour traffic and combine a number of short trips into one long one.

Keeping Your Car Fit

Load: remove roof racks and other accessories you're not using to lighten the load.

Servicing: service your car regularly – a finely tuned engine works better.

Tyres: check your tyre pressure frequently. If tyres are not properly inflated they wear out more quickly and you can use 3–4 per cent more fuel.

Oil: keep your oil topped up. If you're disposing of waste oil, don't throw it down the drain, contact Oil Care (see Transport Weblinks).

Making and Breaking

It's a commonly held belief that cars take more energy to make than they use during their lifetime. If this were the case it would mean we should all hold on to our cars for as long as possible, putting off the day when we buy a new, more efficient model. Actually, it's not true. Of course the ratio varies depending on how much a car is driven, when it was made and how fuel-efficient it is, but the ball-park figure is that the energy used in the life of a car is about 10 per cent to make it,

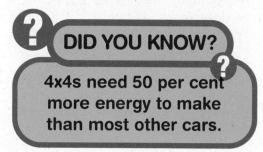

DID YOU KNOW?

4x4s need 50 per cent more energy to make than most other cars.

5 per cent to dispose of it, and 85 per cent to run it. So if you have a car that is more than 10 years old, you should get it off the road as soon as possible.

There are two conflicting trends in making new cars. On the one hand there's a lot of effort being put into using light-weight materials, such as aluminium or plastics rather than metal; on the other hand, cars are getting heavier because they contain more extras such as satellite navigation systems. It would certainly be worthwhile reviewing how many add-ons you really need – and to cut out those you won't ever use.

Surprisingly, cars may be the most recycled product we discard. This is largely because metal from cars has been recycled for years, and legislation now requires that 80 per cent of the materials in a car are recycled and a further 5 per cent must be collected to reclaim energy.

Each car component raises different issues, as follows:

- **Metals:** 98 per cent of the metals in cars is recycled. They're shredded in huge machines and used by the steel industry and resmelting plants, so they may actually go back into making new cars.
- **Plastics:** more plastics are used in cars today, which is an advantage because they're incredibly light. However, relatively little car plastic is recycled because it's generally not cost effective.
- **Tyres:** even though tyres make up a fraction of a car's weight, they've been a huge problem. In many places vast, ugly and polluting stockpiles have self-combusted and gone on smouldering for decades. In 2006 it became illegal to dump tyres in landfill – all 50 million discarded annually have to be recycled, reused or reclaimed as energy.

- **Oils and fluids:** it's estimated that up to 50 per cent of the 20,000 tonnes of oil removed by motorists is handled improperly (see Oil Care in Transport Weblinks), and car recyclers don't always remove as much as they should. One litre of waste oil is sufficient to contaminate 1 million litres of water.
- **Batteries:** battery cases account for a significant proportion of plastics recycled from cars – the recycling rate for car batteries is more than 90 per cent.
- **Glass:** very little glass from car windows is recycled because it's extremely low value and therefore not considered worthwhile. This should improve as recycling laws are tightened.

Don't take too much notice of manufacturers' claims on the recyclability of cars – they're simply doing what's required by law. But if you can find out what recycled materials have been used in manufacturing your car, that's something to boast about. To date, there are no manufacturers who will commit to using a high percentage of recycled materials – let's hope this changes.

POWERING MOTORS

Petrol vs Diesel

When people are considering what sort of car to buy, the question of whether to go for a petrol or diesel engine is often high on the list. Greener motorists might also be wondering whether to run their cars on chip fat or fuels made from crops. Here are my views on filling your tank.

Most cars run on either petrol or diesel. The choice between them is not clear cut as their environmental credentials change depending on where and how you drive. Petrol-engine cars are much cleaner than they used to be, because since 1992 they have to be fitted with a catalytic converter, which removes the most harmful emissions. Diesel cars produce fewer of these emissions in the first place and are more fuel-efficient, so you get more miles to the gallon.

The main problem with diesel is that when burnt it produces very fine particles of soot, known as particulates (petrol cars do too but not as much). These are not a problem for global warming, but they are a health hazard, causing asthma and other respiratory diseases. Particulate traps, designed to catch the soot, are not yet mandatory, even on new cars.

So this means that if you're driving a lot on motorways or live in the country, you're probably better off with a diesel car – if you get a new one make sure it's fitted with a particulate trap. You'll be producing less greenhouse gases, and even without a particulate trap the sooty emissions will be widely dispersed and not so much of a problem. If, on the other hand, you live in the city or do most of your driving in urban areas, you'd be better off with a petrol-engine car.

Gas Fuels

You may have heard that liquefied petroleum gas (LPG) – the same type of gas that's used in gas cylinders – is the cleanest fuel. To date it's mainly been used for car fleets and commercial vehicles, because they need to be specially adapted. Although the emissions are cleaner, the advantages are becoming less clear as the new top-of-the-range petrol and diesel cars match its environmental performance.

Most of us know that when we break wind (to put it politely) we produce methane. Cows also produce a lot of it. What you may not know is that methane gas is also produced by the breakdown of oil and coal and can therefore be a fossil fuel. In this form it is known as 'natural gas' and is a key ingredient in gas supplies to our homes. Where 'natural gas' is used in cars, it's referred to as compressed natural gas (CNG), and is even cleaner than LPG and also good for fuel efficiency.

BP TARGET NEUTRAL

BP has set up an initiative enabling people to directly support projects that reduce the CO_2 they produce while driving. Their advisory group has impressive credentials and it's simple to sign up to the scheme. For most people the cost will be about £20 per year, calculated on the basis of how far you drive and the fuel efficiency of your vehicle. It cost me about half that as I drive about 10,000 miles a year at around 52 mpg.

www.targetneutral.com

FUEL CONDITIONERS
There are quite a number of companies selling fuel additives that claim to improve efficiency and clean up emissions. Approach these with caution. My advice is that you'd almost certainly be better off keeping your car in good condition with clean oil and pumped up tyres – and driving carefully!

It's popular in some countries, such as Argentina, Pakistan, India and Italy, but is not yet widely used in the UK.

As I've mentioned in the section on Household Waste, methane is also the main gas emitted from rotting materials such as sewage, kitchen waste and silage. In this case it's referred to as 'biomethane', and it makes an excellent fuel for cars and other vehicles – as well as for heating and electricity. This is covered in more detail on page 186.

Electrics and Hybrids
Electrics
On the face of it, electric vehicles sound like the answer to all our problems. They produce no emissions from the exhaust pipe and are extremely quiet. In California they became very popular in the fight to reduce smog, primarily caused by exhaust emissions from the millions of gas-guzzling cars.

The power – and therefore the pollution – for electric vehicles comes from centralised power stations. But it's not just a case of shifting the pollution – there is actually less of it, even though the power comes from a coal-fired power station. It's even cleaner if batteries are recharged using solar or wind power.

Most of us have seen electric-powered milk floats and golf buggies, but the main reason they aren't more popular is that they need to be recharged by plugging the vehicle into a source of electricity. This takes time, and the range of an electric car is limited.
That's where hybrids come in.

ELECTRIC SCOOTER
If you simply want to do some short journeys around town, an electric scooter might be the answer. See Scoot Electric and Vectrix UK in weblinks

G WIZ and NICE ELECTRIC CARS

Smaller than a Mini Metro, these two new electric cars are already buzzing around London. Averaging the equivalent of 600 miles to the gallon, they're certainly the greenest cars on our roads – and you don't have to pay the congestion charge. But remember to stay in town because they go for less than 50 miles before needing recharging from mains electricity.

CONGESTION CHARGE
Hybrid vehicles were exempt from the congestion charge in London, but from 2008 it's planned that exemptions will be based on the fuel efficiency of cars rather than the technology. This makes much more sense. Whilst most hybrids top fuel efficiency tables, the four-wheel drive Lexus hybrid certainly doesn't.

Hybrids

Hybrids are relatively new on the car scene. To date, only petrol versions are available, although diesel versions are planned. The clever thing about them is that they recharge the electric motor while you're driving, so you should get more miles to the gallon.

The 'green' credentials of hybrids have made them hugely popular, despite the fact they cost several thousand pounds more to buy than a non-hybrid equivalent. However, a hybrid vehicle is only a better environmental option when it increases fuel efficiency. And the truth is that it's quite possible to find non-hybrid cars that are more fuel-efficient.

You may have heard that the batteries used by hybrid cars take so much energy to make that they offset the fuel savings on the road. Actually, although hybrid technology does use more energy in production, it's relatively insignificant in the overall life of a car.

My view is that the interest in hybrids is largely positive. It's dramatically raised the profile of fuel-efficient technologies and demonstrated how successful they can be. I predict further innovations will follow as car manufacturers realise there are so many drivers wanting planet-friendly cars, as opposed to petrol-heads who want 'sexy' vehicles that can go from 0–60 in a few seconds!

STOP START

It really bothers me that people sit chatting in cars without turning the engine off! You don't get any miles to the gallon if you're stationary – you're producing nasty emissions and getting nowhere. If you think you'll be stopping for more than nine seconds, you should turn the engine off. Research also shows that warming up your car by turning it on for more than 30 seconds is a waste of time and fuel – it warms up better if you drive it.

One new technology takes care of this for you. 'Stop Start' cars automatically switch off whenever you stop – even at traffic lights, where electricity from the battery kicks in as soon as you put your foot on the accelerator. Clearly, the fuel savings for this technology will be far greater for urban drivers or anyone who spends a lot of time in traffic jams, but these cars are still not as good as hybrids.

Hydrogen Futures

You may have heard that hydrogen is the fuel of the future. It certainly looks that way with cars. And hydrogen-powered cars won't just be switching from one fuel to another – they'll be saying goodbye to the internal combustion engine too. Instead of burning hydrogen gas it'll be used in fuel cells, which are similar to batteries. The only emission from your exhaust pipe will be water, so like electric vehicles they'll be particularly welcomed in cities and towns.

The tricky bit is how the hydrogen is produced. It isn't sourced in the same way as oil, coal or gas, but needs to be extracted from water and fossil fuels. Whatever the process, energy is needed to produce the hydrogen. The upside is that any sort of energy can be used, including renewable energy.

If you were to take a full tank of petrol and make hydrogen for a fuel cell, you'd be able to drive further on the same amount of fuel, therefore producing less emissions, including CO_2, for each mile travelled. Clearly, if the hydrogen is made using renewable energy such as wind or solar power, the benefits would be greater, although it's important to remember that renewable power is not without its drawbacks (page 22).

It's actually quite difficult to quantify the benefits of switching to hydrogen fuel cells, because it depends not only on how the hydrogen is produced, but also on what you're comparing it with. It won't come out as well against the cleanest petrol product as it will against a really dirty fuel that's been transported thousands of miles across the world. The great thing is that using hydrogen will give us a realistic alternative to oil.

We may also see new countries becoming key players in the energy stakes. Huge hydrogen farms could conceivably be set up in the dust bowl of Africa, using solar power; many of the poorest countries are not short of sunshine.

Five years ago car manufacturers were wondering if they could make fuel cell cars that work as well as normal cars. Now they've cracked that problem, they're working on making them durable, reliable and cost-competitive. But it's still likely to be at least ten years before we see thousands, perhaps even millions, of hydrogen cars on the road.

Biofuels

There's a real buzz in the air about biofuels. Made from crops or other plant matter, they sound like the answer to all our prayers for a replacement to fossil fuels. But before we get too excited, I have to sound a note of caution: the environmental impacts of a massive switch to biofuels could be absolutely horrendous, even in relation to climate change.

There are three main types of biofuel:

1. **Bioethanol**, an alcohol, made through fermentation of starchy crops such as wheat, sugar cane and potatoes. Essentially a petrol replacement.

CAUTION!
Car manufacturers advise that you should only buy biofuels from suppliers who meet EN590 standards. These don't apply to vegetable oil bought from supermarkets, which may damage your engine.

2. **Biodiesel**, which is made from oily crops such as rapeseed, soya or palm oil.
3. **Biomethane**, which I've mentioned above, is a gas produced by rotting materials.

Bioethanol and biodiesel

Although the pros and cons of bioethanol and biodiesel are not identical, they are similar. I'm concerned that they're being touted as a green alternative to fossil fuels, with both investors and governments over-promoting their use. So what are the issues:

CHIP FAT FUEL
Waste chip fat from fish 'n' chip shops all over the country is being used as car fuel. It needs minimal processing to make it into biodiesel, and exhaust emissions are similar to ordinary diesel fuel, but if it's used without processing the emissions are really filthy. It's also worth noting that any guarantee on your car will be invalidated if you use more than 5 per cent alternative fuel. Otherwise, I'd say this is a good use of a waste material.

- **Land space**
  Apparently, to grow enough fuel to power all the transport in the UK, we'd need to plant every single inch of the country with crops. And on a global scale we'd need five to six times more land than we already use for growing food.

- **Food crops**
  Replacing food crops with fuel crops on a large scale would inevitably lead to food shortages, even if this isn't yet a problem. Even where surplus crops grown in the UK are used, we should consider whether this could be forcing countries overseas to grow more crops and clear land to do so.

? DID YOU KNOW? ?

If all the corn grown in America was used for biofuels it would supply fuel for less than 4 per cent of the cars and trucks on American roads.

- **Rainforest destruction**

  I've already covered the devastating impacts of the palm oil industry (page 49) on the rainforests of the Far East. A doubling in demand for this destructive crop, to be made into fuel, would make a bad situation considerably worse – huge new plantations from cleared rainforests would be inevitable.

- **Intensive agriculture**

  Crops grown for biofuels will need to be cheap for them to work economically. This means they're likely to be grown on a huge scale, without great consideration for their environmental impact. Another issue is that the rise in demand for crops for fuel will inevitably lead to a rise in the use of GM crops (page 42).

- **Energy balance**

  Indirectly, over half of all the energy used in agriculture is for fertiliser production. Yet more energy is required to transport crops to centralised plants to be processed, and more again to take the fuel to where it's being used. Variations in all these factors can make the difference between biofuels reducing overall greenhouse gas emissions and actually adding to them.

- **Cost**

  The Government is subsidising biofuels on a per litre basis. But the discounted price will still work out more expensive because currently a car will go only two-thirds of the distance on bioethanol as it would on ordinary petrol.

Supporters of ethanol claim that it will save 60–65 per cent of greenhouse gases compared to conventional petrol, taking into account crop growing, transport and manufacture. They also say that we currently export 3.5 million tonnes of wheat from the UK each year – enough to run 5 per cent of the country's petrol from ethanol. The wheat is apparently low grade, not suitable for food, and grown on land that has been taken out of food production. Whatever the rights or wrongs, biofuels are going to be an integral part of our fuel mix. The

? DID YOU KNOW? ?

From crops grown on one hectare of land you can run a car three to four times further on biomethane than you can on biodiesel or bioethanol.

Government has ruled that by 2008 all petrol and diesel should contain 5 per cent of plant-derived fuels. Most people won't notice any difference because there'll be no need to adapt our cars or make any changes to the way we drive, but when this happens, we as consumers must ensure we're getting a biofuel mix that helps the planet rather than destroys it. We need to demand that:

- no palm oil or soya should be imported for biofuels
- all crops used in biofuels in the UK should be home-grown
- farmers growing crops for biofuels should abide by strict environmental standards
- biofuels should be processed in small, local plants to minimise transport impacts
- producers provide certified information on the greenhouse gas savings of their fuel.

Waste-powered Cars

The brilliant thing about using biomethane as a fuel is that the process of extracting energy from it actually reduces its potency as a greenhouse gas. What's more, once the gas has been siphoned off, the remaining composted material retains its nutrients and makes an excellent fertiliser. This saves yet more energy. Another plus point is that biomethane stacks up well in terms of clean emissions. Apparently, it produces substantially less CO_2 and other emissions, including particulates, than any other fuel.

With all these positives, you'd imagine the world would be simply humming with waste-powered cars. Actually there are very few. In the UK there's only one company working on developing this technology for cars (Organic Power Ltd – see box), and a few others focusing on farm-scale exploitation of biomethane.

ORGANIC POWER

Organic Power is a small company, but it may be able to contribute to a big reduction in greenhouse gas. The company has developed a process for using organic waste to produce methane as a clean energy source for fuel. Chris Maltin, the eco-entrepreneur behind the company, says the potential is huge. He's hoping to make this more available in the UK, although to date he's been focusing his attention overseas.

www.organic-power.co.uk

In Sweden they've taken things a lot further. In the west of the country the city of Göteborg has created a booming market for biomethane, developing the infrastructure to support biomethane cars, buses, waste trucks and even a train.

Realistically, biomethane is not going to replace petrol and diesel on a huge scale. Vehicles would need to be adapted and a whole new infrastructure of biomethane pumps set up. But it does have enormous potential as a staple fuel for public transport systems, car fleets, farm vehicles, and indeed all public service vehicles. Like decentralised energy, biomethane offers lots of small-scale solutions, which compounded could make a big difference. Support it if you can.

CAR TECHNOLOGIES AND FUELS

Biomethane
My Rating 9
Pros: an alternative to fossil fuel; can be sourced from waste; actually reduces greenhouse gas impact of methane; clean emissions compared to other fuels; good fuel efficiency; better performance than liquid fuels with a higher octane rating; quieter.
Cons: infrastructure for biomethane is non-existent; requires cars to be converted; lack of Government support.

Electric car
My Rating 6–8 (depending on electricity source)
Pros: no tailpipe emissions; reduced overall emissions; quiet vehicles.
Cons: electricity generation impacts; limited range; needs recharging.

Hydrogen fuel cell
My Rating 6–8 (6 if hydrogen is made from fossil fuels; 8 if made from renewable energy)
Pros: clean emissions – only water from exhaust; more efficient technology than internal combustion engine; alternative to fossil fuels; hydrogen is an effective way of storing surplus energy; hydrogen can be made from renewable energy; significant support from car manufacturers and investment community.
Cons: widespread introduction of fuel cell technology is at least ten years away; hydrogen still needs to be made using energy; most hydrogen will be made using fossil fuels; requires change in transport infrastructure.

Compressed natural gas (CNG)
My Rating 5
Pros: cleaner emissions than either diesel or petrol; good fuel efficiency; natural gas reserves will outlast oil and petrol.

Cons: cars need to be made to run on CNG fuel; not yet widely available in the UK; more expensive; problems associated with fossil fuels.

Hybrid car
My Rating 5
Pros: maximises efficiency of traditional fuels; demonstrates the popularity of fuel-efficient technologies.
Cons: more expensive; still uses fossil fuels; other technologies will achieve same fuel-efficiency improvements.

Liquefied petroleum gas (LPG)
My Rating 4
Pros: generally cleaner emissions than either diesel or petrol.
Cons: cars need converting to take LPG; not widely available; problems associated with fossil fuels.

Bioethanol
My Rating 4
Pros: alternative to fossil fuels; can use surplus wheat crop in the UK.
Cons: takes land out of food production; less fuel efficient than petrol and diesel; promotes intensive agriculture; greenhouse gas benefits variable and not certain.

'Stop Start' cars
My Rating 4
Pros: doesn't waste fuel when car is stationary; improved fuel efficiency.
Cons: not as efficient as hybrids; savings chiefly relate to urban driving conditions.

Biodiesel
My Rating 3
Pros: an alternative to fossil fuels.
Cons: takes land out of food production; less fuel efficient than petrol and diesel; promotes intensive agriculture; greenhouse gas benefits variable and not certain; the use of palm oil and soya for biodiesel could result in massive destruction of the rainforests and other precious habitats.

Diesel engine car
My Rating 3
Pros: widely available; more fuel efficient; less greenhouse gases than petrol cars.

Cons: more sooty emissions than other cars; no legal obligation for particulate traps; much higher nitrogen oxide emissions; problems associated with a fossil fuel.

Petrol engine car
My Rating 2
Pros: widely available; catalytic converters clean up emissions; fewer particulates than diesel; better in urban areas.
Cons: polluting emissions; fewer mpg than diesel; more greenhouse gases; problems associated with a fossil fuel.

IN THE AIR

We Love to Fly

Thank heavens not everyone in the world flies
as much as the Americans – it would mean
about 100 times more planes in the sky.
Yet although Europeans fly half as much as
the average American, we still fly ten times
more than people living in Asia, including
the Japanese.

From an environmental perspective, the really
horrendous thing is that there's no stopping the
growth in flights: we're building more and more
airports and runways, the cost of flying is
getting cheaper all the time, and more countries
are becoming wealthy enough to join the great
flying bonanza. Meanwhile the airline industry is
being given huge subsidies to keep going;
they're even exempt from most international
treaties on climate change, which require every
other industry to make dramatic cuts.

From this we might assume that the
environmental impacts of flying are not

significant. Actually, as you will almost
certainly be aware, it's quite the reverse: the
impact of air travel is huge. So let's look at
what's going on in our skies.

Climate Change Impacts

Have you ever stared into a blue sky
criss-crossed with white plumes? Or watched
these contrails (that's what they're called)
disperse into wispy cirrus clouds? Perhaps
you've wondered where in the world people
are heading in the air-conditioned cabins
high overhead.

Actually, where the planes are flying to is not
as important as what happens to the contrails
and clouds they leave behind. Sadly, it's been
discovered that these greatly exacerbate the
climate change impacts of aircraft emissions.
It's rather complicated, and scientists are not
yet in agreement as to exactly how much
damage they're causing, but it's estimated

DID YOU KNOW?

Aviation generates nearly as much CO₂ per year as all the human activities in the whole of Africa.

that if you include aircraft plumes, as well as CO_2 and other pollutants from air travel, they're responsible for between 4 and 9 per cent of the climate change impacts of human activity. And the growth in greenhouse gas emissions from flying around the planet has more than doubled since 1990.

What can be done?
• Techno fix
Given that technology has made such strides in the last 50 years, I was surprised to discover that today's passenger aircraft are no more fuel efficient than they were half a century ago. Although there have been efficiency improvements to jet engines, if you compare a typical aircraft of the 1950s with those flying today they'll be travelling about the same distance on the same amount of fuel.

Over the next few decades there are likely to be some efficiency improvements, but these will apparently be pretty insignificant. So it's unlikely we'll be able to find a quick technical fix to the climate change impacts of air travel.

• Clipping wings
This means the only option is to reduce the amount of flying across the globe. More specifically, we can reduce the growth of air travel, which is predicted to be responsible

for a whopping 40 per cent of human climate change impacts by 2050. If you're planning a family trip to Mauritius or Marrakesh, the cost of travel is likely to be a deciding factor. You're not alone – most of us are tempted by the lure of cheap flights, which means that air fares need to be higher if we're going to reduce air travel. This might make sense, but it's not easy putting it into practice.

Travellers don't like paying more or feeling unable to afford to fly, and airlines hate the idea of having their wings clipped. Governments aren't very keen either, because they're fairly sure that taking measures to raise airfares won't win votes – although a recent poll showed they may be wrong about this.

• Taxing times
Airlines have been getting away with a pretty good deal in relation to fuel costs – and in making commitments to reduce their climate change impacts. You'll be aware that the Government receives a big slice of revenue from motoring in the form of fuel tax and VAT on top of that; by contrast, aircraft fuel is four times cheaper than car fuel because it is entirely free of tax. Frankly, this is ridiculous.

The tax we do pay in the form of Air Passenger Duty is tiny compared to the benefits airlines get from fuel tax and VAT exemption. And it's predicted that even a tax on aircraft equivalent to one-fifth of what motorists pay would have the effect of reducing CO_2 from air travel by only 10 per cent.

My view is that the Government should be bold and tax fuel equally for cars and planes. This would apparently increase fares by roughly one-third, and it's estimated that it would reduce the number of people travelling to and from the UK from half a billion to a more moderate 315 million. It would also eliminate the need for new airports and runways, as well as a general expansion of aircraft facilities.

The airline industry will continue to wriggle. They'd prefer an emissions trading scheme, which would allow them to buy their CO_2 quota from other industries that find it easier to cut pollution. Presumably they favour this idea because it wouldn't be as effective at reducing air traffic. In which case it's unlikely to be as good for cutting emissions, either.

Is Air Fair?

Whichever way you look at the figures, air travel, compared to any other form of transport, is by far the biggest climate change menace. It's simply not fair for fares to go on getting cheaper and for airlines to go on being let off the hook in terms of making reductions in emissions.

The following interesting facts about air travel may help you decide where you stand:

- One return flight to Australia from the UK is equivalent to the climate change impacts of heating, cooking and lighting an average house for nearly three years.
- Mile for mile, short-haul flights create more emissions because of the extra fuel needed for take-off and landing.
- On average, for every minute that an air passenger is airborne they're responsible for the emissions of enough CO_2 to fill 167 party balloons.
- Britain emits more CO_2 from aircraft than any other country in the world apart from the US.
- An area the size of Ireland would need to be planted every year to offset the world's aircraft emissions.

- On average, people with second homes take a return flight six times a year.

If all this bothers you, clearly the best option is to stop flying. However, I suspect there aren't many of us prepared to take that plunge.

So why not ...?
- see if you can reduce the number of flights you take
- try holidaying in the UK
- take a train ride across Europe instead
- set up tele-conferencing facilities for work so you don't need to travel
- forget second homes and timeshares
- pay to carbon offset the CO_2 impacts of your travel
- oppose airport expansions and new runways
- support the introduction of fuel tax and VAT for airlines.

TRANSPORT WEBLINKS

Airport Watch
Opposes the expansion of aviation and airports likely to damage the human or natural environment.

www.airportwatch.org.uk

Alliance Against Urban 4x4s
Campaigns against gas-guzzling 4x4s, particularly in urban areas.

www.stopurban4x4s.org.uk

Association for Commuter Transport
Supports organisations wanting to reduce the number of cars on-site by the introduction of a Travel Plan.

www.act-uk.com

Aviation Environment Federation
Campaigns on the environmental impacts of aviation.

www.aef.org.uk

Brompton Bikes
Quality range of folding bikes sold through dealers.

www.bromptonbicycle.co.uk

Carplus
Provides information on lift sharing and car clubs.

www.carplus.org.uk

Carshare
Provides information on car-sharing schemes all over the country.

www.carshare.com

Cyclists Touring Club (CTC)
Largest cycling membership organisation promoting cycling and campaigning for better cycling conditions.

www.ctc.org.uk

Energy Saving Trust
Gives advice on energy saving for cars, fuel and transport.

www.est.org.uk

Energy Saving World
Sells folding electric bikes.

www.energysavingworld.co.uk

Environmental Transport Association (ETA)
Alternative to the AA or RAC in offering
breakdown service and support for motorists
and cyclists. Also campaigns for a sustainable
transport system.   www.eta.co.uk

Freewheelers
Free service linking drivers and passengers
in order to share the cost of travel and reduce
car usage.   www.freewheelers.co.uk

Friends of the Earth (FoE)   www.foe.co.uk

Green Car Guide
Provides information on the most
eco-friendly cars.   www.green-car-guide.com

HACAN
Campaigns on behalf of those who suffer
from living near aircraft flight paths.   www.hacan.org.uk

Lifecycle
Helps people take up cycling and offers
cycle training.   www.lifecycleuk.org.uk

Liftshare
The most established car-share organisation
in the UK, aiming to encourage and enable
more efficient travel. √   www.liftshare.org

Low Carbon Vehicle Partnership
Promotes low-carbon transport solutions.   www.lowcvp.org.uk

Oil Care
Provides information on your nearest waste
oil recycling facilities.   www.oilbankline.org.uk

Organic Power Ltd
Developed methane-powered cars.   www.organic-power.co.uk

Powabyke
Sells electric bikes.   www.powabyke.com

School-run.org
Online facility to help parents find others to share the school run, including by bike and on foot.

www.school-run.org

Scoot Electric
Sells electric scooters with ranges of between 16 and 25 miles and fuel cost equivalent to 1,000 mpg.

www.scootelectric.co.uk

ShareAcar.com
Car-sharing network for the UK.

www.shareacar.com

Streetcar
Pay-as-you-go car club currently operating in and around London, but expanding to other areas.

www.streetcar.co.uk

Sustrans
Encourages people to walk, cycle and use public transport through practical initiatives such as developing a network of cycle lanes.

www.sustrans.org.uk

Transport 2000
Campaigns to reduce the environmental and social impact of transport by encouraging less car travel and more use of public transport, walking and cycling.

www.transport2000.org.uk

Vectrix UK
The high-performance electric scooter sold by Vectrix is the first of its kind, has a range of up to 70 miles and a top speed of around 60mph.

www.vectrix.co.uk

Vehicle Certification Agency
Car fuel database providing information on fuel efficiency and tax bands for different cars, funded by the Department of Transport.

www.vcacarfueldata.org.uk

5 Personal Matters

COSMETICS and TOILETRIES

I suspect that most bathrooms in the country have far more bottles, potions and lotions than are needed – mine included. In part this is because most of us buy lots more than we're ever likely to use, but it's also down to the extraordinary array of products that many people consider to be vital: hair sprays, nail extensions, skin fresheners, knee moisturisers, and so on. Perhaps this is because we have been taken in by the glamorous images in glossy magazines and on posters: the stick-thin models, lustrous hair and perfect complexions, seemingly achieved with a little help from the beauty industry, have led us to believe that we too can be transformed from frogs into princesses.

Beauty is big business. But this glitzy world has done very little about its environmental impacts. Some companies have begun to look at reducing packaging, but there's still room for improvement on this front! Aside from chocolates, make-up and perfume, bathroom products are probably the most over-packaged items we buy – hardly surprising, because their visual appeal is a vital part of this image-led business.

It would therefore be pointless to give you a list of mainstream cosmetic brands and recommend one over another. The most important thing you can do as a beauty consumer is not to buy too much, and finish up all those half-empty bottles and pots of creams sitting in your cupboard so you don't need to buy replacements.

Another concern of mine is the move to put 'use by' dates on cosmetics. I've been using the same lipsticks, mascaras and other make-up for years and they never seem to go off. I'm not convinced there are serious health issues involved, but I'm absolutely certain it will encourage people to be even more wasteful.

> **TOP TIPS**
> • Buy what you'll need • Finish the pot or bottle • Buy certified products • Avoid wasteful packaging

Green Beauty

The really confusing thing is that 'green' beauty, which is still very much a niche sector, is not particularly focused on the environment either. The main selling point tends to be that they use 'natural' or 'healthier' ingredients. But as I've already pointed out, the word 'natural' doesn't necessarily mean something is either healthy or green. Actually, it's pretty meaningless – it just sounds good!

Consider, for example, which shampoo you would select: one described as being made with real lime and basil, or one using synthetically produced lime and basil flavours. Most of us would find the first shampoo more appealing and assume its eco-credentials would be better too. But plant-based products could use just as much energy and as many chemicals as synthetic ones, if you take account of what's used to grow and transport them.

So what about the health hazards of cosmetics and toiletries? From preservatives to foaming agents, a whole host of ingredients are raising hackles, and there are some fiercely opposing views on how much of a problem they really are. Some of the mainstream brands have removed ingredients simply because they're controversial.

I have to admit this isn't high on my worry list. But I wondered if I should change my view when I discovered that 60 per cent of what we put on our skin is absorbed into the bloodstream.

Organic Personal Care

You might imagine that 'organic' shampoos or hair care products must meet the same sort of criteria as organic cabbages or cakes. You'd be wrong – it's still possible to label beauty products or textiles as 'organic' without any formal certification.

PALM OIL

Growing palm oil can be extremely destructive to rainforests (page 49). Palm oil is widely used in lipsticks, soaps, skin and hair care products, so this is an issue for the beauty industry too. The Body Shop was one of the first companies to take part in an initiative to source sustainable palm oil. Ask other cosmetics and toiletries manufacturers if they're members too.

HANGING AROUND

From an environmental perspective, perhaps the two most contentious ingredients are phthalates (pronounced 'thalates') and artificial musks. The concern is that they hang around in the environment for a long time and build up in the body tissue of animals, leading to birth defects and fertility problems. Phthalates are commonly used in beauty products such as hair sprays, nail polish, moisturisers and perfumes, whilst artificial musks are found in smelly soaps and scents. Greenpeace is campaigning against these ingredients – you can find out which companies are using them and which have switched to alternatives on its website (see weblinks).

BUY BALMS

Oil-based balms are less wasteful than lotions, which are water-based. There's less packaging needed and less energy used in transport.

Help is at hand. In 2006 the Soil Association certified their first soap, having developed relevant standards. Products can be fully 'organic' if at least 95 per cent of their ingredients are organic, or they can say 'contains organic ingredients' if at least 70 per cent of their ingredients are organic. There are other organic certifiers but none are as rigorous. Clearly the main environmental benefit of using organic ingredients is that it encourages more organic agriculture.

Fair Care

There are also a number of initiatives that encourage fair trade and community support. The beauty industry is ideally placed to participate in schemes of this sort because it usually buys relatively small quantities of any one ingredient and so can cut out the middle-man and work directly with farmers. This means that payments go directly to producers and their communities, perhaps helping locals profit from conserving natural habitats rather than destroying them. For example, the Body Shop buy Brazil nut oil from the Kayapo Indians in the Amazon, which helps them preserve large areas of rainforest.

SMALL COULD BE **BIG**

Did you know that many sun creams and other skin care products contain minuscule particles known as nanomaterials? These tiny particles are silently creeping into our bathroom and household products without our prior knowledge or consent.

To date, there are no laws governing the use of nanomaterials, and no independent safety tests have been carried out. Like GM technology, this could be another case of using people as guinea pigs – the health and environmental impacts are difficult to predict.

Technically, some nanomaterials can be very useful. They're excellent at blocking out sunlight, hence the widespread use in sun cream; they're also used in medical bandages to keep wounds sterile, and even in plastic storage containers to keep food fresh. It's a whole new world most of us are unaware of.

But worryingly, it's not known how long the nanomaterials will go on working. What might happen in a sewage works with nanoparticles attacking the bacteria that break down our waste? And what about sun lotions washed off into the sea – will they start 'protecting' crabs and cuttlefish from sunburn?

At the moment we don't know. Some campaigning organisations say we should slow down the introduction of this technology until we know a whole lot more about it. UK groups are aware of the issue but have not yet launched any consumer campaigns. However, I believe that the technology of making things very small could become very big.

Animal Testing

In 2009 there will be an EU-wide ban on animal testing of cosmetics but there won't be a complete sales ban until 2013. The Humane Cosmetics Standards is the only internationally recognised scheme that verifies that no animal testing has taken place: all companies using the logo have to be able to show they haven't tested any products on animals since a particular cut-off date. The British Union Against Vivisection (BUAV) regularly updates its *Little Book of Cruelty-Free*, which lists companies that don't use animal testing.

CHEMIST'S SHOP

Hair Care

You only have to go into a chemist's to see how much people invest in their hair. I do little more than wash mine on a weekly basis and go to the hairdresser no more than three times a year, so it's difficult for me not to see many hair care products as a waste of resources.

But if you're a fan of hair sprays, you'll probably be convinced that aerosol sprays work better than pump-action sprays. Here's the eco-dilemma. On the one hand nearly one-third of an aerosol is taken up with a propellant, which might be considered to be wasteful. On the other-hand the can produces a finer spray so it may actually last longer.

And what about shampoos? Apparently, the more you wash your hair, the greasier it gets and the more it needs washing. Some people have tried not washing their hair at all and found that after a few weeks it feels fine. I'm not recommending that, but it would certainly be an eco-friendly approach.

Then there's the issue of how much shampoo to use. The story may be apocryphal, but shampoo sales were supposed to have soared after a brainwave from a marketing executive who claimed they could double sales of shampoo with one extra word on the pack. The word was: 'repeat'. Thereafter most people lathered their hair with shampoo *twice*; I'm not alone in thinking this is rarely necessary.

Shaving

Electric shaving is less wasteful than wet shaving, with a reusable appliance and no creams. If you do wet shave, use a long-lasting razor and choose shaving cream in tubes rather than aerosols.

Toothpaste

Have you ever wondered which toothpaste packaging has the best eco-credentials? Apparently the plastic ones that stand on their tops are the best, followed by the old-fashioned metal ones that come in a box; worst are the rigid stand-alone tubes because they're the most complex.

Sanitary Protection

Not many women will decide which sanitary protection to go for primarily for eco-reasons.

DID YOU KNOW?

Every year, in Britain alone, we would need to dig a hole 300 feet wide and 300 feet deep to bury used sanitary pads and tampons. 2.5 million tampons, 1.4 million sanitary towels and 700,000 panty liners are flushed down the toilet every day.

But if you do, the first consideration should be the amount of waste produced. Here's an assessment of the main alternatives.

- **Tampons**
  Tampons inserted without an applicator are far less wasteful. If you must have an applicator choose paper or card – and the same with the wrappers. They're not so problematic if you flush them down the loo, although it's better not to.

- **Sanitary pads or towels**
  Thin sanitary pads may be no more wasteful than tampons, but you should use the wrapping for disposal, and never flush them down the loo. You can now get reusable pads made from cotton. The new designs are soft, slim and absorbent and may be less wasteful than disposables, assuming you don't put them in a separate load in your washing machine or increase the wash temperature.

- **Mooncup**
  Most people I've talked to about Mooncup look faintly horrified at the thought of it. This is a funnel-shaped silicone device that you insert in your vagina to catch menstrual fluids. It can be reused regularly for several years, but costs no more than you'd pay in six months for other sanitary protection

products. It's extremely eco-friendly because there's no waste. I wish I'd had one when I was backpacking in South America, where a box of tampons cost as much as a night in a hostel.

What are they made of?
Most tampons and sanitary towels are made of rayon, cotton, or a mixture of both. Rayon comes from wood pulp. There aren't yet any sanitary protection products that have been FSC-certified (page 50) to guarantee that they've come from sustainable, managed forests. This is something to look for in the future and to ask manufacturers and retailers about.

A key issue with cotton is the amount of pesticides used on the crop. There's also the fact that cotton from GM plants is mixed with the non-GM stuff. This doesn't make any difference to the material itself, but it does mean you don't have a choice about whether you want to support the technology or not. Organic cotton tampons are available (made by Natracare) – the cotton will be non-GM and will have been grown with fewer pesticides than ordinary cotton.

BIN IT

Put a bin by your loo so that all tampons, applicators, wrappings and pads have somewhere to go. They can block the sewerage system and make it overflow. But try not to create too much extra waste by using new disposable bags or reams of loo paper to put them in! Cotton buds and condoms can also block the system – bin them too.

Bleaching

Whether rayon or cotton, the fibres need bleaching to remove the impurities, increase absorbency, whiten them and make them fit for use. In the past, many companies used a chlorine bleaching process, which apparently released dangerous dioxins into the environment. This has now been banned. There's little difference between the two bleaching technologies that are now used – neither is a significant environmental hazard. Despite this, some companies are still claiming credit for the bleaching technology they use – I think this is misleading. The issue is the same for bleaching nappies.

Nappies

If you want to use fewer nappies you'd be better off having a girl. By the age of two-and-a-half 90 per cent of girls but only 75 per cent of boys are out of nappies. Clearly this is not something that we can choose, but we do have a choice as to what sort of nappy to buy.

The main choice in nappies is between disposables, which are the most popular, and reusables, which are generally assumed to be the eco-friendly option. But this eco-choice is not as clear as it appears.

Certainly, reusable nappies mean that much less waste is sent to landfill – around 2.5 billion nappies are thrown away in the UK each year (about 7 million a day). This accounts for 2.4 per cent of all household waste. On the other hand, reusable nappies use far more energy in washing and drying and are therefore worse for climate change.

Also, disposable nappies are less bulky than they were: there has been a 40 per cent reduction in the volume of material used in the last 15 years. In part this has been achieved by using an extremely absorbent gel which

soaks up the liquid and keeps the baby dry. However, this gel is made of a plastic material, which doesn't rot and so adds to the debate about nappy biodegradability.

Another issue to consider is that the pulp used in nappies comes from forests. Nappy manufacturers should be making sure all the pulp is FSC-certified, guaranteeing it comes from sustainable sources.

To rot or not to rot

Most people think it would be a good thing for nappies to biodegrade in landfill sites. Disposable nappies are certainly more biodegradable than they were: an unused nappy is around 50 per cent biodegradable, whereas a used one is on average 80 per cent biodegradable. But as discussed earlier, laws covering landfill sites are aimed at reducing the amount of biodegradable waste put into them. The greenhouse gases released from the rotting waste are difficult to capture from this source.

The good news is that nappies can be composted in industrial systems that collect the methane released, which can then be used for fuel (page 186).This approach is being developed in the Netherlands, and there's no reason why it couldn't also work in the UK. Currently, 90 per cent of our disposable nappies end up in landfill sites. I think manufacturers – and local government – should be doing a lot more to change this by helping to set up composting systems for bio-waste, including nappies.

It's in the wash

Whilst the eco-credentials of disposables come down to the design of the product, for reusables it's largely down to the user.

Unfortunately, nappies are a bit of an exception in that they need to be washed at 60°C to get rid of the nasty bacteria. But if you use a disposable liner in a reusable nappy, or put the nappy in bleach before washing, you can put them in a 40°C, or even a 30°C wash like the rest of your clothes. Most of all, avoid using tumble dryers because they'll eliminate any eco-benefit you may have accumulated.

REUSABLE NAPPY TYPES

All-in-ones: shaped, fitted nappies with in-built waterproof cover.

Shaped nappies: similar to all-in-ones but with separate waterproof cover.

Flat nappies or pre-fold: old-fashioned nappies that require folding and separate waterproof pants.

No bags

As we all know, nappies can be very smelly, and a lot of people are meticulous about wrapping them up in plastic bags, sometimes in multiple layers. If you're out and about this may make sense. But at home I think putting them directly into a bucket with a lid, and emptying it regularly, should be enough. And there's absolutely no point in buying degradable bags for your partially biodegradable nappy that's on its way to landfill.

My advice

I'm afraid the choice between disposable and reusable nappies is not clear-cut. You have to decide whether you're more concerned about waste, in which case you'd choose reusables, or climate change, in which case you'd go for disposables.

If you go for disposables, it's worth asking the manufacturer about their policy on sustainable forestry and promoting composting systems. If systems were in place to collect biogas (page 186) from disposable nappies, I think they'd be a clear winner over reusables in terms of their eco-impacts.

NAPPY CHANGE

Although reusable nappies are absorbent, they don't protect the baby's bottom from contact with pee. This means they have to be changed more regularly than disposables to prevent nappy rash.

COSMETICS and TOILETRIES WEBLINKS

Being Organic
Sells Soil Association-certified organic health
and beauty products.   www.beingorganic.com

Body Shop
Cosmetics and toiletries retailer committed
to environmental and ethical principles.   www.thebodyshopinternational.com

**British Union for the Abolition of
Vivisection (BUAV)**
Campaigns against animal testing.   www.buav.org

Forest Stewardship Council (FSC)
Forestry certification scheme used for paper
and wood products.   www.fsc-uk.org

Greenpeace
Campaigns for safer alternatives to some
household chemicals.   www.greenpeace.org.uk

Mooncup
A reusable alternative to tampons.   www.mooncup.co.uk

Natracare
Produces organic cotton tampons.   www.natracare.com

Phyto Trade
Promotes sustainable cosmetic ingredients
from Africa.   www.phytotradeafrica.com

Real Nappy Campaign
Promotes reusable nappies.   www.realnappycampaign.com

Women's Environmental Network
Campaigns on disposable nappies, Sanpro
products, cosmetics, toiletries and other
women's issues.   www.wen.org.uk

FASHION and JEWELLERY

Fashionable Business
Too many clothes

I hate to be a killjoy, but the very idea of fashion is distinctly un-green, as it leads us to dispose of things that are in perfectly good condition simply because they're no longer 'in fashion'. It's wasteful.

Do you buy clothes you hardly ever wear? Apparently, the number of clothing items bought in the UK has increased by at least a third since 2001. In weight, we buy about 2 million tonnes of clothing a year, which including other textiles amounts to 55kg per person. There must be a lot of overloaded wardrobes.

One of the main reasons for this massive increase in clothes buying is that costs have plummeted. Nowadays, if you want to buy a T-shirt for £1 you don't have to go to a second-hand shop – you can buy it new. Cheap imports from the Far East have turned our fashion industry upside down and are partially responsible for a complete collapse in textile recycling in the UK. To get any value from waste clothes they have to be shipped abroad.

The Salvation Army is the biggest collector of old clothes in the country. They say that only 1–2 per cent of what they get is sold through

DID YOU KNOW?

In the UK we buy an average of eight T-shirts per person per year.

CLOTHING TIPS

- Buy only what you need
- Buy second-hand or recycled clothes
- Pass clothes on to friends and relatives
- Buy and sell clothes on Ebay
- Hire or lease clothes where possible
- Buy good-quality clothes
- Try hemp and organic materials
- Avoid clothes that need dry-cleaning
- Choose easy-care clothes
- Only put clothes in the wash when they're dirty
- Wash clothes at low temperatures
- Do away with ironing
- Avoid tumble dryers like the plague!

their shops. Even if you take your clothes direct to a charity shop, only about 15 per cent will be sold on through the store; if they're sorted in the Ukraine more than 80 per cent will be given another life.

Only a quarter of our discarded clothing is collected for any sort of recycling; much of the rest ends up in landfill sites. Basically there's a huge amount of clothing that we don't know what to do with. The big challenge for the fashion industry is to find a solution that saves energy and resources but doesn't cost too much.

More Washing

You might imagine that the biggest environmental impact of the fashion industry is its global nature. Actually, that's not the case. The most significant carbon emissions in the life of a cotton T-shirt or a pair of jeans will be in your home: washing, drying and ironing. In fact if you reduce the wash temperature from 60°C to 40°C, avoid tumble drying and do without ironing, you'll reduce the overall global impact of a cotton T-shirt by half.

So if you're choosing clothes, it's important to consider their cleaning and care requirements. Personally, I think that people do far too much ironing – most clothes can be shaken, hung up to dry and still look very presentable. But then I rather like the current fashion in crinkly shirts that you can dry scrunched up in a bag!

? DID YOU KNOW? ?

It takes ten times more energy to make a tonne of textiles than a tonne of glass.

Dry Cleaning

Dry cleaning is even worse than home laundry. Apart from the energy impacts of taking your clothes to the dry cleaners, you should consider the chemicals used in the process. Perchloroethylene (perc) is the most common dry-cleaning fluid, but there's some concern over its impact on the health of people who work with it. In addition to that – and the really horrid smell – it has long-term pollution impacts if it's accidentally released into waterways.

Now there's an alternative to 'perc' called Green Earth dry cleaning. The fluid is made from a type of silicon, which has also been used in products like shampoos, conditioners, lipsticks and moisturisers for years. It's not

thought to be harmful to human health, is not polluting and has no smell, so dry cleaning workers much prefer it.

Johnson's Cleaners are the biggest dry cleaning company in the UK, with nearly 600 outlets, including Sketchleys and Jeeves of Belgravia. They have converted about half their stores to use the Green Earth product and the others will follow within a couple of years. But very few independent stores have made the switch, and neither have Morrisons, who have dry cleaning facilities in about 100 stores.

If you have to dry clean your clothes, make sure you ask for Green Earth cleaners.

Fair fashion

If you look at the world of 'green' fashion, the key issue for most companies is ethical trade or fair trade. This means they're looking at the impacts on people throughout the supply chain. At one level this means making sure working conditions are safe and healthy: for example, people working in cotton fields or dye houses can be poisoned by the chemicals used. On another level, fair trade helps alleviate poverty by supporting community initiatives, guaranteeing fair prices for goods and helping create livelihoods.

Often a fair trade approach will go hand in hand with a reduced environmental impact. But there's a lot more to be done in cleaning up the world of fashion and textiles – much of which will have little direct relevance to people and poverty.

MORE ORGANIC

Less than 1 per cent of cotton grown is organic, but you can now find it on the high street.

- Levi Strauss has introduced jeans made from organic cotton – Levi Eco.
- Marks & Spencer's range of fair trade organic babywear has been very popular. And 5 per cent of its cotton range will be organic by 2010.
- Tesco has launched a range of organic cotton clothing designed by Katherine Hamnett.

WE NEED MORE HEMP!

Whenever I hear about the virtues of hemp, I wonder why we don't grow more of it. This isn't because I'm a marijuana smoker – it has green appeal. And just to address the drugs issue, you'd have to smoke a roomful of this sort of hemp to get any kind of high.

Hemp is one of the most robust crops grown anywhere. It doesn't mind whether it's hot or cold, is not plagued by insects, and grows faster than surrounding weeds, so doesn't need large volumes of chemicals. What's more, you can get three times more hemp fibre from an acre of land than you can cotton. With lower impacts than any other fibre in terms of energy and water, its eco-credentials are excellent.

It doesn't do badly from a technical point of view, either. New techniques have been found to soften the coarse fibres, and it's apparently four times stronger than cotton, twice as resistant to abrasion, less prone to shrinking and will fade less in the sun.

You might therefore assume that it's hugely expensive. Actually it's 30 per cent cheaper than ordinary cotton and 70 per cent cheaper than organic cotton.

The main reason I've found for the use of hemp not being more widespread is that 'technically the systems are not in place'. I have to ask 'Why on earth not?' I hope that the orange hemp sneakers and skirt I bought recently from Natural Collection will be joined in the future by other hemp additions to my wardrobe.

Material Differences
Cottoning on

Nearly half of all textiles are made from cotton, but there are certain problems with its production. One of these is the massive amounts of pesticides used on the crop – some cotton fields in China, which is the world's biggest cotton producer, are sprayed an average of 20 times a year. And in America, cotton crops take up 4 per cent of agricultural land but use a quarter of the country's insecticides.

Another problem is water. It takes an average of 10,000 litres to produce one kilogram of cotton. In some areas the vast amount of water used has had disastrous consequences: the Aral Sea in Russia has shrunk to a quarter of its original size, in large part due to cotton cultivation.

The widespread use of GM in cotton production is also a contentious issue – it's now used on about 20 per cent of cotton crops and about 80 per cent of what's grown in the US. The aim of its introduction was to reduce the amount of chemicals used, but there are doubts over whether this has actually been achieved. In fact it's feared that GM cotton crops may have led to the growth of herbicide-resistant super-weeds.

Organic cotton uses fewer pesticides and is GM-free; farmers fertilise with manure and use natural pest deterrents. One problem they haven't managed to address, however, is the large quantities of water needed. But most organic cotton is produced in areas where irrigation is not needed. Growing organic cotton also takes up more land because of lower yields.

Organic standards for cotton include restrictions on chemicals used in processing, reductions in energy and waste, labelling specifications, and even requirements relating to materials used for accessories, such as buttons, buckles and zips.

Polyester

Nearly a third of all textiles are made from polyester, which is produced from oil. Making it is a pretty energy-intensive business: between 3–5 times more energy is used to produce a tonne of polyester than a tonne of cotton.

But it's not as simple as that because the total energy used in the life of a polyester garment may actually be similar to one made from cotton. Less energy and water are used to dye polyester and to clean it once you get it home. There's also the advantage of not needing land for crops and not using huge quantities of pesticides.

Rayon or viscose

Another popular fibre is rayon, or viscose. It's actually made from wood, so sustainable forest management is an important issue. Rayon production is both energy-intensive and uses lots of toxic chemicals. However, one of the main companies producing this

FLEECES FROM PLASTIC BOTTLES

One of the best uses for waste plastic bottles is to make them into fleece jackets.

Patagonia was the first clothing company to do this, and over 13 years they have used 86 million plastic bottles.

material has come up with a far more eco-friendly alternative: Tencel (which is the brand name for lyocell).

Tencel recycles the chemicals during the manufacturing process so none are wasted, sources wood from sustainably managed forests, and has minimised its impacts throughout production. It's a pity it's more expensive than ordinary rayon because otherwise it would be more widely used – look out for the Tencel label in clothes.

Woolly thinking

Given that 'greens' are often referred to as the 'woolly jumper brigade', you might think the eco-credentials of wool were impeccable. Not so. Almost all the wool used in clothes comes from Merino sheep in Australia, reared specifically for their fleece rather than for their meat. The hotter climate means that Australian sheep have had to adapt by producing finer wool. Wool from British sheep, on the other hand, is coarse and therefore only good for carpets.

The real issue is the amount of energy and water used in washing and treating wool before it's made into a jumper, a suit or a pair of socks. Wool uses far more of these resources than either cotton or polyester.

The greatest benefits of wool come from its quality and, rather surprisingly, its high price. If you're going to invest in a real wool suit, you're not going to throw it away after a couple of outings. A cheap, synthetic alternative is likely to wear out faster, prompting regular replacements and therefore more resources wasted. Equally, there's a benefit on the washing front too – most people don't wash their woolly jumpers nearly as often as they would a cotton sweatshirt.

CHILDREN'S CLOTHING

Comic character motifs and designs on children's clothing are typically made from PVC, phthalates and other unpleasant chemicals. M&S was the first major retailer to remove all these chemicals from children's clothing.

A good tanning

Leather is usually a by-product of the meat industry, but its eco-credentials aren't that great. Transforming hairy animal hides into a soft and flexible material that can be used for shoes, belts, trousers and other clothing is a pretty noxious business.

The tanning industry is made up of thousands of small operators, many of whom have been working leather for decades, some for centuries. Getting them to clean up their processes is a hard task because it inevitably means increasing costs and reducing profits. It's far easier to get bigger operators to make the sort of changes needed to remove the heavy metals and chemical horrors from their waste streams.

True colours

In the Middle Ages, hatters (people who made and dyed hats) often used some pretty nasty substances in their colour-fixing dyes. They didn't wear protective clothing and some of them absorbed so many toxic chemicals and heavy metals that they became deranged. That's where the expression 'mad as a hatter' comes from.

Today, up to 8,000 different chemicals can be used in the production and processing of textiles – for dyeing, treating, printing and finishing. In fact the whole process of making and using dyes is one of the most polluting industries on the planet. A key part of the problem is the amount of dye left in the water after use; an awful lot of it still gets flushed into waterways without being treated.

Apparently, the global textile industry discharges around 40–50,000 tonnes of dye into rivers and streams every year, as well as hundreds of thousands of tonnes of salt, which is also used in the process. And let's not forget the huge quantities of water needed for dyeing clothes – colouring just one T-shirt will use between 16 and 20 litres of water.

You might imagine that there is very little that we, as clothes buyers, can do about this problem. Not so. Marks & Spencer, which sells between 10 and 12 per cent of all the clothes in this country, is leading the way amongst fashion retailers in setting restrictions on chemicals and standards for pollution control for clothes being sold through their stores.

However, it appears to me that there are very few other retailers who care about the pollution caused by the clothes they sell. This is chiefly because it's not something that we as customers can see – most of us are blissfully unaware it's going on. I think we should be asking retailers like Top Shop, Gap, Burtons, Jigsaw, Asda and Tesco what they're doing to clean up their clothes supply chains. Money talks, and green consumers should be looking at not only what they buy with their money, but what they give away, how they manage it, and of course where they invest it.

DID YOU KNOW?

About 40 per cent of fabrics are dyed more than once because the colour isn't quite right first time round.

FILTHY GOLD

I discovered that the process of extracting the gold for my wedding ring will have resulted in 20 tonnes of rocks and debris being discarded. The wastefulness of this process is staggering – it's estimated that ten thousand times more ore is mined than is refined into gold. And gold mining is one of the dirtiest industries around, commonly using cyanide, arsenic and mercury. Apart from the pollution and scarred landscapes, it's also responsible for displacing thousands of people from their homelands and destroying livelihoods.

More than half of all mined gold comes from indigenous people's lands.

Apparently, there's enough gold already mined to last for at least 50 years. So one has to ask why this filthy industry has to go on destroying and plundering the land – 2,500 tonnes are extracted annually, and 80 per cent of this is used for jewellery. Green Karat, an American company, sells only recycled gold. We should be challenging UK jewellers to do the same. They need to clean up their act.

DIRTY DIAMONDS

I'm afraid the diamond industry is no better – it may be even worse. Similarly, the industry produces huge amounts of waste and uses vast quantities of water. In many places the diamond industry has had a serious impact on wildlife as wetland areas have dried up.

About one-fifth of world diamond production comes from alluvial mining, which means digging up riverbed deposits. The diamonds are usually buried deep in the riverbed or high in the banks, so extracting them can be incredibly disruptive. Tonnes of material are removed and river eco-systems are violated.

Despite the environmental impacts of diamonds, world attention has predominantly focused on its human impacts. 'Conflict' or 'blood'diamonds, where the profits are used to fund corrupt governments, rebel military forces or arms,

have been a big issue for the industry, so much so that almost all diamond producers have signed up to a code committing them to responsible sources.

The problem is that there's not yet a system in place to trace diamonds on the market back to where they've been produced, so you can't be sure you're not supporting bad practices. There's also an issue with child labour and horrendous working conditions – the diamond industry still has some way to go on this.

There are alternatives. The first is to avoid buying mined diamonds at all – they're hardly a necessity! Another option is to buy synthetic diamonds – there aren't many people who can distinguish them from the real thing.

FASHION and JEWELLERY WEBLINKS

Beyond Skin
Vegetarian and vegan designer shoes made
in Britain and produced to minimise human and
environmental impacts and ensure animal-welfare
standards

www.beyondskin.co.uk

Clean Slate Clothing
Sells fair trade and organic school uniforms.

www.cleanslateclothing.co.uk

Eco Fashion
Sells eco-fashion.

www.eco-eco.co.uk

Enamore
Makes clothing from natural organic textiles
(including hemp) and recycled materials.

www.enamore.co.uk

Green Earth Cleaning
The most eco-friendly dry-cleaning fluid.
Should be used instead of 'perc'.

www.green-earth.co.uk

Green Fibres
Sells organic clothing and bedding.

www.greenfibres.com

Green Karat
American company that only sells recycled gold.

www.greenkarat.com

Johnson's Cleaners
The UK's largest dry-cleaning chain, in the
process of converting all its outlets to
'Green Earth Cleaning'.

www.johnsoncleaners.co.uk

Junky Styling
Remakes stylish clothes from second-hand.

www.junkystyling.co.uk

Marks & Spencer
Largest fashion retailer in the UK, leading
the way in reducing pollution from dyes
and chemicals.

www.marksandspencer.com

Natural Collection
Direct mail catalogue selling hemp and other
'eco-friendly' clothing.

www.naturalcollection.com

Patagonia
Proactive campaigning company that makes
a wide range of sports clothing, including
some from recycled materials.   www.patagonia.com

People Tree
Fair trade and ecological fashion brand that
is widely sold in the UK, including at Top
Shop in Oxford Street, London.   www.ptree.co.uk

Salvation Army Trading Company
Largest collector of clothes and textiles
for recycling.   www.satradingco.org

Terra Plana
Describes itself as the most innovative
sustainable shoe brand in the world. Uses
recycled materials and chrome-free leather
in many of its products.   www.terra-plana.co.uk

Vote Hemp
An American organisation campaigning for
more industrial hemp.   www.votehemp.com

MONEY and FINANCE

Helping Hands

If you're going to give money to charity, I think you can generally have more of an impact by donating to small grass-roots organisations – less money will be eaten up by administration and overheads.

Another consideration should be to look for projects designed to provide long-term solutions. Rather than just repairing existing damage, it can be far more effective to help local people benefit from conserving what's already there. We can all see that if your livelihood is dependent on the rainforest, you're not going to be chopping it down.

If you do give to charity, make sure they get Gift Aid, which means they can claim tax back on anything you give them. This is extremely simple – you just have to sign a form.

Affinity giving

Another way of giving is through affinity cards – credit cards that give a small proportion of what you spend to a charity. Most of the main environmental organisations will have signed up to one. At the moment the only way of finding out what's available is to check with either the organisation you wish to support or with credit card companies – they have lists on their websites.

But beware: I received a flyer for a Capital One credit card; I could choose between having a picture of a beautiful tiger or a monkey on it, but it didn't come with any affiliation – what a wasted opportunity. Credit cards are generally made from PVC, but the affinity cards for both WWF and Greenpeace are PVC-free. You can support

Greenpeace through the Co-operative Bank and WWF through MBNA.

Banks and Building Societies

The greenest bank in the UK is Triodos, whose principal idea is to invest in sustainable business enterprises. Unfortunately we can't all switch our everyday banking to Triodos because it doesn't offer personal current accounts, but their savings accounts include ISA investments, a Young Saver and a Charity Saver.

The Ecology Building Society is also founded on green principles. Its investments are made in eco-building projects, low-impact lifestyles and energy efficiency. Anyone can take out a savings account, but mortgages are offered only on buildings that fit their eco-criteria.

For current accounts, the Co-operative Bank is most widely recognised for linking its values with its investment and lending criteria. And it has followed this through with a wide range of innovative eco-initiatives, from turning plastic cups into garden furniture, to selling mortgages which include money going to carbon-offset projects (page 19).

Perhaps the most exciting sustainable banking initiatives are coming from HSBC. In 2006 it became the first carbon-neutral bank, which in theory at least means its global operations are not contributing to global warming. It achieved this by making significant energy-efficiency improvements, switching to renewable energy suppliers, and carbon-offsetting.

HSBC has also taken the lead in applying sustainability guidelines to investments and lending relating to forestry, fresh water, energy and chemicals. And another high street bank, Lloyds TSB, insists that companies requesting loans above £50,000 have to go through an environmental check before a loan is agreed. Quite often this will actually mean these companies have to clean up their emissions before being able to borrow money.

The unusual thing about the banking sector is that there's not much they can do to 'green' the products they sell. But it's clear they're beginning to recognise that there's a lot they can do in relation to their operations, and particularly to conditions applied to any investments they make, where they have a huge influence.

At the moment it's not easy for customers to make eco-comparisons between banks and building societies because it's hard to get the

DISCLAIMER!

Isn't it tedious that anyone who makes even the vaguest financial recommendation has to make a lot of noise about how little notice you should take of it? In that spirit I'm telling you that I'm not a professional financial advisor and nor do I wish to be. Whatever I've written is simply my opinion and should be taken as such! Having said that, before you apply your values to investment decisions, it would be wise to sort out the basics of money management. A good place to start is **www.moneylaidbare.info**

relevant information. I predict it will get a lot easier. You should challenge your bank and ask them what they're doing – if you're not satisfied, switch to another institution that's using their power for good.

Insurance

If you're looking for car insurance, try out Co-op's Eco Insurance, launched in 2006. It offers a 10 per cent discount for the most fuel-efficient cars, and will offset 20 per cent of your car's CO_2 emissions by investing in tree-planting and renewable energy schemes, as well as paying repairers more than other insurers if they recycle as much as possible.

For annual travel insurance, household buildings and contents insurance, Naturesave pledges to put 10 per cent of your premium towards environmental projects.

Investment

Buying stocks and shares is very different to buying potatoes and plums. You can't pick them up and look at them, and quite often it's difficult to get any comprehensible information at all. Part of the problem is that the industry is governed by very tight controls about what they should and shouldn't say about products – see my disclaimer.

If you've decided to adopt a greener lifestyle, it makes sense to carry your approach through to your investments. There's lots of choice and, most important, 'green' investment doesn't mean you have to compromise on performance. You can put your values into practice and expect good returns too.

Which type of fund?

If you want to take account of environmental, social or ethical issues, the funds to look for are known as Socially Responsible Investment (SRI) funds.

There are three main types:

- **Ethical**
  These funds are also referred to as screened funds. Negative criteria may include avoiding investments in alcohol, animal testing, arms or gambling, but some have positive criteria too.

- **Best practice**
  The idea of these funds is to select companies that are leading the way in their business sector. Fund managers can then encourage good initiatives and signal their concerns about poor practices.

- **Opportunity**
  Some funds are set up to make the most of opportunities created by environmental problems. So they might invest in companies that have developed pollution control technology, or those that will get a business boost from the impacts of climate change.

In reality, many funds will have elements of all three approaches. As an investor it's really important to decide where you stand before you start – for example, you should recognise that if you're adamant you want to screen out all companies in a certain sector, this will be much more limiting than taking an opportunity-led approach.

Remember that investment is always going to be a blunt instrument in terms of promoting change or even following your principles. This is chiefly because there are very few companies who'll be doing only 'good' things. Far more likely is that companies developing cleaner technologies will also be involved in activities you're not very keen on. For example, Scottish Power is a big investor in wind power, but they also own coal-fired power stations. My view is that you have to be pragmatic and not too restrictive in your selection criteria.

Advice

If you don't have big sums to invest, you should be able to do without a financial advisor. The UK Social Investment Forum (UKSIF) has a website called Investability, which will help you along the way. Another excellent site is run by the Ethical Investors Group and helps you prioritise your concerns and directs you to funds that fit your criteria.

For anyone with larger sums to invest, or if you want to set up an SRI pension policy, I'd recommend getting some advice. Many financial advisors nowadays have some experience of these issues, but if green criteria are a high priority for you, try out one of the specialist SRI advisors (see Money and Finance Weblinks). Even company pension schemes can include SRI criteria – ask yours what they're doing and check out the Fair Pensions website if you want to know more.

TOP GREEN FUNDS

- **Aberdeen Ethical World**
- **Friends Provident Stewardship**
- **Hendersons Global Care Growth**
- **Impax Environmental Markets (IT)**
- **Insight Evergreen**
- **Jupiter Ecology Fund**
- **Jupiter Green (IT)**
- **Merrill Lynch New Energy (IT)**
- **Norwich Union/Morley Sustainable Future Funds**

IT = Investment Trust

Recapturing Childhood

POSITIVE PARENTING IN THE MODERN WORLD

Mildred Masheder

Mildred Masheder provides wise advice on every aspect of childhood.

With many inspiring contributions from parents, who have written to her about their parenting experiences, she invites us to help our children recapture this special time of their lives, which seems to have been lost in recent years.

'Mildred Masheder has long since established herself as a commentator of rare clarity and wisdom on these matters. This new book is a powerful and straightforward challenge to us all to put our intelligence to work for the sake of our children, to recover the space they need and the care they need.'
Dr Rowan Williams, Archbishop of Canterbury

'Mildred Masheder... helps us navigate through the complexities of childhood today to discover practical ways in which we can help children, and by doing so, help everyone.'
Bob Reitemeier, Chief Executive of The Children's Society

'It seems not a week goes by without alarming revelations about the effects of modern lifestyles on children's learning, behaviour and mental health. But perhaps the media's interest in the topic will at last stimulate politicians, parents and society in general to look for ways of ...providing a 'good childhood' for the next generation.

For this they'll need the advice of people who really understand children, Mildred Masheder is such a one.'
Sue Palmer, author of *Toxic Childhood*

'For me, the power of the book is that it is based on current research and includes a broad-range of parent opinion.'
Dr Neil Hawkes, senior education adviser

Cover photo: Children at play in an earlier era (c1980)

GREEN PRINT

ISBN 978-1-85425-095-7

9 781854 250957

Positive Childhood: Educating Young Citizens

A Resource Book for Teachers and Parents of Young Children

Mildred Masheder MA, Ac.Dip.Ed. is a former primary teacher and senior lecturer in child development and multicultural studies at the University of London. She has subsequently held research fellowships exploring peaceful conflict resolution and cooperation with young children. She has organised workshops to international audiences for over 40 years. She is an active member of Human Scale Education, Gandhi Foundation, World Education Fellowship and WCCI.

'A welcome reminder of our responsibilities here, and a stimulus to thought and action' Dr Rowan Williams, Archbishop of Canterbury

'Brilliant! This was my first reaction when I read Mildred Masheder's book' N Hawkes, Senior Education Adviser, Oxfordshire

Published by Green Print an imprint of Merlin Press

In a world that values marketable achievements, the human dimension of child development is apt to be neglected. Mildred Masheder once again addresses the development of values and skills that make life worth living in POSITIVE CHILDHOOD.

This journey is designed to be fun, with active learning and participation. There are many ideas and suggestions in each chapter, and resources, games and activities are also listed in the bibliography.

197x124mm; 160pp, EAN 97818542509410 pbk ISBN: 1 854250949 £9.99

Carrier's Cart to Oxford

Growing up in the 1920s in the Oxfordshire village of Elsfield

140pp ISBN 978 1902279 28 2 40 photographs. With line drawings by Susanna Masheder.
The Wychwood Press, Charlbury.

This is a picture of vibrating village life in the Oxfordshire village of Elsfield, seen through the eyes of a child growing up in the 1920s. It is a realistic account of her family life on the farm and in the village, and of her schooling. It depicts a bygone age when village children roamed freely in the countryside, making the fields, the farm buildings and the road their playground.

'I am delighted to commend Carrier's Cart to Oxford as an absolutely fascinating, absorbing social history of village life in the 1920s. This delightful history may be favourably compared with well-known works such as Lark Risk to Candleford and Cider with Rosie". DR NEIL HAWKES, former Senior Education Adviser for Oxfordshire.

To obtain copies of any of the books, please contact the author: Mildred Masheder,
75 Belsize Lane, London NW3 5AU, Tel. 020 7435 2182
Add £2.00 p&p.Email: sales@positivechildhood.net Web: http://www.positivechildhood.net

---

Mildred Masheder's eagerly awaited new book, **Re-capturing childhood, Positive Parenting**. will be available in 2007.

LET'S PLAY TOGETHER

This is an exciting illustrated collection of over 300 games and sports which put co-operation before competition and make everyone a winner! Each game is coded to indicate at a glance the age groups most likely to enjoy it. People with disabilities can take part too: suitable games are specially marked. You will find traditional party games, circle games, musical, board and guessing games, games for the lively and energetic, for the drama-minded or the artistic, nature games and parachute games. There are also a number of co-operative sports and a selection of games from around the world. Playing Games will never be the same again

Also available in French - Third Edition Price £8.99 pbk ISBN: 1854250132

LET'S CO-OPERATE (VIDEO)

This is a lively and colourful video film illustrating many of the co-operative games in 'Let's Play Together'. It includes popular games such as 'Dragon's Tail', Sharks, and 'Cat and Mouse'. The video is most informative as well as pleasurable to watch and can encourage parents, teachers and club leaders to try out the more adventurous parachute games.

Price £10.00

LET'S CO-OPERATE

This is a book containing many ideas for parents and teachers to experience with their children. There are sections on: A positive self-concept; creativity; communication; co-operation, getting on with others and peaceful conflict resolution. Each heading has its own age with a paragraph or two on the educational approach to the particular theme and the book is lavishly illustrated with photographs and drawings.

Also available in Japanese and French. Price £8.99 1854250906

FREEDOM FROM BULLYING

This is essentially a practical book to help teachers and parents to work with their children to prevent bullying in the school situation, also to deal with it when it occurs. The conclusion is that with everyone co-operating, both in the long and the short term, whilst we cannot completely eradicate bullying from our schools, we can free a great majority of pupils from this scourge which has for so long been the plague of countless generations.

Price £8.99 pbk 1854250922

LET'S ENJOY NATURE

This is a book to help parents and teachers and their children to get in touch with nature and to care for the planet. It contains over 500 ideas for activities and 150 illustrations, including: making things from nature; conducting experiments; growing plants; nature games; seasonal celebrations; exploring the countryside and conservation in the home and the environment. Children from ages 3 to 14 will find plenty of scope for enjoying the natural world and as they grow older will be encouraged to take an active role in helping to protect the planet from the many dangers which threaten it.

Price £8.99 pbk 1854250841

Add £2.00 p&p.Email: sales@positivechildhood.net Web: http://www.positivechildhood.net

INVESTING FOR CLIMATE CHANGE

Perhaps you're wondering what on earth you should do with your money in anticipation of the global impacts of climate change – I certainly am. If there is a cataclysmic collapse of the stock market – and the whole capitalist system – the painful answer is that there's almost nowhere safe to put your money. However, there are some real investment opportunities created by climate change.

The most obvious sector in which to invest is renewable energy – clearly the world will soon be looking for fossil fuel alternatives, such as solar, wind and wave power. And think of water – it's predicted that supplies will drop by a third over the next 20 years whilst demand will go on growing. So water management and waste-water companies will be hot stocks. In fact cleaning up waste of any sort is going to continue to be good business, particularly the recycling side of it.

And don't forget green transport. Already you have to wait several months to buy a hybrid car (page 181). I'd certainly prefer to invest in companies spearheading the development of fuel-efficient transport technologies rather than those selling sports cars to boy racers or 4x4s to city dwellers. The same sort of choices can be made about buildings: would you want to invest in developments that haven't put energy efficiency high on their list of priorities?

If you want to invest in these technologies you should put your money in a fund such as Jupiter Green, Hendersons or Impax.

You can also look out for small companies in these sectors floating on the Alternative Investment Market. But if you're wary of the stock market, or just want to take a different approach, you can invest in Triodos Renewables – your money will finance renewable energy projects that benefit local communities.

PEAK OIL

Turbulent stock markets may be experienced even before the effects of climate change really hit. And the culprit could be what's known as 'peak oil'. Effectively that means when the world wakes up to the fact that we're running out of oil.

The concern is that many of the oil-producing countries are committed to producing far more oil than they actually have in their reserves. And when the stock markets believe this all hell could break loose: oil prices could hit the roof, share prices could plummet, and world

economies could go into a tail spin – a bit like the Wall Street Crash in 1929. We just have to hope that people won't start throwing themselves out of their office windows.

Those people who see this coming predict it will happen very soon – within the next ten years. But even they are not certain how the world will react. The positive thing is that anyone who's invested in companies concerned with climate change is likely to be on a better footing than the rest.

MONEY and FINANCE WEBLINKS

Co-operative Bank
Offers full range of banking services with eco-criteria, including Greenpeace affinity credit card.

www.co-operativebank.co.uk

Eco Insurance
Offers car insurance which supports and promotes eco-motoring.

www.ecoinsurance.co.uk

Ecology Building Society
Offers savings accounts and mortgages that promote green buildings and eco-renovation.

www.ecology.co.uk

EIRIS
Provides information on ethical investment and will give tailored advice to private investors on the ethical make-up of their portfolio.

www.eiris.org

Equator Principles
A banking initiative applying social and environmental criteria to finance.

www.equator-principles.com

Ethical Investment
Association of financial advisors promoting SRI.

www.ethicalinvestment.org.uk

Ethical Investors Group
Independent financial advisors focusing on SRI funds. Lots of information on its website to help you choose the best fund for your values.

www.ethicalinvestors.co.uk

Fair Pensions
Campaigns for responsible investment of pension funds.

www.fairpensions.org.uk

Gaeia Investment
Independent financial advisor specialising in SRI funds. Website provides lots of information to help you choose the right fund for you.

www.gaeia.co.uk

HSBC
Find out more about HSBC's environmental
track record.

www.hsbccommittochange.com

Investability
Helps consumers choose investments that
reflect their values.

www.investability.org

Lloyds TSB

www.lloydstsb.com

MBNA Europe
Offers affinity cards to support WWF and the
National Trust.

www.mbna.com/europe/creditcards

Naturesave
Offers travel, buildings and contents insurance,
with 10 per cent of premiums going to
environmental projects.

www.naturesave.co.uk

Triodos Bank
Green savings bank that also offers share
issues in sustainable or ethical
business enterprises.

www.triodos.co.uk

UK Social Investment Forum (UKSIF)
Promotes socially responsible investment in
the UK.

www.uksif.org

GIFTS AND OCCASIONS

Give Again

My eldest son worries that someone might notice that they're receiving the wrapping paper they used back again. But it's amazing what you can do with some nifty cutting and a bit of extra Sellotape.

When it comes to presents there are lots of recycling opportunities. Apart from reusing old cards and wrapping paper, there's no harm in giving away things you're not going to use, especially if they're going to be better appreciated by the new recipient. It's certainly preferable to letting unwanted gifts lie around for years before eventually chucking them out. If you don't know anyone who'd like what you have, try selling it on Ebay or giving it away through Rag and Bone (see Gifts and Occasions Weblinks).

DID YOU KNOW?

It's estimated that 83 square kilometres of wrapping paper end up in our rubbish bins each year.

Eco-Horrors

Whether you shop through catalogues, high street stores or shopping centres, it's mind-boggling how much rubbish is for sale. Now, I do appreciate that not everyone has the same view of what's useful and worth buying as me, and it's important not to be a killjoy, but I'm sure that most of us could save a lot of money and waste by being more selective about the gifts and gadgets we buy.

Buying from an 'eco-catalogue' certainly helps, but don't imagine that this'll get you off the hook completely. They still sell some pretty wasteful stuff – I'm not convinced that you'll be doing much for the planet by buying a shower timer, even if it's made from recycled materials. And the benefits of replacing your mouse and computer screen with one made out of bamboo are dubious too!

Have a Green Christmas

Apparently each of us (including children) receives an average of 17 Christmas cards per year. That amounts to 150 million items a day, and a total of 20,000 tonnes of extra rubbish taken to landfill sites. Is it really necessary to send a card to friends and neighbours you see all the time? I think we should be far more selective about who to send cards to. And if you really can't kick the habit, why not send them by email instead? That saves resources, waste and fuel for delivery.

Christmas lights are another shocker – particularly the increasing trend for lighting up houses like festive beacons. I have to admit that I've frequently taken my children to see the really over-the-top displays, and we find them quite exciting. But this is a pleasure I would happily forego on eco-grounds. It's a dazzling example of energy wastefulness.

A few lights on your Christmas tree are excusable because they don't use that much electricity. But remember to turn them off when you're not around – you don't need a festive atmosphere when you're asleep. And if you're buying new lights, look out for LED ones because they're widely available, last a long time and are energy-efficient.

MY TOP 10 ECO-GIFTS

My friend Amanda thinks my idea of 'gifts' is completely potty. She's not convinced there are many people who'd be happy getting a battery recharger or an energy-efficient light bulb as a present! You decide. Gifts are listed in alphabetic order rather than by a desirability rating.

Battery rechargers
Make the switch to rechargeable batteries.

Eco-Kettle
An energy-efficient kettle.

Electrisave
Check how much energy you're using with this brilliant monitoring gizmo.

Energy-saving light bulbs
I often take an energy-efficient light bulb as a gift when I go out to supper. You might think I'm weird, but it's been surprisingly effective at getting people started.

Fold-up electric bikes
If you haven't switched from car to bike because you're not keen on pedalling uphill, try an electric bike – with the added benefit of being able to carry it onto trains and buses.

Hemp fashion
Look out for great clothes made from hemp – the greenest textile on the market.

Recycled products
Whether it's clothing, stationery, bags, glasses or flooring made from children's Wellington boots, go for products made from recycled materials.

Solar lights and accessories
You can now get a wide range of products using solar power, from toys and phone chargers to calculators and garden lights.

Water-powered clocks
Look out for water-powered clocks that don't need batteries.

Wind-up gadgets
Another way of avoiding batteries is to go for wind-up radios, torches and toys.

If you buy an artificial tree and use it year after year, it's far greener than buying a real one and discarding it. If you're desperate for the real thing, then see if you can find one with roots and replant it. Failing that, make sure it gets recycled – most councils will chip and compost trees and use them as a mulch or soil improver.

CHRISTMAS CARD RECYCLING

In 2006 the Woodland Trust's Christmas card recycling scheme collected and recycled 82 million cards, which meant 1,630 tonnes of rubbish diverted from landfill.

Retailers taking cards included WH Smith and Tesco.

Don't Say It With Flowers

Many cut flowers sold today have so many chemicals sprayed on them that they might as well be plastic. And their blemish-free appearance and lack of smell mean that sometimes it's hard to tell the difference. I'm not the greatest fan of cut flowers – I'd far rather be given something to eat, something practical, or at the very least something beautiful that lasts more than a few days.

There are several reasons for my aversion to this most popular gift. The first is the massive amounts of pesticides used – about 200kg per hectare of flowers under cultivation. This is more than for any other agricultural crop. Apart from leaving nasty residues on the flowers themselves, chemical sprays have been shown to have horrendous consequences for flower workers – one survey showed that around half of them suffered from pesticide poisoning.

BETTER FLOWER OPTIONS

- Dried flowers
- Silk flowers
- Local, seasonal flowers
- Pick your own
- Beautiful vegetables
- Or maybe no flowers?

Another concern is the air miles they run up. Around 30 million flowers are flown to the UK from Kenya each year, each of them making a journey of 4,000 miles. This alone is responsible for 33,000 tonnes of CO_2 wafting into the atmosphere. Other flowers may be even worse because some are flown in with their roots in a bucket of water – think of the extra weight and therefore extra fuel that entails. Even locally grown flowers from greenhouses are just as bad because of the energy needed to heat the greenhouse.

Around three-quarters of all cut flowers bought in this country are sold in pre-pack bunches through supermarkets. And I was rather surprised to observe that even a specialist organic supermarket was selling non-organic flowers.

If you're still a determined flower fan, why not try dried or silk flowers that last for years. Or if you want to avoid the pesticide plague, you could choose organic flowers. And now you can get local, seasonal flowers too. Best of all, if you have the space, is to grow your own. Even flat-dwellers can enjoy pot plants, but you have to remember to water them or you might as well have gone for the cut variety after all.

GIFTS and OCCASIONS WEBLINKS

Centre for Alternative Technology
Lots of unusual eco-friendly gifts available
through its shop and catalogue.

www.cat.org.uk

Cut Outs
Sells products made from recycled materials
and aims to raise awareness of reducing,
reusing and recycling.

www.cutouts.net

Ecotopia
Sells a wide range of eco-products, including
bulk detergents.

www.ecotopia.co.uk

Energy Saving World
Sells a wide range of energy-saving products.

www.energysavingworld.co.uk

Freecycle
If you want to give something away or find
something for free, have a look at what's
available near you.

www.freecycle.org

Friends of the Earth (FoE)
Provides 20 top tips for a 'green' Christmas.

www.foe.co.uk

Green Shop
Extensive range of eco-products available at
its shop in Bisley, Gloucestershire, or by
mail order.

www.greenshop.co.uk

Green Weddings
Wedding service offering advice on all
aspects of the ethical and environmental
impacts of the occasion.

www.greenweddings.org.uk

Hippy Shopper
Lists lots of weird, wacky and innovative
product ideas and tells you where to
find them.

www.hippyshopper.com

Natural Collection
Sells household products, cosmetics,
toiletries and fashion.

www.naturalcollection.com

Nigel's Eco-store
Sells eco-friendly products online.   www.nigelsecostore.com

Rag and Bone
Provides a forum for giving things away that
are too good to be thrown away.   www.rag-and-bone.co.uk

The Organic Flower Company
Sells organic flowers.   www.tofc.co.uk

Wiggly Wigglers
Sells seasonally selected, UK-grown cut
flowers which they'll send by courier.   www.wigglywigglers.co.uk

Woodland Trust
Organises a Christmas card recycling scheme.   www.woodland-trust.org.uk/cards

GREEN PUBLICATIONS

Ecologist Magazine
Monthly environmental affairs magazine.   www.theecologist.org

Ethical Consumer
Monthly magazine providing information on
social, ethical and environmental products
and services.   www.ethicalconsumer.org

Green Consumer Guide
Environmental news site – it has no
connection with *The New Green
Consumer Guide*.   www.greenconsumerguide.com

Green Guide Online
Publishes green guides, including *The
Directory for Planet Friendly Living* and *Green
Guide for Christmas*.   www.greenguide.co.uk

Why Organic?
Soil Association magazine and
consumer website.   www.whyorganic.org

GREEN DEATH

Horrible as it may be, I think it's really important to make plans for your death whilst you're still compos mentis – even more so if you're concerned about green issues. Lots of decisions about funerals, coffins, burial and cremation are governed by convention, so if you want something a little unusual, like a bamboo coffin or a shallow burial, your relatives and friends need to feel comfortable that they're doing something you'd like.

DEATH TIPS

- Donate your organs
- Say no to embalming
- Remove all jewellery and gold teeth before burial or cremation
- Dress minimal in death
- Choose natural fibres such as hemp for clothes
- Select a 'green' coffin
- Give cremation a miss
- If you're buried, find a site that will be used for other purposes.
- Do without a headstone

FEED THE BIRDS

When there weren't so many of us on the planet, our bodies were generally eaten by wild animals. Nowadays this approach is pretty rare – and it looks like it might die out altogether.

The Parsis in India leave their dead on open platforms where they can be eaten by vultures – a very swift and efficient form of recycling.

Unfortunately vulture populations have been decimated over the past 20 years – down from 85 million to just 3–4,000. The reason for this is thought to be an antibiotic commonly given to cows, sheep and goats. Birds that eat animals that have been treated are poisoned and die.

I hope the Parsis come up with another way to bring life from death.

Body Matters
Going under

It might be difficult to live a perfect green lifestyle, but it appears that it's even harder to die with minimal environmental impact.

One problem is that there are an awful lot of us – around 600,000 people die annually in the UK. Another is that as one of the larger mammals, it takes quite a lot to get our bodies to rot and become mulch. 'Ashes to ashes, dust to dust' is not strictly accurate as it takes a minimum of 75 years for a body in a coffin to rot – and in some soil conditions the corpse may still be intact a century later.

One important factor in decomposition is that we're buried so deep in the ground: six feet under there is very little air and therefore no worms and pretty few microbes working away at turning us to mulch. In fact we don't actually turn into useful compostable earth at all – the gruesome reality is that we slowly rot or putrefy, rather like a vase of flowers when left too long in water.

Say 'no' to embalming

I think the idea of embalming is rather grotesque – to make a dead body look more alive and to preserve it in perpetuity. The reality is even worse. Blood in the body is replaced with a poison – usually formaldehyde – coloured red to give the corpse a pink hue. The problem with this is that although the body will eventually rot, it takes a lot longer to do so, and meanwhile the formaldehyde leaches out into the earth and contaminates the soil – or, in the case of crematoria, adds to pollution from emissions.

Bodies will last several weeks in a refrigerator – it's usually possible to make funeral arrangements in this time. If a body must be kept for longer, deep-freezing is an option. Perhaps the only time embalming of any sort might be needed is when bodies have to be flown back to another country; however, alcohol could also be used.

Surprisingly, embalming bodies is still common practice in the UK. One person I spoke to suggested cynically that this might be because funeral companies recommend it so they can charge more for their services. The two leading funeral companies in the UK, Co-op and Dignity, both embalm as standard practice – they call it 'hygienic treatment'. You can say you don't want it, but you may feel uncomfortable with your decision if they say that the body won't look as nice.

Apparently there is now a more 'environmentally friendly' embalming solution made from seaweed. My view is that it's better to give it a miss altogether.

The fiery furnace

One thing that's always annoyed me about crematoria is that coffins are burnt along with the dead bodies. The main reason for this is

that crematoria are designed in such a way that they need a stiff board underneath the body to manoeuvre it into the furnace. But a recent survey shows that around half of all crematoria will accept body bags or shrouds, as long as there's a plank to support them.

Some crematoria actually offer discounts for 'green' coffins because they'll burn quicker and cause less pollution. Emissions from the furnaces are a real problem. In the past the big issue was PVC linings in coffins, but these are no longer allowed. Now mercury emissions from tooth fillings and dioxins are the biggest headache.

Apparently 11 per cent of the mercury contamination of North Sea fish comes from crematoria, and it's estimated that this could escalate to nearly a third within the next decade, because of the huge increase in the number of fillings in today's older generations. By 2012 crematoria in the UK will be required to have pollution-control equipment, which will stop these emissions. This is extremely expensive and will still leave them with large quantities of mercury to dispose of.

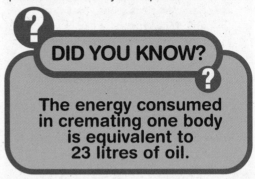

DID YOU KNOW?

The energy consumed in cremating one body is equivalent to 23 litres of oil.

I wondered if it wouldn't be simpler to remove all mercury fillings before cremation. This has been considered but was felt to be impractical and insensitive – and it would only solve part of the problem. Certainly I think crematoria should be obliged to remove gold fillings and make sure there's no jewellery left on the deceased before they're cremated. Just think of all that gold going to waste that could be recycled.

Apart from the toxic pollution from crematoria, there's the energy and climate change impacts to consider. There have been some experiments looking at reclaiming the heat generated, although this may not be so easy because to be really useful the furnace would need to be operating continuously. I wonder if crematoria could produce hydrogen for fuel cells (page 186) because this could be done on a more ad hoc basis.

But the brutal reality remains: burning our dead is an environmental disaster. And trying to contain emissions is going to be financially crippling too. Instead we need to rethink our whole approach to the disposal of bodies.

Freeze-dried bodies

It's not yet possible to be freeze-dried in this country, but it could be soon. The idea behind it is to make the corpse into mulch as quickly as possible.

The body and coffin are exposed to liquid nitrogen, which makes them extremely brittle and dry – a mechanical vibration then causes them to fall apart. The end result is dry granules, rather like instant coffee, which are put in a cornstarch coffin and buried in a shallow grave. Like leaves or other plant debris, the body (now only 30 per cent of its original weight) will become mulch in six to nine months, so it's ideal for tree-planting.

This approach could be a 'green' alternative to either burial or cremation – it certainly gets rid of the problem of emissions. And one of the good things about it is that the nitrogen is a by-product from making pure oxygen for use in hospitals, aeroplanes and so on.

I wasn't so impressed by the fact that you would effectively need two coffins – one that is freeze-dried with you and one for your remains. This is apparently out of 'respect' for mourners, but I assume they don't actually see you going into the liquid nitrogen, so perhaps you could manage without one of them.

Laid to rest

Until about 1850 graves in churchyards were reused. Grave-diggers would work their way across the churchyard burying people and then start again once they had used up the space. Nowadays reusing graves is illegal in Britain, although not in most of the rest of Europe. As a result we're running out of space.

The whole idea of graveyards, with individual plots and headstones acting as an eternal resting place, needs to be reconsidered. Inevitably there's fierce resistance when proposals are made to dig up old graves, reuse burial plots, or even bury bodies on top of each other – you can fit up to three coffins in a six-foot hole. A lot more popular is the idea of natural burial grounds – there are now over 200 of these in the UK. Generally they require eco-coffins or ashes and offer plots in nature parks, woodland sites, or even areas that will subsequently be used for grazing animals.

STORING BONES

One idea for burial is to replace the hard clay soil that is prevalent in most of the country's graveyards with sandy soil – this would dramatically increase the speed of decomposition. The bodies could be put into shallow graves for a limited period, say 20 years. After that the bones would be removed and the plot used for someone else. This is common practice in Germany.

The best sites won't allow headstones, will specify local tree species, not mow the grass more than twice a year, and have a detailed plan to encourage wildlife. But be warned: if the site is too manicured, it's not going to be much use for anything but bodies – to my mind that rather defeats the object of a 'natural' burial ground.

Given the problem with space on earth, you might think it's a good idea to be propelled into outer space. I think this is the most selfish approach to body disposal possible. The climate change impacts of space travel are horrendous.

Coffin Talk

'Green' coffins are now available from most funeral directors and make up about 5 per cent of all coffins sold. But deciding which is greenest and which suits you is not easy. Here are some of the options:

Solid wood coffins *My Rating 1/10*
Solid wood coffins, for example made from oak, are not that common nowadays. They're expensive and probably the worst environmental option because you're wasting beautiful wood, just to bury it in the ground. If you do choose a wood option, make sure it's FSC-certified (page 91).

Pine wood coffins *My Rating 5/10*
Simple pine coffins are an improvement on hardwoods because pine grow a lot faster, but again you need to make sure they're FSC-certified.

Wood chip coffins *My Rating With Formaldehyde 3/10; Formaldehyde-free 8/10*
Most coffins today are made from wood chip – waste wood bits stuck together with formaldehyde. If it weren't for the toxic glue (I'm not aware of any formaldehyde-free wood chip coffins), This would be a good use for recycled materials.

Cardboard coffins *My Rating 9/10*
There's a tremendous variety of cardboard coffins, but most of them come in a flat-pack arrangement for self-assembly. You can get them in plain cardboard, or white ones that can be painted or drawn on. Either way, for a lot of people it feels quite brave going for something so basic. Make sure they have a

high percentage of recycled waste.

Willow coffins *My Rating 7/10*
Willow is harvested from the tree crowns, which grow back within the same season. One tree can go on being reharvested for about 35–40 years.

Bamboo coffins *My Rating 8/10*
Bamboo is like grass – it regrows rapidly when it's been cut. Interestingly, bamboo is one of the best plants for producing oxygen and absorbing CO_2, which makes it climate change friendly. And in case you're worried about bamboo coffins being imported all the way from China, the makers have worked out that each coffin uses the same amount of fuel being shipped to the UK as it would being driven three miles in a car.

Ecopods *My Rating 9/10*
I love the shape of these coffins (see pic below) – they're designed like a seedpod. They also have good green credentials as they're made from recycled paper stuck together with a plant-based glue. Even though the painted ones use Ecos paints (page 88-90), the extra materials do dilute their eco-credentials. These coffins were hand-made and expensive, but they've recently started being mass-produced so prices should come down.

Reusable coffins *My Rating 7/10*
The idea of these coffins is that you put the body in a very basic cardboard coffin and insert that into a beautiful hand-crafted outer coffin that everyone sees. When it comes to burying the body, a flap opens and the inner container slips out. This is a neat way of getting round people's concerns about 'lack of frills' cardboard. The downside is that the coffin has to be collected from the crematorium in a fuel-thirsty hearse, and presumably cleaned after use.

Memorial drape or cloth
Another good idea for overcoming concerns about the visual impact of basic coffins is to use a 'pall', a decorated drape or cloth used to cover the coffin. Rather like a baptism robe, this could be handed down from one generation to the next. Another idea is to add an embroidered emblem for all those who have used the same cloth; some people include pockets in which letters are left for the living.

My Will

Although I've always liked the idea of being eaten by vultures or other wild animals, I do appreciate that's not very practical nowadays. My main objective is to turn my body into nutrients as fast as possible – and with a minimal amount of packaging. With this in mind, the freeze-drying process may be a good option – or shallow burial in a well-run woodland site. Ideally, I'd do without a coffin, but I have to admit that I'm rather a fan of the Ecopod. Perhaps I could be indulgent at the moment of parting and go for one of those. I'd certainly like to have a tree planted on my remains and a memorial on the Internet.

GREEN DEATH WEBLINKS

Association of Natural Burial Grounds
Run by the Natural Death Centre. Full details
of over 200 sites can be found in the *Natural
Death Handbook*.   www.anbg.co.uk

Bamboo Eco Coffins
Sells bamboo and willow coffins.   www.ecoffins.co.uk

Ecopod
Makes Ecopod coffins.   www.ecopod.co.uk

Eternal Reefs
Creates artificial reefs that incorporate ashes
from crematoria.   www.eternalreefs.com

Forest Stewardship Council (FSC)
Sustainable-wood certification scheme.   www.fsc-uk.org

Gone Too Soon
Memorial website.   gonetoosoon.co.uk

Green Endings
Arranges funerals throughout London and
M25 region.   www.greenendings.co.uk

Green Undertakings of Watchet
Specialists in woodland burials and natural
funerals, offering services in South
West England.   www.funeraldirector.com/maps/
                                                    southwestmaps/greenundertakings

Memory Of
Memorial website.   www.memory-of.com

Natural Death Centre
Provides extensive information on 'green'
funerals and funeral services, which can be
found in their *Natural Death Handbook*.   www.naturaldeath.org.uk

Native Woodland
Offers native woodland burial sites.   www.nativewoodland.co.uk

Organ and Tissue Donation
Official website for organ and tissue donation.   **www.organdonor.gov**

Promessa
Swedish company pioneering a
freeze-drying process.   **www.promessa.se**

Woodland Burials
Offers woodland burials with or without
funeral services.   **www.woodlandburials.co.uk**

Conclusion: The Way Forward

How Many Planets

I was born in 1961. It's an unusual year because if you write it on a piece of paper and turn it upside down it still reads 1961. The frightening thing is that in the 45 years since my birth the world itself has turned upside down.

Perhaps the most startling fact is that just over four decades ago everyone in the world could have lived the same lifestyle as people in the UK – now we'd need three planets for this to be achieved. And if we all wanted to live like an average American (thankfully not all of us do!) we'd need six planets. Even on a global scale human beings are using more resources every year than the Earth can produce. How much longer can this go on?

The main reason for living beyond our means is quite simple. It comes down to the number of people on the planet and how much we consume. Some people worry that there's too much attention paid to what we consume and not enough to how many there are of us – and I have some sympathy with this view. I believe we should be taking measures to reduce our global population – at the very least try to limit its growth. I'm also aware of how ferociously contentious this issue is, so I'm thankful that my focus is on what we as individuals can do, both in our own lifestyles and through technology.

CAVIAR QUESTION

Consider this. It's quite clear that the plight of sturgeon, the fish from which caviar is produced, hangs in the balance. We could respond by trying to manage fish stocks, maintain their habitats and severely restrict the sales of caviar. But another reaction might be to say, 'What the heck, sturgeon are going to die out anyway, so I might as well eat as much caviar as possible before they do.' These contrasting approaches were put to the vote at a conference for luxury brands that I attended recently – and the audience was split almost 50:50!

Top Dos and Don'ts

The positive thing is that there's far greater awareness of the problems we face today than there has been in the past. Not so good is that there's a huge difference in opinion over how we should respond. What is becoming clear though is that the longer we wait, the more serious the problems are going to get. We should be doing something right now. And part of what I hope to demonstrate is that there's an awful lot we can do – and that doesn't just mean recycling.

The New Green Consumer Guide is full of ideas, but on the facing page are my top dos and don'ts.

DO

- Fit energy-efficient light bulbs
- Insulate your house
- Wash your clothes at low temperatures
- Use rechargeable batteries
- Buy local, seasonal food
- Share car journeys
- Recycle as much as you can
- Fit water-saving devices to your lavatories
- Invest your money responsibly
- Make a will that includes a green funeral
- Buy products made from recycled materials
- Check for FSC certification on wood and paper products
- Take up cycling and walking
- Print on both sides of a sheet of paper
- Get a reusable shopping bag
- Switch to a 'green' electricity supplier
- Buy top energy rated appliances
- Have a shower rather than a bath
- Repair products rather than replace them
- Buy an energy monitoring device
- Turn lights off when you leave a room
- Put an insulating jacket on your boiler
- Reuse gift wrapping paper
- Buy organic produce
- Eat wild food
- Ask fashion retailers what they're doing to reduce pollution from dyes and chemicals
- Reduce or eliminate your air travel

DON'T

- Buy bottled water
- Buy food or goods that have come by air
- Buy too many clothes
- Leave your computer, TV and other equipment on stand-by
- Buy gold or diamonds
- Fly to your holiday destination
- Eat too much meat
- Buy black-listed fish
- Drive a gas-guzzling car
- Keep your house hotter than you need
- Use a tumble dryer
- Install air conditioning
- Throw away unwanted gifts
- Make your lawn look like a carpet
- Worry about weeds (too much)
- Bother with air fresheners
- Get an Aga if you haven't already got one
- Buy gas log or coal fires (fake fires)
- Upgrade your mobile phone too fast
- Buy disposable cameras or barbecues
- Buy incandescent or halogen light bulbs
- Drive fast and erratically
- Use peat or buy peat-grown plants
- Buy over-packaged products
- Get cremated
- Buy duty-free alcohol that needs to be carried on a plane.
- Buy cut flowers
- Leave your car engine running
- Overheat your house (or office)

Making a Difference

If there's one point above all others that I'd like to make, it's that consumers do have the power to change things. Those who challenge this say that consumers aren't radical enough and will never be able to do enough. Some argue that only governments can make changes on the scale that's needed. I profoundly disagree.

Individual actions do make a difference, particularly when multiplied by millions. Even more important is the fact that what we do is a very strong indicator of what we believe. And both businesses and governments respond to public opinion – they have to because otherwise we wouldn't buy their products or vote for them. So if consumers don't change their behaviour, businesses and governments won't either.

But we have to face up to the fact that there'll never be universal support. Any significant measures taken will mean there are losers as well as winners. Those who are genuinely hard done by need to be compensated, but many others simply have to accept that they must change their ways. And that can be hard.

£ LOSERS

The Chancellor increases airport tax. One family of five were reportedly 'devastated' by the extra £200 a year it would cost them to fly to Florida twice a year to 'check on their holiday property'. Should we feel sorry for them? I don't think so. Far better for the planet if they sold their holiday house and took their vacations closer to home!

MY TOP 20 WISH LIST

It's tempting to believe that the solutions to our problems have yet to be found. I don't think this is the case, and have drawn up a 'wish list' of 20 things that could be done and that would make a difference. The biggest obstacle to making these changes is a lack of motivation. That's where green consumers come in: if we demonstrate our support for these sorts of initiatives we can make them happen. If lots of us work together, writing letters, greening our shopping habits and making our views known, we'll be using our vote as consumers (and citizens) to change the world for the better.

1. **Switch to decentralised energy**
    Instead of large-scale centralised power stations, whether coal, gas or nuclear, we should be setting up a system for home-produced energy from a range of sources.

2. **Source more energy from the sea**
    If we put more investment into wave and tidal power, we could get a sizeable part of our energy needs from the sea.

3. **Use methane from rotting waste**
    There's huge untapped potential for using gases released from rotting waste to power vehicles and heat buildings.

4. **Change electricity charging**
    Let's pay power companies more money if they sell less electricity, and encourage them to charge high energy users more per unit of electricity rather than less.

5. **Green building policies**
    All new buildings should be super-energy- and water-efficient.

6. **Demand energy-efficient lighting**
    All new light fittings should work with energy-efficient bulbs.

7. **Introduce water meters nationwide**
    Water meters should be fitted in all UK households.

8. **Make cooling climate-change friendly**
    Cooling gases used by transport vehicles, supermarkets and other retailers should be climate-change friendly.

9. **Recycle computers and electronic waste**
    No computer or electronic waste should end up in landfill sites – almost all can be recycled.

10. **Protect forests**
    Draconian measures should be introduced to protect forests from agricultural expansion, such as from soya or palm oil.

11. **Source sustainable fish**
We should only be able to buy fish from sustainable sources.

12. **Legislate for fuel-efficient cars**
All new cars should be required to do at least 50 miles per gallon.

13. **Limit car air conditioning**
Car air conditioning should be an expensive optional extra in new cars.

14. **Provide incentives for low-impact travel**
Innovative, low-cost public transport systems should be introduced throughout the UK, as well as incentives for car-sharing schemes.

15. **Stop airport expansion**
No new airports or runways should be built.

16. **Increase the cost of flying**
Tax aircraft fuel in the same way as fuel for cars so that airfares are significantly more expensive.

17. **Ban air imports**
Stop importing any products, whether fruit, fish or flowers, into this country if they come by air.

18. **Grow more hemp**
There should be a large-scale switch from cotton to hemp for use in textiles.

19. **Use old gold and synthetic diamonds**
No new gold or diamonds should be mined – use old gold and synthetic diamonds.

20. **Green death**
Legislation should be revised to allow freeze-drying bodies, shallow burial and the reusing of graves.

LAST WORD

You may have your own wish list or even just one innovative idea that might help the planet. Email me on **julia@juliahailes.com** and let me know what it is. I'll try to respond to each one (unless I'm inundated!). And I'll select the ones I like best and post them on my website: **www.juliahailes.com**

Glossary

Acid rain	Rain that has become acidic from pollution.
Biodegradation	Process in which micro-organisms break down organic matter into smaller, simpler fragments.
Biodiesel	Diesel fuel made from plant sources.
Bioethanol	Alcohol made from plant sources and used to supplement or replace petrol.
Biofuels	Fuels made from plant sources and animal waste.
Biogas	Gas made from plant sources, including rotting organic waste.
Biomethane	Methane gas made from plant sources, including rotting organic waste.
Bovine spongiiform encephalopathy (BSE)	An infectious degenerative brain disease occurring in cattle, often referred to as 'mad cow disease'.
Brominated flame retardants	Materials used to resist or inhibit fire, particularly when applied to electronics, clothes and furniture.
Bycatch	Animals or fish caught by accident in fishing gear – primarily in nets.
Cadmium	A toxic heavy metal used in products such as batteries, televisions and some plastics.
Carbon	A non-metal element that occurs in all organic compounds.
Carbon dioxide (CO2)	The main greenhouse gas, formed during breathing, burning and rotting.
Carbon monoxide (CO)	Highly poisonous gas formed by incomplete burning.

Carbon neutral	Producing no more carbon dioxide (or other greenhouse gases) than is absorbed either by growing a fuel crop or by carbon offsets.
Carbon offsets	Compensating the greenhouse gas emissions from an activity, product or service by emission reductions from projects elsewhere.
Carbon rationing	Limiting the amount of carbon emissions that people or companies are entitled to.
Carbon sequestration	The removal and storage of carbon.
Carbon sinks	Wherever carbon is stored, for example in oceans, forests and soil.
Carbon capture and storage (CCS)	Collecting greenhouse gases and pumping them under land and old oil and gas fields deep under the ocean floor. This is still at an experimental stage.
Chlorine	Gas or liquid that is widely used to purify water, as a disinfectant and as a bleach.
Chlorofluorocarbons (CFCs)	Family of inert chemicals that were widely used in refrigeration, air conditioning, as aerosol propellants and for packaging, but which were found to destroy the ozone layer
Chromium	A toxic heavy metal used in stainless steel, leather processing and some glass.
Climate change	Changing weather patterns, particularly relating to global warming, caused by human activity.
Compact fluorescent lamps (CFLs)	Energy-efficient replacements to incandescent (ordinary) light bulbs, that are also referred to as low-energy light bulbs.
Compressed natural gas (CNG)	Natural gas compressed so that it can be used as a liquid fuel.

Dioxins	Highly toxic compounds produced by industrial processes as well as forest fires and volcanoes.
Ecological footprint	The land and water area required by a human population to produce the resources it consumes and to absorb its wastes, using available technology.
Embodied energy	The energy used to make and transport a product.
Enzymes	A protein that encourages a biochemical reaction, such as dissolving fats on clothes or speeding up fermentation.
Fossil fuels	Fuels such as oil, coal and gas, formed in the ground from the remains of dead plants and animals.
Fuel cell	A technology that produces electricity through a chemical reaction similar to that found in a battery.
Genetic engineering	The science of changing the DNA of a plant or animal to produce different characteristics.
Genetic modification (GM)	Altering the genetic material of living cells or organisms.
Geothermal	Relating to the heat generated in the centre of the Earth.
Global warming	A gradual warming of the earth caused by increased levels of greenhouse gases.
Global warming potential (GWP)	Measurement used to show the different impacts of greenhouse gases in terms of their effect on global warming.

Greenhouse effect	An illustrative way of describing global warming, whereby the gases trapping the heat work in a similar way to a garden greenhouse.
Greenhouse gases	Gases that trap heat in the Earth's atmosphere and therefore cause the greenhouse effect.
Hormone-disrupting chemicals	Chemicals that prevent hormones in our bodies working properly.
Hydrocarbons (HCs)	Family of compounds containing carbon and hydrogen in various combinations – found particularly in fossil fuels.
Hydrogen	The lightest and most abundant gas in the universe, but found on Earth chiefly when combined with oxygen as water.
Hydrofluorocarbons (HFCs)	Chemicals used to replace ozone-depleting chlorofluorocarbons, but they are still significant greenhouse gases.
Landfill	A site where household and industrial waste can be buried.
Light-emitting diodes (LEDs)	Long-lasting energy-efficient alternative to ordinary light bulbs.
Liquefied petroleum gas (LPG)	Mostly propane and butane, these gases are extracted from fossil fuels and can be used for cooking, refrigeration and cars.
Mercury	Highly toxic heavy metal that is released from the Earth by mining and burning fossil fuels, and used in products such as thermometers, dental fillings, batteries and fluorescent lights.

Methane	A colourless, odourless gas that is a key component of biogas, produced by rotting waste. It is also a clean fuel, but when emitted to the atmosphere it is a powerful greenhouse gas that is between 20 and 24 times more powerful than CO_2.
Methyl bromide	A gas or liquid which was widely used as a pesticide until restrictions were introduced because of its ozone-destroying capabilities.
Nanotechnology	Engineering done at an atomic scale resulting in minuscule technologies.
Nitrogen Dioxide (NO2)	A colourless gas often used as an anaesthetic – it is also a powerful greenhouse gas being 310 times more powerful than CO_2.
Nitrous oxide (N2O)	A mixture of NO and NO2 implicated in health problems and smog formation.
NOX (oxides of nitrogen)	A mixture of NO and NO2 and implicated in smog formation.
Organochlorine	Any hydrocarbon pesticide that contains chlorine, including DDT.
Organophosphates	Toxic chemicals used in pesticides that have been shown to damage the human immune system.
Ozone	A form of oxygen, which at ground level is an air pollutant in the form of smog, created by the reaction of certain pollutants with sunlight.
Ozone layer	Layer of ozone found 12–30 miles above the Earth's surface that filters the sun's ultra violet rays, acting as a natural sunscreen.
Particulates	Fine, solid particles found in car and industry emissions.

Phosphates	Chemical compounds which were used in detergents to break down fats – still used in fertiliser, toothpaste and baking powder.
Phthalates	Man-made chemicals primarily used in plastics as a plasticiser.
Plasticisers	Oil-based substance that when added to plastic makes it flexible, resilient and easier to handle.
Polybrominated biphenyls (PBBs)	Group of chemicals widely used as fire retardants in electrical products such as computers and TVs.
Polychlorinated biphenyls (PCBs)	Synthetic chemicals that were widely used in paints, inks and electrical equipment, but which have been found to be carcinogenic and weaken the immune system.
Post-consumer waste	Waste produced by offices and homes.
Polyvinyl chloride (PVC)	Plastic made with chlorine, which may release dioxins when burned.
Smog	Air pollution produced by a reaction to sunlight.
Solvent	Fluid in which something dissolves.
Titanium dioxide (TiO2)	A white powdery substance used as a whitener in a vast range of products, including paints and detergents.
Volatile organic compound (VOC)	Any organic compound that evaporates at room temperature, including solvents found in paints, alcohol and petrol fumes.

ABOUT THE AUTHOR
JULIA HAILES

Ham Hill

The memorial column on Ham Hill, in Somerset, is etched firmly in my memory. I could see it from my bedroom window in the house where I grew up. From boarding school, where I went from the age of eight – and from London, when I left home at 18 – I would frequently return and spend both sunny and rainy afternoons running up and down the quarry hills of this iron-age fort that dominates the surrounding countryside.

When I returned to live in Somerset in 1995, I moved to the National Trust house at Tintinhull (pictured right), which is still in the shadow of Ham Hill but on the other side to my childhood home. Two of my three sons were born in one of the upstairs bedrooms, during our 10 years renting the house.

Although I have no wish to be cremated, I have sometimes thought about having my ashes sprinkled on Ham Hill. I now realise that by the time I die it may be possible to have my freeze-dried remains spread about under a pile of leaves somewhere in the vicinity – so I will have come full circle.

World Travel

Soon after school I spent a year in Paris – not 'down and out' but earning money from busking, selling flowers and even one job which involved dressing up in silver foil to sell frying pans and another making 'pooper scooper' gloves for Parisian poodles! When I returned to London my career was no less eclectic. I sold teddy bears in Selfridges, shirts and jumpers door to door, and spent a few months working as an industrial pudding cook at Metal Box factory.

But it was my time travelling in South and Central America that really got me hooked on environmental issues. I was horrified to see rainforests being chopped down, vast slum areas spreading as rural populations moved to cities and, on a more personal level, my fellow crew members on a luxury racing yacht chucking all the boat garbage into the sea!

Of course, many of these trips involved flying. At that time there wasn't anything controversial about this. Now the impact of air travel on climate change is making us think whether zooming around the planet in this way is acceptable. Here's the quandary – on the one hand the experience of travelling may be switching more people onto the perils of global warming. On the other, our travelling habits are making the problem worse.

The Green Consumer

I came back from Central America via the
east and west coast of the States. Having
learned to roller skate down Broadway in the
rush hour, I continued in London, this time
from North Kensington to Barnes, where I
was working with John Elkington. He and I
joined forces in 1986, setting up a company
called SustainAbility and subsequently
writing the original *Green Consumer Guide*.
This book went on to sell over a million copies
worldwide. I believe that if we hadn't written
it someone else would have – it was the right
book at the right time. John's idea was that
businesses would be more 'green' if they
knew that this would bring them more
customers. I saw it from the other direction –
if most people knew the environmental
impacts of their shopping habits, they'd
make 'greener' choices.

What neither John nor I had anticipated was
the response from the business world.
As consultants, we were besieged by
companies saying they recognised the
importance of environmental issues, but what
could they do? This was particularly apparent
amongst the supermarkets – it may surprise
you to hear that even at this time they were
busy appointing environmental advisors to
get them up to speed.

The Current Climate

It's nearly 20 years since the publication of *The Green Consumer Guide*. In the intervening period, I have written a number of books on the theme, worked as a consultant for companies including British Airways, ICI, Marks & Spencer and Procter & Gamble, and given speeches all over the world. Having left SustainAbility I am now freelance – or, in modern parlance, a 'portfolio' worker. As I often find myself explaining, I have lots of hats but they're all green.

A couple of years ago my family moved to a Victorian farmhouse, which I'm still eco-renovating. Some of my experiences are included in *The New Green Consumer Guide* – for example re-using a friend's kitchen units and my struggles to find suitable energy-efficient light bulbs. However, I've got lots more to do and will be posting progress reports on my website – www.juliahailes.com. There'll also be news of my consultancy work and speeches – this year has already been extraordinary both in terms of the world waking up to environmental issues and, as a result, people wanting me to do things. I'm run off my feet.

But I haven't lost sight of Ham Hill – I've just moved to yet another side!

Somerset, February 2007

INDEX

Page numbers in **bold**
denotes glossary reference

ACKNOWLEDGEMENTS

My biggest thanks must go to Amanda Mitchison, who has been absolutely brilliant as both a sounding board and first draft proof-reader.

I would also like to thank John Elkington, with whom I co-wrote the original *Green Consumer Guide*, as well as seven other books, and who inspired and encouraged me to write *The New Green Consumer Guide*.

Others who have been immensely supportive include my agent Sara Menguc, my editor Kerri Sharp, Giles Gibbons from Good Business and Rosie Boycott, who has written the Foreword. And a special thanks to those I've interviewed: Hugh Fearnley-Whittingstall, Pen Hadow and Kevin McCloud.

Writing The New Green Consumer Guide has been incredibly time-consuming. As a single mother of three energetic boys – Connor (12), Rollo (10) and Monty (8) – this has meant a considerable amount of help on the home front from friends and family. My heartfelt thanks go to my mother, Minker Soames, my sister Amanda Campbell, my brothers, Mark and Charles Hailes, and my friends, particularly Helena Barrowcliff, Ed Bryant, Mike and Isabelle Davies, Lorna Denny, Adam Laurie (who rescued lost data on my computer), Laura Pentreath, Totti Shaw, Annette and Stephen Smallwood, Jay and Trina Turvill, Tricia Walsh, Helen Williams, and Martin and Lisa Young.

Also thanks to Mike and Valerie Hoare and Anne Howell, who has helped me keep my house from becoming too chaotic without complaining about my eco-instructions! Of course I mustn't forget my wonderful boys who've had to put up with me being 'in the office as usual'.

An enormous amount of research has gone into this book, and much of it was conducted through long conversations on the telephone. I'm tremendously grateful to all those I've talked to – and in many cases shared draft copy with – for sparing their time and expertise. I should point out that even with all this brilliant advice and input, the opinions expressed and mistakes made are entirely my own. And I apologise to anyone who has helped me but whose name I may have missed from the list below, and anyone whose name I have misspelled.

Thank you to (in alphabetical order by organisation or by first name where no affiliation is listed):

A – C

Absorbent Hygiene Products Manufacturers Association (AHPMA) – Tracy Stewart; AEA Energy & Environment / Marketing Transformation Programme – Dr. Kevin Lane & Charles Gaysford; Alternative Vehicle Technology (AVT) – Robert Fowler; Anita Roddick – Founder of the Body Shop; Asda – Dominic Burch; Bamboo Coffins (SAWN) – William Wainman; Banana Link – Alistair Smith; Bath University – Philip Shields; Baxi Potter – Ian Stares; BBC – Jeremy Bristow; Benchmark Furniture – Sean Sutcliffe; Bio Thinking – Edwin Datshefki; Body Shop – Jan Buckingham; Brendan Sewill – Air travel expert Bridport TLC – Leon Edwards; British Aerosols Manufacturer's Association (BAMA) – Paul Jackson; British Plastics Federation – Mercia Glick; British Wind Energy Association (BWEA) – Chris Tomlinson, Michael Hay; Brompton Bikes – Emerson Roberts; Building Research

Establishment – Roger Hitchin, Chris Roberts; Bulmers Cider, part of Scottish & Newcastle UK Ltd – Richard Heathcote; Cambridge University – Julian Allwood; Campaign Strategy – Chris Rose; Carbon Neutral Company – Jonathon Shopley; Care Group – Peter Stokes; Centre for Alternative Technology – Peter Harper; Centre for Sustainable Energy (CSE) – Mark Letcher; Chartered Institute of Waste Management – Tina Benfield; Combined Heat & Power Association – Syed Ahmed; Compassion in World Farming (CIWF) – The Global Benefits of Eating Less Meat; Composting Association – Jeremy Jacobs; Co-operative Group – Michelle Vernon; Croydon Crematorium – Garry Schone.

D – H

Department of Trade & Industry – Peter Cottrell & Paul Hallett; Department of Transport – Dave Williams; Digital Link – David Sogan; DM Hall Surveyors – Andrew McFarlane; Earthcare Products – Nick Cox; Ecology Building Society – John Lee; Ecos Trust – Caroline Cameron; Ecover – Alistair Lidstone & Peter Malaise; Edinburgh Centre for Environmental Management – Richard Tipper; EIRIS – Mark Robertson; Electrans – Mike Jarman; Elm Farm Research Centre – Christopher Stopes; Energy Advice Centre (Bristol) – Mike Wilcox; Energy for Good – Saffron Myhill-Hunt; Energy Savings Trust – Jenny Abelman, Andrew Amato, Alex Veitch, Danielle Wyatt; Environmental Change Institute (Oxford) – Catherine Bottrill, Tina Fawcett, Chris Jardine; Ethical Investors Group – Lee Coates; Ewen Cameron – aka The Lord Cameron of Dillington; Federation of Environmental Trade Associations – Terry Seward; Food Climate Research Network (FCRN) – Tara Garnett; Forest Stewardship Council – Nick Cliffe; Freedom Foods – see RSPCA; Friends of the Earth – Ed Matthews; Fuel Cells UK – Sylvia Grieves; Geoscience – Dr Robin Curtis; Green Car Guide – Paul Clarke; Greenfinch – Michael Chesshire; Green Moves – Julian Brooks; Green Paints – Alan Beaven; Greenpeace – Ben Ayliffe, Doug Parr; Green Spirit Fuels – Arthur Llewellyn; Haller Foundation – Louise Piper; Hendersons Global Investors – Nick Robins; Heuga Home Flooring – Patrick Riley (Interface Carpets); Historic Futures – Tim Wilson; Holden & Partners – Giles Chitty; Horticultural Research International – David Simpson; HSBC Bank – Francis Sullivan.

I – R

International Institute for Environment & Development (IIED) – Zoe Lelah Wangler; Imperial College – David Hart; Institute of European Environmental Policy (IEEP) – Malcolm Ferguson; Interflush – David Wilks; Johsnon Matthey – David Jollie; Johnson Seafarms – Alan Bourhill; Johnsons Cleaners UK – Andy Taylor; Jonathan Baird – Cut flower expert; Josephine Fairley – Green beauty expert; Joulesave – Chris Robinson; Jupiter Asset Management – Emma Howard-Boyd; Kate Fletcher – Green fashion expert; Ken West – Green burial pioneer; Livos – R_diger Filbrich; Loch Duart – Andy Bing; Low Carbon Vehicle Partnership – Greg Archer; Malcolm McCall – Architect; Manolo Calderon – Coffee broker; Marks & Spencer – Mike Barry, Rowland Hill & Phil Patterson; Marine Conservation Society – Bernadette Clarke & Dawn Purchase; Mercury Recycling – Graham Mitchell; Microgen – Adrian Richardson; Micro Power Council – Jane Vaus; Morrisons plc – Ellen Malinski; Nanoforce – Ata Yoosefinejad; National Hazardous Waste Forum – David Luckin; National Society for Clean Air (NSCA) – Rob Pilling; Natural Building Technologies – Neil May; Natural Death Centre – Mike Jarvis; Natural History Museum – Andrew Parker; Novozymes – Ture Damhus; Npower – Robert Harper &

Nick McHugh; Organic Power – Chris Maltin; Pesticides Action Network – Clare Butler-Ellis; Peterton – Peter Brann; Philips Lighting – Robert Hall & Peter Van Strijp; Phytotrade – Rosie Abde-Collins; Procter & Gamble – John Bailey, Forbes Macdougall, Cathy Rogers; Promessa Organic – Susanne Wiigh-Masak; RDC – Gary Griffiths; Recoup – Lucy Shields; Rio Tinto – Tom Burke; RSPCA – Freedom Foods – Dr Julia Wrathall & Suzi Browne (PR).

S – Z

SAB Miller – Alan Knight; Sainsbury plc – Alison Austin & David Meller; Sally Bagenal – Founder & former CEO of the Organic Milk Suppliers Co-operative Ltd (OMSCO); Salvation Army – Garth Ward; Shell Fish Association of GB – Peter Hunt; Simmonds Mills – Adele Mills; Sky TV – Ben Stimson; Society for Motor Traders & Manufacturers – Steve Franklin; Soil Association – Sara Hathway; Sony – Kieran Mayers; Stuart Martin Architects – Stuart Martin; Sue Pollard – Independent Researcher & Consultant; Sustain – Kath Delmeny; Sustainable Building Supplies – Matt Robinson; Swedish Heat Pump Organisation (SP) – Roger Nordman; Synnogy – Sylvia Baron; Tesco plc – Andrew Slight; Tetrapak UK Ltd – Nicola Mann; Thames Water – Richard Aylard, Terry Bane, Brian Crathorne & Mark Terrell; Tim Brown – Environmentalist & emissions expert; Tomato Growers Association – Gerry Hayman; Triodos Bank – Charles Middleton; UK Social Investment Forum – Penny Shepherd; Uniross Batteries – Simon West; University of Southhampton – Charles Banks, Sonia Heaven; Vital Earth – Arnie Rainbow; Visit London – Charles Secrett; Waitrose plc – Jess Hughes, Gill Smith; Warmcel – Jasper Meade; Warwick University – Professor Ralph Noble; Whispergen – Mike Small; Woolmark – Malcolm Campbell; Waste Resources Action Plan (WRAP) – Chris Davie, Nicola Ellen, Patrick Mahon & Maggie Newton; World Wide Fund for Nature (WWF) – Andrea Kaszewski & Becci May.

Photographs on pp.9, 58, 67, 128, 138 © Kerri Sharp, with thanks to Mike Slocombe for loan of camera. Photographs of Tintinhull House and Ham Hill on p.244 © Chris Spracklen – Martock. Author photograph p.245 © Pauline Rook Photography.

The Haller Foundation: I would like to give a special acknowledgement to Dr Rene Haller, who has been an inspiration to me. His truly innovative and creative thinking and approach to environmental conservation has been applied to rehabilitating land and community initiatives in Kenya. But the lessons from this can be replicated in many other situations, including by businesses and governments. I have helped set up a charity, The Haller Foundation, to promote Rene's work and to spread his ideas. Please support us if you can: www.thehallerfoundation.com